Breaking the Code Of Codependence

~ Becoming Conscious
Through
The Transpersonal

D0973121

BREAKING

THE CODE OF

Codependence

Becoming Conscious

Through

The Transpersonal

Sharon Joy Ng Hale, Ph.D.

Third Edition

For more information contact:

Wu Chi Creations
1010 Foxchase Drive Suite 315
San Jose, California 95123
wuchicreations@sbcglobal.net
www.wuchicreations.com

ISBN 0-9786884-0-6
ISBN 13: 978-0-9786884-0-0

Book cover design by Kameron L. Montgomery

This book is dedicated
to all
who seek
to find
their
truth

Contents

(Part I reviews the literature on research into codependence. It outlines theories regarding etiology and the personality characteristics of the codependent identity)

Chapter Two: Understanding Codependence

Chapter Three: Society's Child

Chapter Four: Gender and Codependence

Chapter Five: 12-Steps and Recovery

(Part II outlines how we take in reality, the various forces and perspectives in psychology that allow an individual to understand codependence through multiple psychological lenses. It addresses the changes in consciousness, perception and behaviors that are necessary if one is to heal from codependence. Codependence is proposed to be a personal mythology in need of revision. From the information gained in Part I of this book, the reader is prepared to "see" codependence as a condition born from patriarchy and the sociocultural conditions that result in behaviors that are labeled as codependence. The reader will come full circle in this exploration of codependence to understand that there is a path to healing. Transpersonal theories and techniques are introduced that provide the reader with a roadmap to journey the path of healing)

Chapter Eight: How Consciousness Works

Chapter Nine: What is My Mythology?

Chapter Ten: Work to Be Done

Preface to the Second Edition

Breaking The Code of Codependence identifies the many factors associated with the construct of codependence. The characteristics and behaviors of codependence are described and explained by providing psychological explanations for how these behavioral patterns develop. This book proposes that there are factors in society, culture and our families that may contribute to making a person more at-risk for behaving in codependent ways.

It also provides the means for a person to transcend these factors so that one can heal from codependence. The means by which this is achieved is to evolve consciousness. This is the path of the **Transpersonal**. By understanding the nature of consciousness and how we form our realities, we are able to emerge from these codependent patterns and awaken to a deeper sense of who we can become.

This transpersonal framework explains how you can become conscious of the **personal mythology** that has resulted in codependent relating. By identifying the familial, cultural, and societal factors that have contributed to our perception and the way we see the world, we can raise our consciousness and begin to make choices that empower us rather than sustaining the dysfunctional ways we have related with others.

We begin to understand that the way we see ourselves may not be accurate. By examining the influence of our cultures and society upon our perceptions of appropriate gendered behaviors, it becomes clear that who we are may not necessarily fit into the prescribed role we were given. Codependence becomes the result of being misunderstood and unknown for who we truly are at the core--by others and ourselves. What we learned as children is translated into our adult lives and unless we consciously identify and examine those factors that led to our tendency to behave in codependent ways, we are likely to continue the patterns.

What has to change is our consciousness. Our self-perception is too often formed through the eyes of others, including the influences of societal and cultural labeling. We may not even know who we really are because we have been too busy trying to be what others have expected of us. The good news is that we CAN evolve our consciousness and learn from the past to form a healthier relationship to others and ourselves that encourages consciousness evolution and continued growth.

As this book will reveal, the path to awakening and living from a more expanded form of consciousness can help us heal. Evolved consciousness is more compassionate and less judgmental. It provides us with a more receptive consciousness that allows us to consider different alternatives to the way we interpret experience. Consciousness expansion provides us with more choices of perception that allows for more flexibility and happiness in life.

To expand consciousness one needs to first identify the constrictions in place. As we identify the parameters we have applied to our thinking and perceptions, the boundaries that have formed our reality become clearer. Evolving consciousness means we have to be willing to consider what we have not considered up to this point. We have to be willing to "let go" and just **be**.

Awareness and awakening require a commitment to owning our reactions and perceptions. Awakening is to become conscious of the repressed, suppressed, and disowned aspects of self. Waking up to our potential requires opening to unknown regions of our emotions, memories and psyche without retreating to safer, more familiar strategies.

Clinicians have a valuable part to play in the process of helping others heal from codependent relating. Those helpers must also be on a journey of their own to evolve their consciousness however. We can only help others traverse territory we ourselves have traveled. Whether you are reading this because you suspect you may be under the influence of codependence, or whether you are hoping to help others in the clinical setting, this book outlines a path to healing from codependence. It is not just about recovery, but is written to help you and others to awaken to your potential and evolve your consciousness to a greater state of awareness—to heal.

A detailed examination of the personal myths guiding relationship formation, choice, role assumption and responsibility is part of the process that helps uncover the underlying myths that translates into codependence. Understanding that the role models available in our life may be inadequate to help provide an identifiable route to travel in interrelationships, can spark the creativity to imagine what can be possible.

Relationships provide us with a unique opportunity to tap into the strengths, resources, and creativity within. When problems arise in relationships, each partner is called to look within. Willingness to be uncomfortable without blaming is to turn within for the answers. We learn to trust and depend on ourselves for our own truths. The challenges for interrelating are great, and yet, call upon the strength inherent in human nature to rise above the common reactions that we express. Being aware of the potent power of archetypal reaction, we can fill the unconscious template with a sense of individuality and unique response. Awakening the unconsciousness to live more consciously is empowering.

Learning to trust our inner wisdom is to empower us to create the kinds of relationships we want. By adhering less to societally sanctioned characteristics we assumed would bring health, wealth, and happiness, we can evolve our definitions of *appropriate behaviors* and contact the creative co-creator within. Desiring, choosing, and forming a conscious relationship guided by individuality, rather than social prescription, is a self-loving act. Commitment to a conscious path of love is one that nurtures and encourages our spiritual growth and soulful purpose as well as that of our partner.

As a tradition, marriage, its rites, rituals, and expected gender role splitting need revision. Today's couples are more concerned with achieving a spirit and soul filled relationship. Economic security is not enough. As couples seek intimacy, each can do so by determining which stories they are bringing to the relationship. A true spiritual partnership can be forged that encourages growth, intimacy, passion, individuality, love, care and commitment.

Dr. Sharon Joy Ng Hale
June 2006, Second Edition

Preface to the
Third Edition

This updated third edition includes new and exciting information that augments and supports the basic premise of this book: that we can heal from codependence. Research published since the last edition has been incorporated throughout the book. We consider the ideas of Mc Grath et al (2011) who propose that codependence can be likened to *pathological altruism*. Briefly defined, it likens codependence as a construct that describes "the willingness of an individual to place the needs of others above him or herself to the point of causing harm, whether physical, psychological, or both, to the purported altruist" (Mc Grath et al 2011). Also, with the recent revision of the *Diagnostic and Statistical Manual of Mental Disorders (DSM-5)* and the inclusion of *Premenstrual Dysphoric Disorder* to this revision, an update to Chapter 5 was necessary because in the last edition I had written about the concerns among feminist when PMS was first being considered for inclusion in the DSM-IV-TR. Now that it has been incorporated into the DSM-V, we will have to see how this new category impacts females.

The Holyoake Codependence Index (HCI) has been added to Chapter One expanding the list of codependence assessment tests (Dear, 2002; 2004; Dear & Roberts, 2000; 2005). The HCI was developed because a lack of psychometrically sound instruments to measure the phenomenon has hampered research into codependency (Mc Grath & Oakley, 2011). Developed by Dear & Roberts (2000), HCI is the only assessment device for codependence that was "deliberately developed not to contain items that confound the measure with other variables, such as self-esteem or emotional distress" (Mc Grath et al, p. 56).

From the field of **interpersonal neurobiology** we are learning that parents or caregivers are essential to the healthy development of our brain. From the contemplative practices we witness changes in brain physiology and structure through meditation. There is much to share regarding the importance of attuned communication experiences with caregivers as we are growing up. These types of experiences lead to an integrated left/right hemispheric coherence that increases our ability to attune with others, to be more flexible in our responses, and to ultimately change our everyday habitual responses into conscious, flexible and complex responses to life. What is important about these findings for our exploration of codependency is that it provides support to my earlier contentions that it is possible to go beyond recovery into healing from codependence. Through attuned communication we can develop the areas of our brain that did not develop sufficiently as a child, learning and experiencing "feeling felt" and interacting with others in ways in which they will "feel felt" as well. These types of interpersonal interactions are important to our mental well-being and enable us to have conscious relationships that meet our needs and in which we are happy.

These new insights into the bodymind connection are encouraging and are effectively reshaping the landscape of how we understand the importance of early relationships and the development of our full capacity for love and fulfilling relationships. Added to Chapter Two is Dr. Dan Siegel's (2001, 2011, 2012) work on Interpersonal Neurobiology that reveals the essential elements for secure attachment: collaboration, reflective dialogue, repair, coherent narratives, and emotional communication. Without these five basic elements being present in a caregivers interactions with the infant, the developing child's brain will not develop the left/right brain integration that allows for the development of coherent narratives of our lives and the ability for emotional regulation and flexible responses. Interestingly, the most robust predictor of the attachment classification of a child is the coherence of the parent/caregiver adult's autobiographical narrative (Siegel, 2001). When our parents/caregivers are securely attached, they can provide the kinds of experiences needed that lead to our secure attachment with them.

"(I)ndirect analyses...suggest that attachment classification are determined primarily by relationship experiences and not by genetic inheritance" (Siegel, 2001). This informs us that parents are very important to the secure attachment and full development of a child's capacity to love, be happy, and feel fulfilled. This does not mean that we blame our parents for our problems, but that it infuses us with a compassion for our parents' own limitations to provide us with the type of experiences that we needed for a secure attachment style.

From the work of Richard Davidson (2008) at the University of Wisconsin-Madison, we are learning more about the neurological changes that occur during meditation, especially *Mindfulness* meditation. This type of meditation refers to a calm awareness of cognitions, sensations, emotions, and experiences that cultivates a nonjudgmental awareness of the present moment (Ng, 2013). Mindfulness engages the mind by intentional reflection upon concepts such as *awareness, acceptance, release, attention,* and *nonjudgment.* It alters our relationship to our thoughts.

Beauregard (2012) reminds us that we have the capacity for volitional control of our emotions that result in a corresponding calming of the amygdalar activity in the brain. The *amygdala* is a small almond shaped structure, close to the hippocampus deep within the brain. It is part of the limbic system. The *amygdala* and hippocampus work together to help us remember if we need to fear an object, person or situation based on past experience. This is great for general survival on the African plains, but when the *amygdalar* activation gets associated with a particular situation, our basic warning system may stay on high alert for anything that resembles that fearful or dangerous situation even when the danger has passed. It is associated with *implicit memory* and will feel as if the danger is present in the current moment although the activation of the *amygdala* is due to the past memory. Our brain does not know the difference between the "reality" out there from the "reality" we create with our minds. Learning self-regulating techniques such as *reappraisal* and *cognitive distancing* reminds us that our physiological responses are due more to our perceptions than the situations themselves (Ng, 2013, Apr/May).

Because we know that the brain continues to change throughout life (known as *plasticity*), we now understand that we are not doomed if we emerged from childhood with *insecure* or *anxious attachment*. These types of attachment styles indicate that the critical interpersonal elements necessary for an integrated Self were lacking in the *holding environment* of the individual as a child, but with attuned therapy and efforts of the individual to change their brain through meditative practices and changing negative thought patterns, it is possible to develop the capacity for more flexible and complex responses as well as better emotional regulation, both hallmarks of an integrated brain. The brain's plasticity continues throughout our lives therefore our efforts to "change the brain" are worthy endeavors in hopes of our ability to truly evolve into our potential and engage in more meaningful relationships.

Dr. Sharon Joy Ng
October, 2013, Third Edition

♥

Introduction

In the late 1970s, the term *codependent* came into usage among substance abuse treatment professionals. These therapists were trying to understand the climate in which substance abusers lived. In this process these therapists identified a pattern of behaviors in the partners of their clients that appeared to hinder recovery efforts by the drug user in recovery. Consequently, the focus of concern moved from the substance abuser to the family members, this pattern of behaviors became known collectively as codependence. The behaviors of codependent family members were characterized as having an extreme external focus and a "need to control" others because these family members seemed to be driven by the need to control the substance abuser's drug habits. Ironically these care-taking attempts came to epitomize the meaning of what has been described as codependence.

The prefix "co-" can be defined as "with or necessary for the functioning of." Codependence therefore refers to the partner or spouse of a person who is chemically dependent (Greenleaf, 1984). In the literature, codependence is characterized by a list of symptoms that range from an extreme need for control to emotional numbing. According to these different sources, codependence stems from an exaggerated sense of responsibility for the well being of others. By getting others to comply with the codependent's "controlling" behaviors, the codependent gains a sense of being needed and valued. As will be explained in a later section of this book, these tendencies are developed in the childhood environment when a person learns that if love is not forthcoming, being needed or gaining approval are at least second best to feeling love.

It is in the childhood environment that most people learn to act in codependent ways. When love is not given, children seek approval. When we are not validated for our true individuality, we develop a "false self" that hides who we are and who we can become. When we grow up and seek love within an intimate relationship, we mistake our ability to "get others to change for the better" as being valuable—we gain self-worth. When we are successful at getting others to act and do the things we feel are best for them, we feel needed. In the case of substance abuse, we feel needed and important if we can only get the drug abuser to stop abusing. This perpetuates the denial of our own selves because we are so concerned with what is best for others that we never take the time to discover what is best for us. Consequently, this creates a distorted relationship to our sense of personal will power. Codependence predisposes a person to invest inordinate amounts of energy in the effort to improve other people's lives in our search for a semblance of self-worth (Cermak, 1986).

Defining Codependence

Melody Beattie (1987, 1989, 1997) defined codependence as primarily a condition of relating with others, or interrelating, that resulted in

> ...lives (that have) become unmanageable as a result of living in a committed relationship with an alcoholic....A codependent...has let another person's behavior affect him or her...and is obsessed with controlling that person's behavior (pp. 30-31).

Others, such as Cermak (1986) proposed that codependence is characterized by:

- Continued investment of self-esteem in the ability to influence/control feelings and behavior in self and others in the face of obvious adverse consequences for doing so;
- Assumption of responsibility for meeting others' needs;
- Anxiety and boundary distortions around intimacy and separation;
- Enmeshment in relationships with personality disordered individuals;
- Three or more of the following: constriction of emotions, depression, hyper vigilance, compulsions, anxiety, substance abuse, excessive denial, recurrent physical or sexual abuse, stress-related medical illness, and/or a primary relationship with an active substance abuser for at least two years.

He felt that these five criteria would assist in the diagnosis of codependence.

Beattie (1987) suggested that codependents were taught to avoid focusing on their own personal feelings and desires so that they didn't upset the existing family system. These types of families taught children that to focus on personal emotions and needs was selfish. These children learned to suppress their real feelings. It also prevented them from being proactive problem-solvers. These

unwritten, silent rules...usually develop in the immediate family...(and) set the pace for (adult) relationships. These rules prohibit discussion about problems, open expression of feelings; direct, honest communication; realistic expectations...being human, vulnerable, or imperfect...(and create a)...habitual system of thinking, feeling, and behaving...that can cause...pain...(leading one)...into, or keep(ing one)...in destructive relationships...(It) can sabotage relationships that may otherwise have worked (Beattie, 1987, pp. 30-34).

3

These early childhood experiences appear as over-learned behavior in adulthood. What was learned so well in childhood carries over into adult relationships and sets the stage for a tendency to relate to others codependently. Subby (1984) believed that the oppressive rules of dysfunctional families create a mistrust of self and others for the codependent.

What is a dysfunctional family? Mellody, Miller, and Miller (1989) described a dysfunctional family as a situation in which adult and child roles are not clearly distinguished. The child may serve as a surrogate partner for one of the parents, or both parents may triangulate the child regarding issues arising between the parents. *Triangulation* is the tendency of one or both parents to use the child as a "middle-man" or mediator between the mother and father. When we are triangulated, we become hyper-vigilant to what we think others are feeling or what we might believe the other person "really" wants or needs. It is an effort to make everyone happy. Codependence makes us more focused on the external cues from others instead of listening to our own wisdom.

Analyzing Codependence

The construct of codependence has been described in a variety of ways with little agreement among the various descriptions. It has been referred to as a behavioral adaptation to a drug or alcoholic environment formed in the family of origin or one's primary relationship (Beattie, 1987). It has also been advanced as a primary disease that is brought into a relationship causing drug abuse in one's partner (Cermak, 1986a, 1986b; Gotham & Sher, 1996; Rice, 1996). Uhle (1994) described codependence as a need to be needed and to seek approval from others. Codependents experience a willingness to suffer (Collins, 1993), a need to be in control, including an urge to change and control others (Fagan-Pryor & Haber, 1992; Wright & Wright, 1991); an inability to maintain clear boundaries

4

between self and significant others (Fagan-Pryor et al., 1992; O'Gorman, 1993); a numbing or denial of feelings (Mannion, 1991; Morgan, 1991; Granello & Beamish, 1998); and, it has even been referred to as *pathological altruism* (Mc Grath et al, 2011).

Not all of these depictions of codependence have been validated but they are listed here to demonstrate that the construct of codependence has many problems associated with it. We are unsure if it really exists yet researchers continue to study it as if it does. Keep an open mind given the confusion at this point in our growing understanding of the codependency. We aren't sure if it is a syndrome or just a collection of problematic behaviors that make is easier to discuss by calling it "codependence." My personal concern with the discourse of codependence is that there is no agreement as to what it is. On the one hand it is described as the "need to control others" or a "numbing or denial of feelings," and conversely, as "pathological altruism." These are quite different behaviors.

Addiction models characterize codependents as being addicted to the addict (Capwell-Sowder, 1984; Wright et al., 1991) while psychodynamic approaches have focused upon dysfunctional early childhood environmental factors that may have resulted in low self-esteem and culminate in codependent relating (Carson & Baker, 1994; Wells, Glickhauf-Hughes, & Jones, 1999). Attachment theorists have described the construct as typifying the characteristics of avoidant or anxious/ambivalent types and provide some indication of how the parenting style can contribute to later codependent development in the children (Carranza, & Kilmann, 2000).

New research in *Interpersonal Neurobiology* (Siegel, 2011) is revealing that insufficient development of the right prefrontal cortex can result from childhood experiences that lack *attunement, collaborative and emotional communication, reflective dialogue, repair of disruptions in the relationship, and coherent narratives.* Without these essential elements being present in our parents or caregivers interactions with us, we likely developed insecure/ambivalent attachments to them that resulted in our impaired ability to have satisfying, attuned relationships with others, and our own children. We are now learning that these deficiencies can be remedied through attuned communications and therapy that focuses on integrating a person's experiences. These and other theoretical approaches all attempt to bring awareness to our understanding of codependence and provide the means to break the code of codependence. These theories are examined more in depth in a later chapter of this book.

The prevalence and popularization of codependence has been publicized through the popular press and media (Gemin, 1997). From this discourse, it sounds as if codependence is really a personal problem. What is advocated in this book however is the disparity between the way the condition develops and the manner in which treatment is assigned. Although codependence develops within the context of relationships, treatment approaches focus upon individual recovery from codependence requiring separation from others. In many ways, this **intrarelationship** approach is insightful to our understanding of the nature of codependence, but it is not the cure all for this type of **interrelationship** problem.

Recovery models encourage establishing boundaries and being vigilant for violations of those boundaries by others. It advocates "letting go" and "letting God." People in recovery are always *working the program.* One criticism of the recovery model is that a person is always "in recovery but never recovered." What appears to be an interrelationship problem is dealt with on an intrapersonal level in this type of setting, which is important to the healing process. In other words, we need to learn more about ourselves first so that when we enter into an

6

intimate relationship with another person, we have a developed *Self* to share. This *Self* differs from the *self* (capital "S" versus the little "s") in that the *self* is really our *ego*. Our *ego* is a truncated version of the fullness that the Self embodies because it is our version that makes us socially acceptable to others. These are the parts of us that we allow others to see, but the *Self* is the actualization of the true inner soulful being that you are. We know who we are, what we want, what we feel, what we think, what we need, what we like or dislike and can share this with our partner. If we have not learned to undo the damage of an unvalidated childhood, then we continue to try to fit into the image that we hold of ourselves or the image that others expect us to be. We are the chameleons.

At some point we must reenter the world of relationships. This is the forum where we learn to become a warrior. Unless we are challenged to use our new found "Self" we never truly know if we have taken that important step into living what we have learned. Without actively engaging in a relationship with another person and allowing ourselves to learn who we are in relationship to this other person, we can never know if the *intrarelationship* healing has been effective in helping us to have a healthy *interrelationship*.

Feminist critics of the construct of codependence are concerned that the recovery movement traditionally focuses upon the "identified codependent" instead of examining the additional contributions to its development that come from societal and political factors. Focusing on the identified codependent simply diverts attention away from the forces in society and the political atmosphere that impact gender related behaviors and how we judge those behaviors. Females are taught to be caretakers and nurturers and have historically not enjoyed the same privileges that are afforded to most males. By simply describing codependence as a personality problem of the individual, many are left unaware that society expects women to be the caretaker and the nurturers as long as they don't carry out that role to the extreme. If we don't acknowledge that codependence is an exaggerated form of the typical roles assigned to females in society, public consciousness will remain constricted about the construct of codependence (Favorini, 1995; Frank & Bland, 1992; Gemin, 1997; Gordon, 1997). It will continue to be seen as a problem emerging from the individual. Codependence is thus understood as an individual problem rather than acknowledging the complexity of this behavioral syndrome that can only be understood if we examine all facets that contribute to its development: lack of attuned interactions during development, gender bias, politics that create division into the "have" and "have nots," societal prejudices, cultural expectations, and more.

Another criticism of the current discourse on codependence is that the societal structures that exacerbate addictive behaviors are not considered in this myopic definition. Hierarchical power structures, common in American society, may well be the primary driving force behind the prevalence of codependence in our society. We live in a patriarchal society. Patriarchy is defined as a social form in which ranking, status, independence, logic, and domination are male-defined and reflect primarily male standards. Peele and Brodsky (1975) believed that such distinctions create an unequal distribution of power within the social, economic, military, and political structures of these types of societies and therefore any deviations from these patriarchal established norms are considered as abnormal or pathological.

If expected gender roles are male-defined there will be a rank ordering to the behaviors assigned appropriate for males and females. In most societies, characteristics associated with the masculine are seen as being more normal than behaviors associated with females. For example, the words "strong, independent and objective" are preferred over the words "weak, dependent and subjective." When behaviors and gender roles are assigned by predominantly male standards, then those roles associated with females are seen as belonging to a minority class in society. This is an example of hierarchical ranking.

Expected roles for females are defined by male standards that reflect this bias. This is not a statement of gender bashing but describes the conditions in society that contribute to a stratification of rank-ordered and preferred behaviors. *Enabling* and *care taking* are terms generally associated with codependence and expected feminine gender role behaviors. As a consequence, a higher proportion of females are diagnosed as codependent. Researchers have suggested that this gender discrepancy arises because males are more likely to be the chemically dependent partner in relationships.

The roles and behaviors expected of females reflect the opposite of that which males are expected to adhere to, but as in the case of codependence, when females carry out these expected gender-role behaviors too well, they are labeled as a form of deviant behavior that needs to be fixed. Whether codependence was originally described to obscure the part that patriarchy has contributed to gender inequality, or whether it more specifically represents a personality disorder that primarily affects females will be further examined in this book.

The pervasive nature of codependence and the confusion regarding its definition, etiology, and diagnosis has created much disagreement about the construct. Current theoretical approaches have proposed a mixture of contradicting or narrowly defined viewpoints regarding codependence, its etiology and treatment. Mc Grath et al (2011) asserted that there is a lack of psychometrically sound instruments to measure the construct of codependence and propose that it "might be better to conceptual(ize) codependency as dysfunctional behaviors to identify, rather than a disorder to diagnose (Mc Grath et al, 2011, p. 53). This echoes earlier writers who argue that the identification of the behaviors that constitute problematic relating would be more helpful in treatment strategies. This book proposes such a re-visioning of the construct, but to see it as a personal mythology in need of revision rather than a mental health diagnosis.

An integrative framework that incorporates the total body of knowledge on codependence would provide a more holistic approach for working with codependence. By addressing the sociopolitical, economic, cultural, theoretical, family of origin, personality factors and feminist concerns regarding how the construct of codependence is framed, a viable path to healing can be identified. Through these considerations, deeper understanding can be achieved and the necessary steps to heal from codependent patterns of relating can occur. There is an emerging revolution in psychology that considers how this can be achieved—the Transpersonal Movement. The Transpersonal takes us into the realm of the mysterious and unseen world of the human being— our consciousness. By learning how we form our perceptions, what happens in the brain as we change the ways in which we view our "reality" we are empowered to heal ourselves. The plasticity of the brain informs us that what happened or did not happen when we were children does not doom us as adults. We have the capacity and ability to change our brain and lives through knowledge that leads us to practices that heal.

Transpersonal psychology is concerned with the different forms of consciousness that humans are capable of experiencing. Briefly defined, transpersonal psychology is concerned with consciousness awakening and consciousness evolution in our lives. It considers our human tendency to behave in archetypal ways.

Archetypes are predisposed patterns of behavior that are unconsciously reenacted in each generation. For example, we tend to follow the patterns of relating in intimate relationships that we had modeled for us by our parents and others in society. Unless we consciously choose to create something different, we will no doubt repeat these patterns.

There are as many archetypes as there are situations, but the focus of this book is to investigate how the archetypal pattern comes to life when we enter into an intimate relationship. We may be an independent, confident person outside of a relationship, but within a relationship, we seem to lose our sense of identity and our direction. Suddenly, the other person's life and well-being is much more important than our own happiness. We do what we can to assure that our partner makes those choices that "we" think are best. Breaking the code of codependence is to understand the many factors that have contributed to this pattern of interrelating.

To see codependence as an *archetype,* or the modern expression of the characteristic ways in which females and males have related to one another for thousands of years, the possibilities for emerging from unconscious adherence to these patterns of behavior happens. Understanding how the dynamics in dysfunctional families can make one more at-risk for later codependent relating, and increasing awareness of the archetypal influences at play, we begin to recognize the patterns in which we are stuck and can then form new ways of relating. As we develop practices to change our brain, we learn to witness our emotions to become the observer. Becoming the observer of our emotional times loosens the neural nets that keep those emotions brewing and at-ready to burst upon the scene. We know that neurons that fire together, wire together (and all the accompanying hormones and neurotransmitters that are released to make up our "emotional cocktail"). Conversely, neurons that no longer fire together will loose their connections to one another (Siegel, 2001, 2011).

Prior to learning about transpersonal psychology, interpersonal neurobiology, and archetypes, we will explore how codependence has been described and defined as well as how it develops from the childhood environment within the family of origin in Part I (Beattie, 1987; Cermak, 1986). We will also examine how society has affected our notions of appropriate gender roles and behaviors that culminate in codependence (Jimenez, 1997; Peele & Brodsky, 1975). Society's contribution to addictive behaviors and gender bias is another perspective from which we can gain a clearer understanding of just what codependence is and how it develops.

In Part II, we will explore codependence from a transpersonal perspective. What is the transpersonal path? Part II examines this emerging fourth force in psychology and places it within the historical development of the discipline of psychology. Transpersonal psychology is intimately involved in explaining how we form our notions of reality and simultaneously provides scientific evidence for perhaps revising the way in which we have come to understand "how the world works."

Most important to understanding codependence and how one can heal from these patterns will be to understand how we form our "**reality**." Is reality all around us simply waiting to be seen or is it something that we actively create? These are the concerns of Part II where we will look at how we come to perceive what we call our reality and at the same time find a path to change the archetypal patterns that have culminated in codependent behaviors.

The transpersonal framework gives us a basic understanding about how codependence can be seen as a condition a person can grow beyond. To expand our individual boundaries and transcend our human nature we can create a broader way of understanding what is happening in codependence. To seek the transpersonal is to seek the unity within the universe and our connection to others. It helps to explain our similarities and tendencies to use consciousness in restricted ways.

Get ready to explore how you can heal or help others to heal from codependent relating. Learn tools to change your perception and your brain. Learn how your consciousness has contributed to the formation of the reality you experience and how to change these perceptions that ultimately help rewire your brain. By educating ourselves and learning the tools to evolve consciousness, we will each have the opportunity to grow and evolve to become the person that we desire to be.

Part I

♥

As mentioned in the Introduction, Part I primarily addresses the phenomenon of codependence. This exploration will provide the necessary information for the reader to enter into the work of Part II, where we will discover how it is possible to view codependence in such a way that leads to change and ultimately, healing.

The information in Part I is valuable in documenting the symptoms, measurement, personality factors, and family of origin situations that contribute to codependence. It further elaborates upon the idea of how codependence is an addiction (relationship addiction). We examine the nature of American society and how the hierarchical power structures inherent within our system may set us up for addictive behaviors. In Part I, we also examine the 12-Steps philosophy and outline the steps to recovery based upon this philosophy. The information in Part I is meant to be descriptive of codependence, but does not offer treatment solutions to the condition. Solutions are offered in Part II.

Part II deepens our understanding by examination of how codependent relating is a natural outgrowth of the ways in which we have come to see our roles in relationships, especially for females but also for any minority group. We learn how to regulate our consciousness and that reality is really the result of our perceptions. We can change! We explore the idea that codependence is but an archetype—a way in which we are predisposed to behave in relationships—that we must unravel and update so that we no longer act in typically human fashion, but in more creative and individualistic ways. Bon Voyage!

♥

Chapter One

The Codependent Identity

Co-dependence is "an emotional, psychological, and behavioral condition that develops as a result of an individual's prolonged exposure to, and practice of a set of oppressive rules—rules which prevent the open expression of feelings as well as the direct discussion of personal and interpersonal problems" (Subby, 1984, p. 26).

These oppressive rules result in what can be described as the symptoms of codependence:

- Difficulty in identifying feelings
- Difficulty expressing feelings
- Difficulty forming or maintaining close relationships
- Perfectionism—too many expectations for self and others
- Rigid or stuck in attitudes and behavior
- Difficulty adjusting to change
- Feeling overly responsible for other people's behavior or feelings
- Constant need for other's approval in order to feel good about self
- Difficulty making decisions—worrying or thinking too much that you get "stuck"
- General feelings of powerlessness over one's life

- A basic sense of shame and low self-esteem over perceived failures in one's life (Subby, 1984, p. 32)

Miller and Miller (1989) divided codependence into five core areas:

- Low levels of self-esteem
- Difficulty maintaining and setting boundaries
- Extreme over-responsibility and over-committing themselves
- Inability to meet personal needs and wants
- Difficulty in living moderately

Although these symptoms are descriptive only they provide a personal checklist for codependents. This provides a way to frame the experiences encountered within relationships. Description is insufficient to adequately address the many issues that form codependence and thus this checklist should serve only as a beginning point. Much analysis and reflection needs to be done in order to work through the ingrained patterns of belief and behavior before healing can occur. The path is a process and it is the process that will lead to healing. The goal may be to be rid oneself of the behaviors and perceptions that form codependent relating, but it is ultimately the discovery process while embarked upon the path that brings healing to the individual.

How Codependence Is Measured

This section provides a brief overview of the psychometric instruments developed and/or used in the clinical assessment of codependence and will be of interest to those who are concerned with the assessment and treatment aspect of codependence. The *Beattie Co-Dependency Checklist* (BCI) represents the earliest assessment device and is a paper and pencil checklist of 114-items based upon the 260 characteristics and symptoms outlined in the book, *Codependent No More*

(Beattie, 1987). Because these 260 characteristics could conceivably fit most of the population, it should not be the sole criteria by which a person determines codependence.

Codependence varies along a continuum and thus warrants a multi-level approach to its measurement (Friel & Friel, 1984). The Codependency Assessment Inventory (CAI) is a 60-item true/false inventory that "...tap(s) into self-care, secrets, self-criticism, 'stuckedness,' boundary issues, family of origin, intimacy, physical health, autonomy, identity, feelings of identification, and over-responsibility/burnout" (Springer et al., 1998, p. 145). This inventory measures codependence taking into consideration the concerns generated by the earlier 260-item BCI. The levels described in the CAI are associated with the severity, length, and total number of codependent symptoms experienced and provides a more individualized picture of codependence in the individual.

In 1990, Spann and Fischer condensed the earlier 60-item scale into the Spann-Fischer Codependency Scale (FSC). This is a 15-item assessment instrument that focuses upon identification of interaction patterns with others. These 15 items collapsed into four major areas of concern: "(1) an extreme focus outside of self; (2) a lack of open expression of feelings, and (3) attempts to derive a sense of purpose through relationships" (Loughead, 1998, p. 88). The fourth area was later added by a subsequent study by Fischer, Spann and Crawford (1991), namely: (4) a focus on care-taking behaviors.

Wright and Wright (1991), who were more concerned with codependent relating as opposed to codependent characteristics, modified the Acquaintance Description Form (ADF) which is "...a multivariate technique for measuring the intensity and quality of personal relationships" (445). The ADF was modified four times in the attempt to refine the scale to reflect a clear differentiation between codependent and comparison subjects resulting in the ADF-C2, ADF-C3, ADF-C4, ADF-C5, respectively (Wright and Wright, 1990, 1991, 1995, 1999). Although the earlier versions placed more emphasis on the "processes within developing and ongoing relationships and de-emphasized personal dispositions...recent data...suggests that a dispositional syndrome...(may be a factor)...in some, but not all, instances of codependent relating" (Wright et al., 1999, p. 530). The differentiation between codependent characteristics and codependent relating (i.e., endogenous or exogenous codependence) are explored in more depth in a later section of this chapter.

Wells, Glickhauf-Hughes, and Bruss (1998) developed a 36-item scale, the Codependent Questionnaire (CdQ). They reduced the 60-items of the earlier CAI through an elimination of redundant and non-personality characteristic items. The CdQ yields a total score and four subscale scores that measure the following aspects of codependence: (a) *responsibility*—the assumption of responsibility for meeting the needs of others to the neglect of one's own needs; (b) *control*—the desire to influence and control the feelings and behaviors of others and oneself; (c) *intimacy*—the difficulty to which one has in establishing an appropriate level of intimacy with others; and, (d) *enmeshment*—the tendency to become involved with personality disordered or chemically dependent individuals (Roehling, Koelbel, & Rutgers, 1996).

The Codependency Assessment Tool is a multivariate tool that measures the five factors that they believe constitute the construct: other focus/self neglect; low self-esteem; hiding self; medical problems; and family of origin issues (Hughes-Hammer, Martsolf & Zeller, 1998a). It has been demonstrated to have high reliability and validity as well.

Another more recent measurement of codependency, the Holyoake Codependency Index (HCI) was developed and validated by Dear and Roberts (2000). This 13-item scale is comprised of three subscales relating to three key themes discussed in the codependence literature: external focus, self-sacrifice, and reactivity (Dear & Roberts, 2000). The HCI measures the extent to which a person endorses codependent beliefs and attributions. Validity for both males and females has been established as well as test-retest reliability for the subscales and the HCI overall (Dear, 2004; Dear et al, 2005). The HCI has been rigorously tested for internal validity in four studies conducted by Dear et al (2005) resulting in further evidence of construct validity for the subscales.

> (T)his index is sufficiently psychometrically sound for research. The index is content valid; the subscale structure is stable across samples and sexes; the subscales are internally consistent and have good retest reliability over 3 wk.; and there is adequate initial evidence of construct validity (Dear, 2004, p. 56)

Other aspects of importance to consider in the assessment of codependence include psychometric measures of parental quality. Following a review of the literature, Fischer and Crawford (1992) concluded that impaired family functioning was a likely precursor to developing codependence. These included such perceptual factors as feeling emotionally supported by one's parents, the extent to which one's parents were involved or uninvolved, the predominant parenting style experienced (i.e., permissive, authoritarian, or authoritative), and the level of parental control exerted. Parental support was defined as the extent to which a person felt his parents supported his unique identity. Parental control represented such tactics as induction, coercion (power assertion), or love withdrawal.

Our Family of Origin

There are many contributing elements to the development of codependence that seem to originate from the circumstances within the family of origin. Gayol (2004) suggested that codependence is a *script* that is transmitted between generations—a *transgenerational script*. A *script*, according to Eric Berne (1972) is "a life plan based on a decision made in childhood, reinforced by the parents, justified by subsequent events, and culminating in a chosen alternative" (p. 445). The *codependence script* is one of "passive behaviors," such as *doing nothing* (denial), *overadaptation* (rescuer), *agitation* (emotional repression), and *incapacity and violence* (expressed internally as psychosomatic disorders or externally by not setting limits on abusive behaviors of others" (Gayol, 2004). The primary means of script transmission is *projective identification*—"one person disowns his feelings and manipulatively induces the other into experiencing them" (Gayol, 2004, p. 317). *Projection* is a Freudian defense mechanism wherein our feelings and thoughts are so unacceptable that we reject them and instead, accuse the other person of having those unacceptable feelings or thoughts. We project what is inside of us outwards onto another, similar to the way old film projectors cast the images from the film onto a distant screen. The screen appears to hold the image, but it is simply a projected image. This functions as a vehicle for transmitting repressed feelings through several generations, especially feelings related to a history of abuse, negligence, or abandonment in the family.

Additional developmental factors add to the mix—having been reared in a dysfunctional environment; learning to numb your feelings; assuming a role in the family instead of being yourself; and being parentified as a child—all increase the risk of behaving in codependent ways as an adult.

Dysfunctional Environment

Mellody, Miller & Miller (1989) defined a dysfunctional family as one that is characterized by a lack of clear boundaries separating adult and child roles. Adult-adult relating and adult-child relating is clear in healthy families, but not so in the dysfunctional one. What familial factors contribute to a greater risk for developing codependency? Cullen and Carr (1999) found that codependence was more likely in families that lacked nurturance, acceptance, support, role clarity and emotional expression. These elements are essential if a child is to achieve a secure attachment style and grow up feeling "felt" by the parents/caregivers (Siegel, 2011). Greater parental mental health problems, parental coercion, maternal compulsivity, authoritarian paternal styles, dysfunctional parenting, repressive atmospheres, physical and verbal abuse, higher levels of control and enmeshment within the family of origin are additional factors that increase codependence (Kottke, Warren, William, & Moffett, 1993). Codependence is also known as "relationship addiction," because the behaviors are compulsive. This will be discussed in the next chapter.

"Survival techniques learned become internalized and part of the individual's personality...Those victimized by prolonged involvement in a family system dominated by addiction problems...experience emotional and interpersonal difficulties far beyond the confines of that system" (Wright et al., 1991). More importantly, research into epigenetics reveals that experience is the trigger that activates our genes and that they don't automatically turn on by themselves (Lipton & Bearhman, 2012). This contrasts with earlier depictions of how we believed that "biology is destiny."

There are optimal times during development, called *critical periods* when certain experiences are required if our genetic potential is to be achieved. For example, we know that there is a critical period for learning language and that without experiences in communicating with others, we cannot develop this potential. Similarly, without certain forms of verbal and non-verbal communication as we develop, our brain will lack the integration of the left/right hemispheric coherency that is necessary for socially attuned and compassionate interactions. "The importance of the first years may be that brain structures that mediate social and emotional functioning begin to develop during this time in a manner that appears to be dependent upon interpersonal experiences" (Siegel, 2001, p. 71). We are finding that in regards to attachment, the brain's plasticity allows for the rewiring and further development of our undeveloped prefrontal cortex that will result in our ability to regulate our emotions better and to move into the plane of possibilities rather than staying stuck in habitual reactive patterns of behavior (Siegel, 2011).

Numbing

Suppression and denial are common defense mechanisms utilized in order to adapt and survive in dysfunctional families. Parker and Gladstone (1996) cited that codependents were more likely to have come from families with highly controlling, non-nurturing parents. Children in dysfunctional families learn to mislabel feelings through the misinterpretation that occurs. Because the child's needs tend to be denied or mislabeled as weakness or betrayal, one views the dynamics within these types of families as normal. The numbing of emotions becomes a way of interrelating that suppresses the open emotional expression that occurs in functional family environments. The problem with numbing is that we end up being numb to everything then—even joy and happiness.

Role Assumption and Parentification

Wegscheider-Cruse (1984) described some of the roles played in these families that included:

- The successful, compulsively achieving Family Hero around which the family staked its claim that it was a normal, healthy family;

- The hostile, rejecting Scapegoat who shuns the family and acts out feelings in an attempt to get attention from a system that was already spread too thin;

- The Lost Child who withdraws from the emotional chaos of family life, has learned to cope through avoidance which devastates the adult in terms of experiencing...(life fully); and,

- The Family Mascot learns to mask his most urgent communications of "love me, want me, accept me" with humor (p. 2).

"These children have not lost their identities, they have never had the opportunity to form them...what children learn in...(the dysfunctional family)... setting becomes the model not only for their own behavior, but for their choice of future relationships" (Greenleaf, 1984, p. 6-7). They grow up not realizing that having an extreme external focus and assuming responsibility for others prevents identification of personal needs. "Dysfunctional families reflect intense forms of denial, repression, distortion, and emotional constriction" (Krestan & Bepko, 1990, p. 221). Children are forced to comply with rules that require the assumption of various personae in order to accommodate. The roles assumed often help to maintain the status quo in the family, yet constrict the full expression of personality.

Social modeling, or learning by what one observes others doing, teaches us strategies that help us to know which behaviors will yield particular results. Through this method and through reinforcement, children learn to either delay or ward off chaos by doing those things that "work" to keep chaos from erupting. They become a part of that child's coping repertoire. The template for *normal* interrelating is learned through these early childhood experiences, even if they are dysfunctional.

Being vigilant to external cues can serve as a filtering device. Incoming information can be used to regulate our actions so that we can choose to act according to acceptable standards. Familiarity falsely guides us, in this case, because familiarity becomes equivalent to normality. When a person acting in codependent ways is able to shape the environment through his or her adjusted behaviors, self-efficacy and self-confidence are increased and reinforces the likelihood that the same behaviors will be repeated again in similar circumstances.

Triangulation is another common occurrence in dysfunctional families. Triangulation occurs when one parent builds an inappropriate relationship with one or more of the children to the exclusion of the other adult in the family. The child is inappropriately seduced into the role of confidant to one or both parents. Without appropriate guidance and role modeling, the child fails to development healthy individual boundaries. The child's needs are always secondary to others in this type of environment. Parentified children generally have parents whose emotional needs were not met while growing up. These parents then grow into adults who are unable to provide appropriate nurturing for their own children.

Parentification is also more likely to occur if one parent is a substance abuser because that parent is emotionally unavailable to the partner. This neglected partner then seeks intimacy from the child(ren) and creates a role reversal where the child feels compelled to take care of the well being of the neglected parent. This is parentification.

Children who are parentified tend to become vigilant for cues of being needed by the parentifying parent. This vigilance leads to obsessive-compulsive behaviors that enable the child to have some form of control over chaos in the family. Controlling others then culminates with alleviating anxiety for the time being. It appears that codependence is more highly related to factors other than drug abuse. Familial environmental factors, such as the inability to express feelings, feeling unaccepted or misunderstood, and one's parenting style, are more highly correlated with codependence.

Wegscheider-Cruse (1984) believed that children in dysfunctional families learn that love is equated with need. Being needed becomes equal to controlling others. This makes it difficult for a child to grow into an authentic and fully functioning human being because through playing a role in the family the child comes to believe that it is better to be needed if one does not feel wanted.

Personality Variables

When a person's behavior arises from identifiable dysfunction resulting from excessive rigidity or intensity associated with definable traits, a diagnosis of codependent disorder is warranted. Cermak (1986) has characterized codependence as a mixed personality disorder consisting of features associated with both dependent, borderline and narcissistic personality disorders (1986; 1991). Support for these criteria has not been strong, however, although there has been some verification that codependence represents a mix of masochistic, or self-defeating, and borderline personality characteristics (Wells et al., 1998). Research has also supported the contention that codependency "reflects a self disorder and (a) relational orientation that revolves around burdensome self-sacrifice and care-taking intended to 'control' significant others" (Wells et al., 1998, p. 34).

Anxious/Ambivalent or Avoidant Attachment Style

Attachment styles depict the relationship of the individual to the primary caregiver(s) in infancy and childhood. In the best of circumstances, a *secure attachment style* is most conducive to healthy emotional and mental well-being in a person. When we are in an environment that fosters secure attachment to our caregiver(s), we grow up with a stable and consistent *core self* that reflects *attuned* and collaborative communication experiences—we felt valued, appreciated, loved, seen and heard by our primary caregiver (Siegel, 2001). "The deepest sense of self-awareness, of core consciousness, may be profoundly influenced by early experiences in infancy even before explicit, autobiographical memory is available" (Siegel, 2001, p 76). Especially in family environments that include child abuse, the child's sense of agency, coherence, affectivity, and even continuity (memory) of the self in interaction with others will be severely impaired.

Typical codependents are anxious, insecure, and avoidant about relationships (Springer et al., 1998). The details regarding *attachment styles* and the importance of attuned interactions with our caregivers will be more deeply explored in the next chapter. Securely attached children appear to emerge from childhood with enhanced emotional flexibility, social functioning, and cognitive abilities. "Suboptimal attachment experiences may predispose a child to psychological vulnerability in par by altering the brain's neuroendocrine response to stress" (Siegel, 2001, p. 77).

Also, we will discuss the neurological deficiencies that are believed to be associated with those who have either *anxious/ambivalent attachment styles* or *avoidant attachment styles* and the prognosis for healing and developing those areas of the brain that allow us to attune with others is heartening. This is good news for those suffering from codependent behaviors. Recent research findings in *interpersonal neurobiology* (documenting the biological/physiological and structural changes in the brain due to interpersonal interactions) and the *contemplative practices* (various forms of meditation) are supporting the effectiveness of meditative types of therapies, informing us that changing our behaviors, thoughts, perceptions, and reactions will subsequently lead to positive changes in our brain and well-being that indicate a more integrated state (Siegel, 2001, 2011; Davidson, Kabat-Zinn, Schumacher, Rosenkranz, Muller, Santorelli, Urbanowski et al 2003; Davidson, 2008). An integrated state is associated with the ability to regulate one's emotional states, having more flexible responses, and greater complexity in behaviors.

Although people with codependent symptoms seem to have an intense desire for merger and reciprocation in relationships, a fear of intimacy is also apparent (Springer et al., 1998). Loughead et al (1998) described codependents as being disordered, avoidant and self-defeating in interrelationships. They are often compliant and self-sacrificing, entering into relationships that are likely to result in hurt and rejection. They appear to want relationships but at the same time are ambivalent about them.

Codependency increases the likelihood that the person will become involved with personality disordered, chemically dependent, other codependent and/or impulse-disordered individuals, which in turn increases the likelihood that enmeshment occurs (Cermak, 1986). The term *enmeshment* describes how those with codependency seem to have a need to orchestrate other's behaviors, but is in fact, efforts towards chaos control. Individuals with codependency are self-denigrating and question their own love-worthiness, making it difficult to trust or rely on others (Springer et al., 1998). They tend to have a strong physical attraction for their partner with intense jealousy and possessiveness accompanied by a fear of abandonment or feeling misunderstood. Considering what we know from *interpersonal neurobiological* research, we would expect this latter type of behavior as representing someone who has an insecure/ambivalent and/or avoidant attachment style (Siegel, 2001). In the brain, the development of some neuronal connections are experience-expectant" and some are "experience-dependent." The neuronal pathways that develop, specifically in the right hemisphere, require collaborative communication, reflective dialogue, repair of breaches to the connection with the caregiver, coherent narratives and emotional communication.

Arrested Ego Development

Cullen & Carr (1999) proposed that codependence represents arrested ego development. From a theoretical viewpoint, this implies that the individual is fixated at a particular stage of psychosocial development that impedes the degree to which one is able to engage in relationships of intimacy with a strong ego or sense of identity (Erikson, 1950).

As children, loving guidance and encouragement is needed to ensure the development of the ego strengths, or virtues, as described by Erik Erikson (1950). He believed that the ego strengths gained at each stage of psychosocial development were essential to later healthy adult well-being. When caregivers provide the type of nurturance that helps the child discover his or her individuality, the foundation is established that provides the kind of support that helps children to enter into healthy patterns of intra- and interrelating.

Healthy ego development requires awareness of personal boundaries. A firm sense of identity is achieved through a healthy inquiry into the values and ideologies learned as a child with a balance between the expression and restraint of the various ego strengths gained in earlier stages of psychosocial development.

Self-Consciousness

Codependents are extremely focused on that with is external to them. This type of focus results in what amounts to self-consciousness. Springer et al (1998) wrote,

> (The) portrait of the codependent is a person with low feelings of self-worth or self-acceptance. They feel little control over their interpersonal relationships and feel as though their interactions are guided by others or by external influences. They are very self-conscious, both publicly and privately and are thus aware of and sensitive to the opinions and reactions of others in social situations (p. 5).

One's awareness and sensitivity to the opinions and reactions of other people is self-consciousness. Self-consciousness can be of two types, private and public self-consciousness. In *private self-consciousness* one tends to focus on the personal facets of self and to have a greater awareness of internal processes than of social processes (Carver and Shaeier, 1985). *Public self-consciousness* describes a greater emphasis on the social aspects of self-identity and is characterized by extreme sensitivity to the opinions and reactions of others. Needing approval shapes behavior and perception stems from what others need and expect which increases anxiety about social rejection in the process (Springer et al., 1998). Being both privately and publicly self-conscious, codependents are hypervigilant to the cues of others which leads to actions that presumably help the codependent gain an increased sense of identity and worth (Cermak, 1986).

Shame Proneness and Lower Self-Esteem

Codependence is characterized by an inability to recognize and identify internal needs and emotional states. This results because codependence keeps a person so focused on the well being of others that the individual is not aware of what is personally meaningful. As discussed earlier, this external focus impedes the flowering of the internally based self and prevents learning what one feels or needs. Feelings are not merely covered up. They are not known.

In dysfunctional families, children grow up without a sense of being valued and validated for individuality. Parental approval takes precedence over being loved. The inability to have needs gratified in the family of origin results in a distorted sense of self worth (Springer et al., 1998). Personal feelings and needs become secondary to everyone else. Choices are made to alleviate discomfort for others, or to ensure that their needs and desires are met. The unfortunate result is a lowering of self-esteem because choices are based more on what one believes others need or want instead of reflecting one's inner truth (Springer et al., 1998).

Hogg and Frank (1992) wrote that "...shame may be the common affective experience underlying all addictive behaviors (p. 371)." Shame makes a person feel as if there is something inherently wrong with oneself. It prevents the free expression of inner emotions and perspective unique to individuality.

Shame differs from guilt because the latter is generally what is felt when we "do" something wrong. Guilt is evoked when one feels disapproval and the *act* is condemned, not the person. With shame, a person believes that the basic flaw resides within. It is a condition that cannot be changed simply through changing one's behavior (Whitfield, 1987). Shame becomes "who one is" and exacerbates a mistrust of oneself and others.

Love becomes reduced to simply being needed. According to this mindset, one cannot be lovable, so approval becomes the next best thing. When one is needed there is a possibility that approval can be earned but this is merely a substitute for love (Beattie, 1986). These early childhood patterns take on a compulsive nature in adulthood because each time the codependent is able to avert a crisis or is able to get one's partner to stop drinking or drugging, the sense of personal value gained in the situation is similar to a drug fix.

Post-Traumatic Stress Disorder

A diagnosis of post-traumatic stress disorder (PTSD) may be a viable description for codependence (Frank & Golden, 1992). Although the term, PTSD, was originally coined to describe the symptoms associated with the aftermath of severe trauma, such as rape, assault, combat, or natural disasters, the diagnosis is now being extended to other circumstances. There is growing evidence that PTSD can result from having lived with prolonged exposure to stressful situations, such as living with the danger or chaos that can be part of families with alcohol, drug, physical, or sexual abuse (Shapiro and Forrest, 1997).

PTSD symptoms, such as flashbacks, anxiety, nightmares, and an exaggerated startle response result because the memory has not been fully consolidated. It has been catalogued as "dangerous" by the amygdala so that each time the person encounters a similar situation or circumstance, the trauma response is repeated. Even a perceived sense of danger is enough to activate the sympathetic action.

The amygdala and hippocampus work together to determine if the current situation is dangerous or if it is similar to past experiences that were dangerous. In PTSD it appears that the memory was not fully consolidated into an explicit memory, but remains as an implicit memory with no frame of reference for when the actual danger was present. If it had been consolidated, the trauma would simply be a memory---in the past and no longer happening. When this happens, our brain reacts as if the anxiety-provoking situation is happening right now rather than sensing it as a memory. With this continued sympathetic arousal, depletion of valuable neurohormones and neurotransmitters is adversely affected that persists for life. In codependence, dysfunction in the family of origin and the constant vigilance to others learned in codependence creates a predisposition towards PTSD symptoms and characteristics.

Interrelationship and Intrarelationship Factors

The importance of interrelationships cannot be over emphasized. As Dan Siegel (2011) relates in his article, "Human connections create the neural connections from which the mind emerges" (p. 72). He describes the two basic processes that shape the developing mind, some of which are *experience-expectant* and the other *experience-dependent*. In the former, development depends upon minimally stimulating the circuits to maintain the neurons and their connections. However, in environments that are toxic, creating excessive stress on the child can lead to the elimination of existing synapses. In the "experience-dependent" conditions, the laying down of new neural circuits is dependent upon experience. We then understand that our brain structure is altered through both the maintenance and strengthening of existing synapses, or by the experience-driven creation of new synaptic connections (Siegel, 2011; Wegscheider-Cruse & Cruse (2012).

When a child grows up in a stressful dysfunctional family environment or does not experience the attuned types of communication and interactions that are necessary for the full development of the orbitalfrontal region of the brain (associated with our ability to regulate emotional and social functioning), we usually think in terms of *attachment* on a psychological level and believe that these children will have *anxious/ambivalent* or *avoidant attachment styles*. Recent research into epigenetics reveals that experience is the trigger that activates genes (Lipton & Bearhman, 2012). This contrasts with earlier depictions of how our genes are our destiny. There are optimal times during development when experiences will determine the unfolding of our genetic potential. For example, we know that there is a critical period for learning language and that without experiences in communicating with others, we cannot develop this potential. Similarly, without certain forms of verbal and non-verbal communication as we develop, our brain will lack the integration of the left/right hemispheric coherency that is necessary for socially attuned and compassionate interactions.

Interestingly enough, many parents have thought that they could optimize their babies chances in life by bombarding them with stimulating sounds, visions, etc. Yet Siegel (2001) reminds us that the

> The importance of the first years may be that brain structures that mediate social and emotional functioning begin to develop during this time in a manner that appears to be dependent upon interpersonal experiences…the orbitofrontal region, central for processes such as emotion regulation, empathy, and autobiographical memory may have experience-influenced development that depends upon the nature of interpersonal communication during the early years of life. Interactions with "older people," with attachment figures, are essential during this time to create the contingent, collaborative communication necessary for the proper emotional and social development of the child…(pp. 71-73).

We are finding that in regards to this deficiency, the plasticity of the brain allows for the creation of new neuronal connections and neural nets that are associated with better regulation of emotions and the ability to attune to others. We move into the plane of possibilities rather than staying stuck in habitual reactive patterns of behavior.

Codependence seems to be rooted in a faulty relationship to oneself that forms from the dynamics associated with living in a dysfunctional family (Springer et al., 1998). It is a way that an individual views oneself rather than characterizing a particular way of responding to others (Wells et al., 1999). The manner in which a child learns to focus upon the needs of others is adaptive but becomes a compulsive way of interacting that interferes with healthy interrelating. The person with codependent behaviors must learn how to relate with others based upon inner truth rather than simply being needed (Wells et al., 1999).

Gender Differences

Some considerations in regards to gender are needed in the assessment and treatment of codependence. The construct of codependence is not gender specific (Springer et al., 1998) but appears more often among females because addiction has been primarily a male problem (Favorini, 1995). Another reason for the greater prevalence of codependence among females may be due to expectation of gender appropriate behaviors, rearing practices, and social constraints that encourage females to exaggerate care-taking behaviors when problems arise in relationships. Females engage in more communal behaviors than do males who act more from a position of independence (Tannen, 1990). Communal behaviors emphasize connection and intimacy, more care taking of others, and giving more attention to the comfort and needs of others than to oneself. When taken to the extreme, these behaviors translate into a fair description of codependence. These ideas will be discussed in further detail in the next chapter where socio-cultural factors are examined to determine their contribution to the greater appearance of codependence in females.

A second consideration pertains to adolescent response to abusive parenting practices (Roehling, Koelbel, & Rutgers, 1996). Males tend to react to abuse by exhibiting antisocial behaviors. This may be due in part to expectations that males are to be tough and to not show emotions that may be interpreted as feminine. When these males are brought into the clinical setting they are generally diagnosed with conduct disorder. Females in the same type of familial circumstance generally respond in dependent, borderline, or narcissistic ways, which is congruent with expected gender role behaviors and codependence.

Males are also more likely to report codependent patterns under different circumstances than do females. Females tend to respond to lower levels of maternal support through codependent characteristics, while males are more likely to be codependent if higher levels of maternal support were experienced (Parker et al., 1996).

Endogenous and Exogenous Codependence

Codependence can stem from endogenous ("coming from within") or exogenous ("coming from outside oneself") conditions (Wright and Wright, 1999). The endogenous form of codependence is described as a personality syndrome in which the codependent is predisposed to forming and maintaining codependent relationships. With this form of codependence, one usually chooses a mate that fosters the expression of these codependent tendencies.

The term *endogenous* refers to the source of codependence as coming from "within" the individual that predisposes the person to act out in codependent ways regardless of the characteristics of the partner or the situation. Endogenous types tend to come from alcoholic or similarly dysfunctional families. The learned codependent pattern of relating makes it more likely that enmeshment will occur, eventually leading to an increased vulnerability towards codependent relating as an adult and a seeming preference for exploitative relationships (Mendenhall, 1989).

Endogenous types appear to have a disposition similar to the characteristics that are tapped when using the FSC assessment device. They are "not only vulnerable to becoming codependent relaters, they are likely to do so to the point of gravitating toward codependent-dependent relationships, or encouraging their development" (Wright et al., 1999, p. 539). They tend

> ...to become involved in repeated dysfunctional relationships...and have a more difficult time changing behavior and relationship patterns in response to therapy. They find it difficult to do things of particular enjoyment, interest or benefit to themselves alone, and have difficulty getting pleasure from relaxed, "non-serious" interaction (Wright et al., 1991, p. 443).

The exogenous type is seen as a complementary identity or role assumed in the course of a problematic relationship. It is a reactionary role that arises in order to cope. Family of origin dysfunction is not necessarily a part of the exogenous type of codependence, however. Exogenous types tend to have been reared in stable supportive homes that encouraged healthy interdependence and a communal orientation (Wright et al., 1999). They are socialized to be compassionate, cooperative, and concerned for the well being of others that perhaps leads to an increased "vulnerability to be manipulated into enabling and care taking roles vis à vis their respective partners, or…into assuming situated identities as inordinately responsible caretakers" (Wright et al., 1999, p. 539).

Endogenous codependence might be viewed as a more deep-seated form. Endogenous types tend to spend more time in therapy focusing upon past problems associated with the family of origin, although current relationship concerns are also discussed. Exogenous types tend to focus more solely upon contemporary relationships in therapy (Wright et al., 1999).

The term para-alcoholic was coined to describe the children brought or born into a dysfunctional environment. **Para-**refers to "like or resembling" whereas the prefix, **co-** describes the relationship of an adult to a user. The term "para-alcoholic" helps to describe the position in which children assume in these families and may therefore represent a more endogenous type of codependence.

♥

Chapter Two

Understanding Codependence

To better understand the development of codependent characteristics, it is helpful to examine personality development as explained in psychodynamic literature. According to this paradigm, behavior arises from the unconscious that drives the person towards the fulfillment of those needs. Freud (1938a) believed that basic human nature is in conflict with the demands of any given culture and society. He described human personality as a dynamic system constantly in motion seeking to reach a relative equilibrium among the needs of the individual, the demands and requirements of society, and the moral conscience of the person. When needs are not adequately met, anxiety results. Behavioral adaptations are strategies formed to address this anxiety.

An alternative explanation that provides additional insight into the roots of codependence comes from the sociocultural theory of Karen Horney (1966). She believed that all behaviors represent movements towards gaining a sense of safety. In a functional environment, one would learn to relate with others in a flexible manner. One's responses would depend upon the circumstances and allow for individual boundary establishment while simultaneously learning the mutual give and take of interacting. When the need for safety necessitates a rigid pattern of response, a child can learn an inflexible pattern of responding that derails this process. Although these behaviors may not consider the needs of the child, a semblance of safety is attained for the time being (Horney, 1966). As behavior that has been over learned, codependent relating begun in childhood is carried into adult interrelationships (O'Gorman, 1993).

Another early psychodynamic theorist, Alfred Adler (1957) believed that humans are motivated to strive towards better adaptation. This motivation comes from an intrinsic sense of inferiority that stems from being human. Human dependency characterizes each person's journey from infancy to death, with an inordinately long period of vulnerability in the early years of infancy and childhood. Adler (1957) saw this basic human condition as indicative of human vulnerability and inferiority in relation to other species. This vulnerability generates feelings of inferiority that motivate a person towards striving for perfection and better adaptation in the developmental process.

Basic feelings of inferiority can develop into an *inferiority complex* however, if one is abused, neglected, or pampered. Neglect and abuse send a message that one is either not worth caring about or that one deserves to be hurt. Pampering causes a similar deepening of a sense of inferiority because it leads to helplessness and insufficient autonomous striving. Without a strong ego, people often turn towards external sources of validation that bolster a sense of superiority.

Human need is motivated by needs for comfort, safety, and pleasure. A simultaneous drive to avoid pain and discomfort exists that compels a person to form adaptive responses and defense mechanisms to accommodate the circumstances imposed by family and

41

society. Behaviors assume a repetitive and compulsive nature when the strategies prove to be successful, regardless of whether these adaptive patterns are rational or not.

Anderson (1994) suggested, "The origins of the disease (of codependence) are thought to be found in early childhood, at which time such people learn a tendency to enter into addictive relationships" (p. 677). In a dysfunctional family, children quickly learn which behaviors result in anxiety reduction or escalation, thereby adapting to behaviors that help ensure survival. This adaptation prevents these children from identifying and expressing their own need for love, safety, warmth, and encouragement because survival is dependent upon damage control.

Much psychic energy is expended towards preventing chaos from erupting. The ability to moderate chaos in the family and to prevent the parents' displeasure, solidifies the strategies necessary for these children to survive. As these strategies serve to diminish the problems within the family, the children continue these survival strategies compulsively. Survival is not synonymous with healthy development, however, but the patterns are set and "functional" within the family of origin setting—they work.

Overall, psychodynamic theories point to the psychological needs that motivate human behavior. Dysfunctional family environments prevent the children from understanding and recognizing personal needs and feelings because survival seems dependent upon reading how others will react to any given situation. In some sense this causes underdevelopment of introspective skills because even when one checks within, it is generally framed in relation to how effective one is in helping and meeting others' needs.

Personality Disorders

Personality disorders are identified and described in the 5th edition of the Diagnostic and Statistical Manual of Mental Disorders (DSM-V). The many disorders that are described in the DSM are helpful in diagnosing psychological problems and provide statistical information about the populations in question. These criteria are also geared towards assisting clinicians to treat the behavioral problems as well. Where codependence is concerned, however, the treatment directions are not clear. If codependence is seen as a personality disorder this implies that one brings to the relationship tendencies that cause and exacerbate substance abuse behaviors in one's partner. This disease perspective has been criticized by feminists and others as a form of "victim blaming" and thus necessitates caution in applying this notion to explain codependence. Nevertheless, the five criteria listed by Cermak (1986) in the introductory chapter of this book are helpful in framing codependent behaviors, and are repeated here:

- Continued investment of self-esteem in the ability to influence/control feelings and behavior in self and others in the face of obvious adverse consequences for doing so.
- Assumption of responsibility for meeting others' needs.
- Anxiety and boundary distortions around intimacy and separation.
- Enmeshment in relationships with personality disordered, chemically dependent, other codependent and/or impulse disordered individuals.
- Three or more of the following: constriction of emotions, depression, hypervigilance, compulsions, anxiety, substance abuse, excessive denial, recurrent physical or sexual abuse, stress-related medical illness, and/or a primary relationship with an active substance abuser for at least two years.

Only modest support for the validity of these criteria has been provided through research. Although both anxiety and boundary distortions are present in both codependence and in some personality disorders, the continued investment of energy to control others in codependence was not substantiated in research conducted by Loughead, Spurlock and Ting (1998). To simply collapse codependence into a personality disorder may be an oversimplification of a more complex phenomenon (Loughhead et al., 1998). For example, Cermak believed that one symptom of codependence was that there is a significant distortion of one's will power that is not evidenced in Dependent Personality Disorder (DPD). Another personality disorder, Avoidant Personality Disorder (APD) is different from codependence because people with APD do not demonstrate the need to control feelings and behaviors or to control others as is symptomatic of codependence. Avoidant personality types also feel no need to socialize with others at work or to have significant interpersonal relationships.

Given these considerations, if the DSM is to be used to describe codependence, it may be best to classify it as a Personality Disorder Not Otherwise Specified (PDNOS). This classification is used when an individual does not qualify for a single personality diagnosis but demonstrates features that together cause clinically significant distress or impairment in relationships or functioning. Yet, much debate still rages over whether the construct (i.e., the symptoms taken together) of codependence is a valid category for the DSM. To date, no clear definition of the construct exists. Codependence is simply a list of characteristics that if take together represent a construct, but not necessarily a disorder.

As one examines the logic of categorizing codependence as a personality disorder it becomes questionable whether it is truly a personality trait gone awry. Personality traits are generally defined as enduring patterns of perceiving, relating to, and thinking about the environment and oneself that are exhibited in a wide range of social and personal contexts. These traits become personality disorders when they are inflexible and maladaptive, causing either significant impairment in social or occupational functioning or subjective distress.

There are problems associated with this perspective because it does not consider how cultural and societal restrictions serve to create behavioral anomalies. This position will be expanded upon in the next chapter where societal factors are considered in current understanding of the construct.

Codependence As Addiction

The emergence of codependence as a form of relationship addiction arose from clinicians working with the partners of substance abusers. Addicts are believed to behave in ways that are characterized by

> ...a lifestyle, a way of coping with the world...a way of interpreting...experience...(in which)...a progressive focusing of all attention on a target—an activity...preempts the expression of one's feelings (Capwell-Sowder, 1984, p. 19).

Van Den Bergh (1991) wrote,

> Addictions arise from a feeling of incompleteness and imperfection...(causing one to)...reach outside of (one)...self to external objects, persons, or situations which...provide a sense of wholeness and completion" (p. 3).

When a person grows up in a dysfunctional family, the inherent sense of inferiority that often develops increases the likelihood that one looks outside of the self to gain a sense of completeness. As outlined earlier, the origins of codependence can be traced back to early childhood. Growing up in a family atmosphere where invalidation, oppression and abuse are a component part of family life, predisposes one towards addictive

45

behaviors (Burris, 1999). Because of the oppression in these families, shame, low self-esteem, and feelings of inferiority motivate codependents to seek relationships in which feeling needed substitutes for feeling love.

Dysfunctional family systems are not very effective environments in which to learn problem solving or communication skills. Messner (1996) wrote that codependents tend to tolerate highly inappropriate behavior probably because boundary violations are familiar. Codependents generally don't recognize when another person has inappropriately crossed personal boundaries. Not recognizing that this has occurred can lead to unidentified feelings of anger, victimization, or guilt.

These early experiences help establish a pattern of a self-destructive attachment to others that often takes on an obsessive-compulsive nature. The thought that one can change or control another's behaviors through careful choices of one's behavior leads to the compulsive behavior that characterizes codependence. For example, if one can simply "make," "convince" or "get" one's partner to refrain from drinking or drugging, then the effect will be similar to getting a "fix" that alleviates anxiety. The codependent's arousal level abates and order is reestablished, at least temporarily. Codependents overreact to external stimuli and under-react to internal cues. This takes on the appearance of being hypervigilant to what others may or may not do. A codependent's behaviors are predicated upon the other person's response.

Because this pattern is familiar, it may be difficult for people to perceive the nature of their codependence.

> (C)odependents must understand how their own behavior and attitudes toward self have kept them in an addictive relationship....(E)nmeshed, enabling, and destructive relationships must be avoided....The hallmark trait is care-taking behavior—the codependent meets the needs of

another before meeting his or her own needs and will do this consistently (Favorini, 1995, p. 827-830).

Codependence prevents a person from being aware of personal needs, believing instead, that another's needs are synonymous with one's own needs. Relating to others in codependent ways happens when an individual assumes an excessive degree of responsibility for another and has been called *interpersonal addiction* (Peele and Brodsky, 1975). Whether codependence is a disease or an adaptation to problematic circumstances depends upon the theory one applies to the behaviors. What is most important are the factors taken into consideration when attempting to understand codependence.

Different points of view have been suggested in regards to the nature of codependence. Cermak (1986a) viewed codependence as a disease that one brought into relationships. Schaef (1987) saw it as a result of personality traits gone awry, while Gotham & Sher (1996) believed it was the result of an addiction prone society. Favorini (1995) felt that "the extension of the disease concept from addiction to codependency is inappropriate" (p. 828). The disease concept of codependence lacks supporting evidence. The other points of view do hold some value to our growing understanding of codependence. Codependent behaviors are learned behaviors and can be transmitted intergenerationally (Gayol, 2004).

Addiction is defined as a physiological process wherein tolerance results from continued use of an external source of chemicals, eventually creating a physiological dependence on the substance. Tolerance describes how the body adapts to certain substances, requiring increased amounts of the drug of choice as use continues. Addiction manifests when the use of a substance turns into abuse because of this physiological process.

47

Addiction is not limited to substance abuse, however. ***Process addictions*** describe people who act out compulsive behaviors in relation to people or experiences. Compulsive gambling, seeking sexual contact indiscriminately, and compulsive shopping or internet usage are being labeled as addictions. Wright and Wright (1991) suggested that codependence is at the core of all addictive behaviors.

Anderson (1997) believed that comparing codependence to substance abuse is not analogous.

> Process addictions…(are)…an interpersonal process that mimics drugs in its effects on people…Alcohol and drug use result in toxic effects of brain dysfunction distinct from compulsive behaviors like shopping" (Anderson, 1997, p. 678).

By extending the concept of addiction to codependence the compulsions of codependent behavior are better understood. As a process addiction, codependence represents being addicted to the addict or to relationships in general. By extending addiction to behavioral processes, such as the need for gambling or to shop, a more objective biological approach to understanding and treating addictions was created. In codependence, the behaviors acted out in relationships are attempts to alleviate anxiety in an obsessive-compulsive pattern that mimics the addictive process.

Recognizing that these processes are analogous to chemical addiction helps explain *why* one gets stuck and remains stuck in codependent patterns. Many of the beliefs that shape and sustain codependent action are outdated and unworkable yet continue because they worked in the past.

Anxiety in codependence is generated through habitual external focus upon elements in the environment that one feels must be controlled. This obsessive activity leads to actions aimed towards shaping or controlling others. Each time the need for control results in diverting an oncoming disaster, the codependent reacts physiologically as if a "fix" has been achieved. Anxiety is lowered.

Attachment Style, Codependence and Interpersonal Neurobiology

The following descriptions represent the various characteristics associated with descriptions of individuals who suffer from codependency and are not meant to label people negatively. Instead, this information can be useful to help individuals or clinicians to be more mindful when developing treatment plans.

The literature on codependence has characterized codependents as being anxious/ambivalent or avoidant in their attachment styles to others as adults (Springer et al., 1998). Attachment and loss were described as important variables in development that could foretell the manner in which a person was able to relate with others (Bowlby, 1969, 1973). Attachment to the primary caregiver is formed early in life and establishes the manner in which that child will relate to others as an adult. There are many situations that can influence attachment style, but disruptions to the continuity, presence, and availability of the caregiver can result in what are termed attachment disorders (Randolph, 1985).

The three styles of attachment have been described as secure, anxious/ambivalent, and avoidant attachment styles (Ainsworth, Blehar, Walters, & Wall, 1978). These styles were observed in a clinical observational study called the Strange Situation. Young children were observed as their mothers left them in the presence of a stranger. The child's initial reactions were observed as were the behaviors exhibited upon the return of the mother. Children who reacted in distressed ways when the mother left the room (e.g, crying, looking towards the door through which the mother departed) and, who later, approached the mother and allowed themselves to be held upon her return, were described as securely attached. *Secure* adults see themselves as liked by most people, easy to get to know, well intentioned, and good-hearted. Children who seemed somewhat disturbed when the mother left, but acted ambivalently when she returned were classified as ***anxious/ambivalent***. Ambivalent behavior was described as perhaps approaching her, but simultaneously appearing to be angry by hitting or pushing her away when the mother tried to console the child. Children who appeared to show no distress upon the departure of the mother and who showed no interest in her upon her return were described as ***avoidantly*** attached. Avoidant individuals fear intimacy, are jealous, and experience emotional swings. The avoidant type acts as if others are not important in life, yet, when in a primary relationship begins to act codependently.

Beattie (1987) wrote that people who act in codependent ways seem to have an extreme need to control others, are out of control, and attempt to control others but simultaneously deny that they do this. Anxious/ambivalent individuals tend to have an obsessive regard for their partners and an intense desire for merger and reciprocation. "More self-doubt, feeling misunderstood, and believing that most people are not as willing to commit, characterize codependence" (Springer et al., 1998). Anxious/ambivalent types reflect more clearly the obsessive/compulsive nature of codependence. Given what we are discovering about the neurobiology of attachment, these types of behaviors would be expected because suboptimal attachment experiences result in behavioral and neurological deficiencies that can be corrected through therapy and attuned communications that encourage integration of the neural structures of the orbital frontal cortex. It is believed that the orbital frontal region "plays a central role of the brain's ability to respond to changes in the internal or external environment with a flexibily adaptive range of behavioral or cognitive responses" (Siegel, 2001, p. 87).

The importance of *secure attachment* is becoming more evident as researchers learn more about *interpersonal neurobiology*. Dr. Dan Siegel (2001, 2011, 2012) professor at UCLA has spearheaded this vein of research that is revealing how certain types of interpersonal experiences during the early developmental years is essential to the formation of secure attachment of a child to its caregiver/parents. The child's sense of self is reflected in the interactions with the caregiver and when these interactions are consistent and mindful, the child "feels felt" and simultaneously learns how to attune to others. This is not new to the field of developmental psychology, but the neurobiological evidence is more recent. *Interpersonal neurobiology* is a term that Siegel applies to the study of the effects of interpersonal interactions and their effect on the brain's physiology and structure. We now know that without the presence of specific types of interactions, we are likely to develop an *anxious/ambivalent* or *avoidant attachment style* with our caregiver/parent(s). These essential factors include: 1) Collaborative Communication; 2) Reflective Dialogue; 3) Repair; 4) Coherent Narratives; and, 5) Emotional Communication.

Collaborative Communication

Collaborative communication that is contingent and attuned refers to such aspects as eye contact, facial expressions, tone of voice, bodily gestures, timing and intensity of responses between the caregiver and child. One can imagine the double messages that can interfere with healthy development of a child's core consciousness when body language reflects a far different message than the words being spoken.

Resonance between the caregiver and child creates a connecting environment that supports the development of a number of domains in childhood such as social, emotional and cognitive functioning. "Such collaboration may be essential in the creation of a coherent and autobiographical sense of self" (Siegel, 2001, p. 78).

Reflective Dialogue

Reflective dialogue helps a child learn skills essential to mindsight—verbally sharing of a focus or internal experience of each person in a dyad. This is where the parent or caregiver attempts to make sense of the signals sent by the child and then communicates this meaning. Sharing of this perceived meaning and the mental state of the caregiver involves emotions, perceptions, thoughts, intentions, memories, ideas, beliefs, and attitudes (Siegel, 2001, p. 79). We attune to others and then provide our own meaning to the situation. This helps our children learn the social skill of attuning to others, which helps them develop empathy. Reflecting upon the situation also helps children to make sense of their own internal experience as well.

Repair

Repair to disruptions in a relationship is healing. When there are breaches to the relationship, the efforts towards *repair* helps children understand that misunderstandings are simply a part of interrelationships. The caregiver needs to stay engaged with the child otherwise prolonged disconnection can lead to disconnections in collaborative communication. Children learn to make sense of disruptions and to create a sense of meaning by understanding one's own and another's mind.

Coherent Narratives

Coherent narratives form an autobiographical form of self-awareness. Through co-construction of narratives, children learn this tool for living that helps them understand both their internal and external worlds. It is interesting that the most robust predictor of a child's attachment style depends upon the nature of the parent's narrative of his or her own life. Those parents who have gaps to their narratives or whose autobiographical stories lack sufficient detail to include both positive and negative events, are likely to interact with their children in ways that impede secure attachment and instead fosters insecure/ambivalent attachment.

Emotional Communication

Emotional communication is the type of communication where positive emotional events are shared as well as negative emotional states without emotional abandonment. Children need to learn that although they or others may experience negative emotions, the relationship is such that the caregiver will stay engaged emotionally with the child.

These five elements are identified by Siegel (2001, 2012) as essential for the fostering of *secure attachment* in children. Understanding the neurobiological implications of insecure/ambivalent or avoidant attachment styles can guide clinicians to form appropriate treatments that will help ameliorate the symptoms of codependence while healing the underlying deficiencies in the person's experiences that can help restore the brain's capacity for fulfilling, complex, flexible and coherent states. The left hemisphere of the brain functions as the interpreter that seeks causal explanations in a linear and logical manner, while the right hemisphere mediates autonoetic (consciousness and the retrieval of autobiographical memory. Coherent narratives are proposed to be a product of left and right hemisphere processes (Siegel, p. 87).

Therapy that focuses on developing *mindsight* skills changes the physiology within the brain allowing for better emotional regulation and more attuned communications (Siegel, 2001, 2010). As we are learning, the brain's plasticity is not limited to when we are young but extends throughout our lives. With the development of greater *mindsight*—to be more objective, more observant, and more open—the areas of the brain that were not sufficiently integrated will develop connections that allow for a more coherent narrative and therefore, greater flexibility and complexity of behavior (Siegel, 2010, 2011, 2012).

The importance of these types of interpersonal interactions during development are emphasized by the following statement by Siegel (2001):

> With some neurological conditions, such as sensory impairment, caregivers may be especially challenged to provide the kind of connecting, collaborative communication that allows the child to "feel felt," make sense of the internal world of minds, and create the capacity for mindsight. In other situations, suboptimal caregiving may not have fostered the development of a coherent sense of a core or autobiographical self. We can view these situations as being the inadequate development of a coherent sense of another's mind within the mind of the child. Such interactions are "incoherent," and fail to facilitate the child's own integrative processes. The fundamental outcome of such nonintegrative states can be seen as an impairment in self-regulation (p. 87).

Arrested Psychosocial Development

Erik Erikson (1950) described healthy ego development as consisting of knowing who and when to trust, the ability to express one's will appropriately in the social context, to feel autonomous and competent within personal limits, and to have a solid sense of fidelity to a personal ideology. Without these necessary virtues, or ego strengths, the individual is more likely to have adapted to these psychosocial crises without successfully resolving the crisis of that developmental period and would therefore experience more frustration, dissatisfaction, ineffectiveness, and overall unhappiness than a person who adequately resolved these stages.

It may be helpful to see codependence as representing an unsuccessful resolution to the Eriksonian stage of adolescence—*identity versus role confusion.* This arrested development underlies the restrictive manner in which codependents relate to their own psyche because the ego-strength of *fidelity* had not been adequately developed. Fidelity is the ability to identify a personal ideology and is formed through active questioning of the values one has been taught by parents and society. When one achieves a firm sense of self through this process, entry into the next phase of psychosocial development of learning to love and to be loved is more likely to result in true intimacy rather than fusing or enmeshment.

Successful identity achievement requires that an individual progresses and resolves the crises of earlier stages (Erikson, 1950). The accumulation of the virtues, or ego strengths, achieved buttresses the ability to successfully resolve subsequent developmental crises. What appears to be arrested in the case of codependence is this ability to know and identify what is *mine* and what belongs to another. Erikson described this crisis in his fifth stage of development during adolescence. The successful resolution of the crisis of identity versus role confusion results in *fidelity*—the identification of one's values, beliefs, mores, and self. Without this ego strength intact, the individual is ill-equipped to handle the challenges presented in the later stages of adulthood.

Codependence becomes most apparent as one enters the young adult crisis of *intimacy versus isolation.* Erikson (1950) believed that successfully resolving this stage would result in the ego strength of *love,* which gives a person the capacity for intimacy. One can love without losing oneself and simultaneously feels loveable. When the crises of prior stages are not resolved adaptively, the subsequent adaptive resolution of later stages is compromised because of a weakened ego. Thus, an early formation of mistrust, shame, doubt, guilt and inferiority, all maladaptive resolutions to the earlier four stages, sets the stage for adult codependent relating.

Young adulthood challenges humans to achieve intimacy, or otherwise, suffer a sense of isolation. The search for identity during adolescence prepares one to achieve intimacy without losing oneself in the process. Fidelity gained in the adolescent stage provides a foundation of a personal ideology by which to live. Having a strong sense of one's uniqueness guides perception and values. This implies that entry into young adulthood requires a strong sense of identity, knowing who one is and what one believes. This helps demarcate one's personal boundaries.

This perspective helps point the way towards healing from codependence. It provides a tentative explanation for the work that needs to be done in order to move beyond codependence. Consideration needs to be given to the earlier ego strengths that were formed in the first four stages of development as well. To simply look at the ideology of a person without exploring the levels of adaptive resolve from the earlier stages may be insufficient to gain a complete understanding of the ego strengths to bolster for the codependent. When the challenges encountered on the road of development are reviewed, this recapitulation of our developmental history can provide a way to identify the ego strengths that need amplification.

Our Relationship to Ourselves

Self-esteem and the ability to value ourselves forms the foundation for the health of our *intrarelationship*, or our relationship to ourselves. Understanding our own needs, desires, temperament, and personality readies us to enter into relationships with the ability for telling our truth and revealing who we are. The basic self is

> directly related to how one resolves emotional conflict, especially with one's own parents....(It is) that part of a person that changes due to internal forces. The beliefs, opinions, convictions, and principles of the basic self are determined by intellectual reasoning and the capacity to project the consequences of one's actions (Fagan-Pryor and Haber, 1992, p. 25).

"Codependence is a form of learned helplessness and comprises a learned behavior system consisting of family traditions and rituals taught from one generation to the next" (O'Gorman, 1993, p. 200). As a child watches, observes and repeats the patterns of interaction within a dysfunctional family the basic self becomes impaired. Discipline that is inconsistent and behaviors that are punished or rewarded in a double-bind manner teaches a child to mistrust what is coming from within. One doesn't "follow those feelings, but rather, the actions of others...(and becomes)...dependent on what is outside (one)...self" (O'Gorman, 1993, pp. 205-206). These patterns are maintained because one invites the pain that is familiar in return for avoiding the discomfort of the unknown. The ability to predict, control, and "shape" reality gives a codependent a sense of value and feeling needed. Saving another person who is behaving badly, the codependent feels worthwhile. Codependents over-learn these adaptations of childhood (Beattie, 1987; Larsen, 1987).

Concern has been expressed that the term of codependence is a label that may not accurately describe what is occurring (Frank and Golden, 1992). It may be more useful to see codependent relating as adaptive responses to a social situation that are exacerbated by societal rules and expectations of gender roles.

> Terms like **posttraumatic stress disorder** are more illuminating and accurate in that they do not burden an already suffering human being with a slightly masochistic diagnosis suggesting complicity in one's own misery" (Frank et al., 1992, p. 6).

How codependence relates to PTSD can be understood by examining the characteristic conditions and symptoms of the disorder. Originally, PTSD was believed to culminate from having survived experiences of extreme trauma such as war, rape, or assault. More recent studies have indicated that this definition excluded too many other obvious sources of the disorder (Shapiro & Forrest, 1997). There is also evidence that physiological changes occur in response to perceived threats in the environment, whether those threats are imagined or real.

PTSD symptoms include nightmares, insomnia, increased vigilance and greater startle effect. This was mentioned earlier, but it bears repeating again. Being continually on-guard activates the autonomic functions of the sympathetic nervous system, which is that part of the nervous system that allows us to fight, freeze or flee when we anticipate danger. Because codependence generally arises from long-term exposure to high anxiety levels experienced in childhood, this creates sympathetic arousal that affects the overall "thermostat" of physiological arousal in the individual. This prolonged activation often leads to depletion of essential neurotransmitters and hormones that keep us feeling well. The codependent's extreme external focus and hypervigilance keeps the person stuck in this aroused state preventing the ability to turn inwards to perhaps hear the inner voice that needs attention.

New information about the neurological correlates to PTSD are helping clinicians form safe, effective and rapid treatment protocols using self help techniques such as Emotional Freedom Techniques (EFT) or Energy Psychology (see the chapter on **Work To Be Done**). We are learning that trauma that has not been sufficiently processed by the hippocampus and amygdala creates an *implicit* memory state for the trauma (Feinstein, 2005; Siegel, 2001). The memory is not fully processed so the amygdala establishes a connection between the activating stimulus and the anxiety experienced. This implies that the connection between the high anxiety state and any similar stimuli is enough to activate the sympathetic nervous system into action again. The person has no idea that this trigger comes from the past and that the danger/anxiety being experienced may be more a product of one's mind than the actual situation at hand because it feels as if the danger is present in the current situation. Our mind does not know the difference between its thoughts and the "reality" out there. If we think it is real, it is (Dispenza, 2008).

♥

Chapter Three

Society's Child

Codependence is primarily a self-diagnosed phenomenon that has come to be understood through its popularization as depicted in the media and self-help industry (Gemin, 1997).

> The mass-mediated discourse of codependency functions to help manufacture the idea of the codependent identity....The discourse of codependency is able to reproduce itself by means of a self-referential process in which the codependent identity serves both as a constitutive element and (has) an effect of a 'discursive formation' (Gemin, 1997, p. 251).

The self-help books that were published in the late 1980s by early writers of the construct, such as Wegscheider-Cruse (1984), Whitfield (1984), Woititz, (1984a), Subby (1984), Friel, Subby and Friel, (1984), and Beattie (1987) helped to establish the popular view of the nature of codependence. Collectively these authors described the patterns of behavior that were being labeled under the rubric of codependence. It was Beattie's (1987) book, *Codependent No More* that served to popularize the construct within the general population, eventually leading to the appearance of many self-diagnosed codependents appearing in the clinical setting for help. Codependence seemed to provide a viable conceptual container for understanding and working in troubled relationships, especially as it applied to chemical dependency (Gemin, 1997).

This growing concern prompted researchers to find answers to the etiology, characteristics, symptoms, and environmental influences associated with the construct. A systems approach in psychology implies that all members within a family unit act in complementary ways to keep the unit in balance. Using a systems approach to understanding chemical dependency, clinicians turned their focus of treatment away from the substance abusers and towards the partners and family members. Subsequently, researchers attempted to determine how these members contributed to the development and maintenance of the substance abuser's behaviors.

Peele and Brodsky (1975) as well as Van Den Berg (1991) outlined how living in a patriarchal, capitalistic society contributes to the development of addiction prone behaviors. In our society, social structures are hierarchical and power is distributed to each based upon conformity to that system. If a person is to be successful, one must learn how to fit into society by learning the ropes. Unfortunately, those ropes are equally available to all. Gotham and Sher (1996) wrote that codependence results from living in this type of society. Addictive behaviors result when blocked opportunities, discrimination, and prejudice keep us from accessing the services and benefits available to those who have power. Feelings of inadequacy and powerlessness result for those on the lower end of the power hierarchy. Addiction provides a means by which one can numb oneself.

As discussed in the last chapter, there are those who believe that codependence is a disease brought into relationships by the codependent who has developed personality traits gone awry (Cermak, 1987; Schaef, 1987). Feminist writers have criticized this perspective arguing that it lacks a more comprehensive look at society and the ways in which gender role expectations and societal structures contribute to codependence (Cowan & Warren, 1994; Gorden, 1997; Miller, 1986; Van Den Berg, 1991).

How Codependence Became Popular

The original literature on codependence was written primarily for clinicians working with substance abusers. To bring these notions to the general public, writers of self-help books compiled this less accessible clinical information to create self-help books for lay people and presented codependence as an individual problem within the person. It simultaneously promoted recovery as the sole responsibility of the codependent through participation in 12-Steps programs. Ironically, codependence emerges when we are in relationships, yet recovery is a solitary pursuit by the person identified as the codependent.

Labeling *interdependence*, or the need for other people in our lives, as part of the pathology of codependence fails to recognize that females are reared to emphasize relationships and to be caretakers of other's emotions (Uhle, 1994). This rearing tends to promote over functioning by females when they enter relationships because they have learned to feel responsible for others. Whether codependence refers to a problem of autonomy (Granello et al 1998), power (Cowan, Bommersbach, & Curtis, 1995), insecurity, learned helplessness (O'Gorman, 1993b), or personality (Cermak, 1986) is not clear because the problem is complex. Besides the consideration of individual and familial factors that contribute to the problem, we must also take into account how society and culture may exacerbate codependence development. Codependent behaviors can be seen as symptomatic of a more foundational problem that emerges from the way in which society is structured.

Context is essential to understanding the social dynamics that are an intrinsic part of codependence (Loring & Cowan, 1997). Gemin (1997) argued that even those opposed to the concept of codependence have contributed to the advancement and popularization of the construct by keeping it alive. By focusing on its nonexistence, codependence exists. Arguments both for and against the validity of codependence serve to perpetuate the current notions regarding the problem. It adds to the discourse being popularized that it represents a disease, is pathological, and is a condition over which the individual has no control.

Current treatment for codependence establishes that it is initially up to the codependent to change in order for other family members to stop their dysfunctional behaviors. By citing the causes and cure for codependence as being the responsibility of the individual suffering from the syndrome fails to address the interdependency of human situations (Collins, 1993; Miller, 1986). It discourages thinking outside an either/or parameter and limits the manner in which codependence is understood. By keeping the focus of cause and cure as the responsibility of the individual, the discourse co-opts sociopolitical criticism of its own premises (Faludi, 1991; Haaken, 1990).

Whether codependence is seen as a disease or as a means to detract attention away from investigating the sociocultural systems of oppression, both sides help to confine public consciousness to the view that codependency is an issue restricted to the realm of the individual. Gemin (1997) wrote,

> The term, codependence, can be seen as dysfunctional in that its discourse keeps its clients in a constant repair mode, simultaneously reinforcing the conditions for interpersonal insecurity by promoting anxiety and fear of others while at the same time promising future deliverance from this state of being. It is able to confer a sense of identity, albeit a dysfunctional one. People are not thought to "have" codependency, but are codependent... one is never deemed "recovered," but always in recovery....This serves to promote a culture of specialized therapeutic experts that struggle to maintain their elite status by continually coding what was once considered normal behavior as pathological, and thus in need of outside intervention (p. 262).

Thus, those who label themselves as "codependent" tend to see recovery as their personal responsibility. They are the source of their own problems. Is this a form of blaming the victim?

Patriarchy and the Addictive Society

The construct of codependence has evolved in a society that encourages and defines appropriate behaviors for each gender. Males are assigned the realm of logos and reason, whereas females are held responsible for the emotional aspects of relating. This translates into a tendency to approach situations from two different viewpoints. Whereas males tend to use logic and reason to procure results in work and relationships, females have a tendency to emphasize relational strategies such as nurturing, connectedness, and expressions of feelings. Femininity is generally defined as

> embodying emotionality, sensitivity, nurturance, and interdependence, whereas masculinity was seen as encompassing assertiveness, independence, dominance, and goal directedness (Hogg and Frank, 1992, p. 372).

Societal expectations contribute to addictive tendencies and a sense of helplessness by establishing expectations of conformity to specific gender appropriate roles and behaviors. For example, from a patriarchal viewpoint, having a strong sense of individuality is believed to be healthier than being relationship oriented. Given this stance, a codependent will only get better if she or he can develop autonomy and independence, which is actually more male-like behavior.

These differences in expectations for males and females create confusion in our attempt to analyze the roots of codependence. Females are reared to establish one set of gender appropriate characteristics, but when these behaviors are problematic, females must conform to being more male-like. This neglects the established relationship-oriented nature that is developed in most females.

By excluding how factors inherent in a patriarchal society contribute to notions of health or dysfunction, biases are perpetuated that may impede a better understanding of individual behavior and social phenomena. Moving beyond the realm of the individual to include the contributions of society and hierarchical thinking provides a more substantial foundation base from which to analyze the situation.

What is Normal Behavior?

Patriarchal definitions of psychological and behavioral health focus upon separation, independence, and autonomy as indicators of a fully functioning person (Collins, 1993; Cowan et al., 1994). These definitions are limiting for all because ideal masculine behavior is generally used as the standard by which all behaviors are measured. The expectations of feminine behaviors are male prescribed and defined with a strong preference for those qualities assigned to the dominant group because they represent the ideal (Van Den Berg, 1991). This may cause males to suppress their feelings, emotions, and "softer" side because it may be seen as "too feminine." For women, the result is to be devalued.

What is defined as feminine is often simply the opposite of what is considered desirable for males. Thus, if behaviors are seen as too different from the standardized norm, they are considered deviant. Predominantly patriarchal definitions give rise to patriarchal solutions that value one mode of behavior over its opposite.

In a patriarchal society, behaviors associated with masculinity are generally held in higher regard than behaviors that reflect femininity. In most cases, this is true whether the judgment comes from a male or a female. By dividing characteristics into feminine or masculine categories, a dichotomy is established that has psychological ramifications. We tend to prefer and judge more favorably those characteristics associated with the dominant group (i.e., males). Females are described in contrast to males. This creates a double-bind situation for females, however, because women are expected to conform to their assigned gender roles that are, by their very nature, a deviation from what is considered "normal."

It therefore becomes apparent that the standards used that measure psychological health in males may be inappropriate when applied to females (Zelvin, 1999). This is a major concern of feminist writers. Defining therapeutic strategies that do not incorporate the effects of socialized differences creates ineffective and biased solutions. When psychological health is at question, the male mode generally sets the pattern for measuring the elements that constitute health. When male standards define the nature of a healthy personality, behaviors that represent the opposite tendencies are seen less favorably.

Codependence and Subservience

Codependent relating is likened to the style of interrelating that is characteristic of individuals from nondominant groups in society, such as minorities and women. Behaviors characteristic of codependence are a consequence of inequality, rather than an individual pathology and originate from lack of power and access to resources as well. It represents the emotional condition of the oppressed and is an adaptation to subservience (Collins, 1993; Miller, 1986). Members of these groups tend to invest much energy into the success of making relationships work. They invest heavily to insure that the quality of relationships with members from dominant groups goes well, which reflects a need for self-protection. Because females form a minority class in society, they are generally more hypervigilant and tend to over-identify with others' feelings and needs instead of focusing upon their own personal needs. Some writers have advanced the idea that codependence is related to *pathological altruism* (McGrath & Oakley, 2011) which the authors define as "a dysfunctional empathic response, a displaced mutual aid endeavor in which the main defect is an inability to tolerate negative affect in the important other" (Mc Grath et al, 2011, p. 57).

Women have been socialized to use power in indirect and subtle ways that reflects low power in relationships (Loring et al., 1997; O'Neil & Egan, 1993). This indirect use of power is based on adaptation, compromise, appeasement and covert manipulation according to some writers (Haaken, 1990). Females stress intimacy and connection with others while males tend to seek status and independence (Tannen, 1990). These differences are formed in the early childhood milieus of the two genders.

By examining the types of games that boys and girls play, it becomes apparent that females are reared to establish symmetry in relationships while males strive to establish asymmetry or hierarchy. Females are elevating their second-class status in relation to males, but feminine behaviors are still viewed as less desirable than male related characteristics. This is demonstrated in the 12-Steps program where independence is seen as being qualitatively better than dependence.

When viewed through the eyes of patriarchy, being more concerned with interdependence, moving towards others to assure intimacy and connection, are behaviors of the *weak*. To be considered strong, the male-defined solution to being codependent is to be ultra independent. In other words, overextending oneself in attempts to connect with others can be remedied through separating from others, becoming more independent, and thus establishing greater autonomy from this viewpoint (Loring & Cowan, 1997).

When traditionally masculine behaviors are taken to the extreme, they are more closely associated with aggression, dominance, and independence. Their tendency will be to behave in more contradependent ways. *Contradependence* is "a behavioral tendency to separate oneself from others to prevent being emotionally hurt" (Andersen, 1992, p. 372). This may be due to the *vasopressin* that is secreted during sympathetic, or fight/flight, arousal in males (Lane, 2006). *Vasopressin* appears to induce males to become more aggressive towards other males. Contradependence may be the expression of the flight response during emotionally distressing events.

Females, in contrast, are more likely to become more nurturing, strive for greater interdependence, and exaggerate their care-taking role. They will do what they can to "fix" the relationship. Interestingly, when sympathetic arousal occurs in females, *oxytocin* is released, rather than *vasopressin*. *Oxytocin* has been called the "cuddling" chemical. It is what bonds a mother to her nursing infant. This may also explain a female's tendency to try to reestablish connection with another when the relationship has been breached. She wants to bond. To label these efforts as codependence is to blame women for carrying out their role too well. Females are at one end of the spectrum and tend to act in codependent ways while males are more prone to detach from others and act in contradependent ways.

From this perspective, both genders lean towards pathology when interrelationships become problematic. The difference lies in the direction that the two genders move in relation to others, but both exhibit an extreme form of expected gender-related behaviors. Male personality disorders reflect a tendency towards rebellion, aggression, and violence while females tend towards the behaviors generally associated with codependence. If codependence is to be understood without considering these differences, there is likely to be a negative impact upon the way addictions, including current definitions of codependence are framed, understood, and treated.

Whether it is appropriate to apply preferred masculine solutions to feminine tendencies is arguable. Lerner (1985) felt that society is more comfortable with women feeling inadequate, self-doubting, guilty, sick, and diseased than to empower women. By using male behavior as the normative standard for mental health, the concept of codependency pathologizes women for internalizing the female socialization message (Bruss & Glickauf-Hughes, 1997). Using labels such as codependence stigmatizes women who are attempting to do their best in relationships through behaviors learned in childhood. It has a discriminating effect and places the blame for unsatisfying relationships on the shoulders of a committed or loyal partner (Loring et al., 1997).

69

Feminists argue that a woman's desire to form connections represents strength rather than a pathological condition.

Who Has The Power?

Cowan et al (1995) saw codependency as a result of the inequitable power hierarchies inherent in American social structures. Hughes-Hammer, Martsolf, & Keller (1998b) recommended that future codependency research needs to focus on the relationship of codependence to power. Traditionally, power has referred to

> ...having the ability to mobilize others to accomplish things, having control over resources, and being able to get things done...influencing others without undue coercion....(There are) two types of power in...society: (a) 'power to' which refers to capacity, ability and implies freedom, and (b) 'power over,' or domination of others (O'Neil & Egan, 1993, p. 54).

Capitalistic societies are based on competition, power and status, which create an atmosphere where there will be a winner and many who lose (Van Den Bergh, 1991). Power, in this sense, is *power over* rather than *power to*. Those with less *power over* others are more likely to develop addictions as a means to cope or numb themselves to the inequities encountered in life.

Those who belong to lower status groups are expected to act in more compliant, sacrificing ways, especially in deference to those who belong to the higher status groups. Conformity is generally held in higher regard and is characteristic of patriarchal capitalism because it promotes the ability to control and to have power over others (Van Den Bergh, 1991). Among those who enjoy higher power and status are those who conform and adhere to societal expectations. People with lesser status generally find it more difficult to gain access to the resources that allow one to wield power in society-

-higher paying jobs, degrees of higher learning, and advancement in careers.

> ...frustration is engendered within capitalist patriarchy as individuals are taught to seek but are not able to acquire that which provides legitimacy and status. Psychologically, over time, that frustration can produce feelings of inferiority and an addiction can develop as a way to numb and deny a sense of powerlessness (Van Den Bergh, 1991, p.4).

In a patriarchal society, males have a clear power advantage, especially those who are not from a minority class. The layering of power in society forms unequal access to opportunities and resources in society. Those who wield more power attain greater dominance. O'Gorman (1993a) wrote, "From the dominant culture's perspective, feeling empathetic and compassionate is to suffer from ineffective thought and action, which jeopardizes one's chances for success" (p. 159).

As we have relied less upon an extended family system, we have become more dependent upon the members of our nuclear family. This puts a larger burden upon only a few people in our lives. Those people take on a more important role in our lives because we have fewer support systems in place to help us through the passages of life. Love, marriage and family come to be the most frequent objects of our addictions.

Peele et al (1975) wrote that a concept of addiction is needed that emphasizes how people interpret and organize their experience. The industrialization of society created circumstances that further encouraged the development of addiction-prone behaviors. Because "dependence (is) a part of an individual's daily experience...a sense of inadequacy and dependence on others (arises)" (Peele et al., 1975, p. 163). The loss of the extended family system, coupled with our increased dependence upon external sources in society, has created a perception that power exists *out there*. This has created a basic sense of impotence and self-empowerment often seems out of reach. Helplessness becomes the norm for many and permeates our interactions.

Addiction is not a chemical reaction, but an experience that grows out of a person's

> routinized subjective response to something that has special meaning...(One)...finds (it) so safe and reassuring that...(one)...cannot be without it. Addictions form from the habits of dependency one learns growing up in a culture that teaches a sense of personal inadequacy, a reliance on external bulwarks, and a preoccupation with the negative or painful rather than the positive or joyous (Peele et al., 1975, p. 6).

From this perspective, dependence is not created through the attributes of a substance such as a drug but forms because of the perspective we hold about our place in society. The layering of power and status in society creates fear and suspicion. We mistrust the system and the people in it. This fosters greater dependency upon our inner circle of friends and family that can translate into codependent behaviors.

Codependence may be more reflective of the problems within society than it is a problem within the individual (Miller, 1986). The structure of societal institutions within patriarchy teaches us that self-sufficiency is difficult to attain, if not impossible for some. One is always dependent upon the services or production of others. There are experts for every aspect of living imagined. With such a layering of power many are left feeling helpless to affect what is needed to thrive and grow in society — medical care, education, or economic stability. Dependency upon experts exacerbates an over reliance on others. People within a patriarchy are expected to seek out advice to accomplish the everyday aspects of living. What occurs in codependence can then be seen as a microcosm of the larger society.

♥

Chapter Four

Gender and Codependence

This is not a chapter on gender bashing. The information presented in this chapter is not meant to divide the two genders but is to help all of us understand the nature of how patriarchy affects both men and women. Similar to a feminist perspective, this chapter is written in the hopes of establishing a vision that promotes the feminist vision of

> nurturance of the self as well as concern with collective well-being. It...values...working collaboratively, collectively and cooperatively; valuing personal experiences, encouraging growth and development; caring for others; building supportive relationships as well as believing in the interconnectedness of people and events (Van Den Bergh, 1991, p. 5).

Contrary to the belief of many people in society, feminists do not view males as the source of the bias experienced in society. It is *patriarchy* that is the underlying problem. Patriarchy is defined as a form of social system in which males set the rules, laws and standards of that society. It is characterized by a rank-ordering of power where hierarchical dominant-subservient relationships are created. Power is vested to those who belong to the dominant group--primarily Caucasian males--while ethnic minorities and women belong to what is considered to be a subservient class. This unequal distribution of power makes addictions, such as codependence and substance abuse, more likely in our society, especially for females or minorities.

Societal structures perpetuate hierarchical perspectives regarding what is deemed normal or abnormal. It establishes which behaviors will be considered deviant. Those members from the upper echelon are able to set the standards and rules for society and thus have an integral hand in defining the characteristics that either lead or are equated with success. This ranking in society creates a situation where there are a few winners and many losers when it comes to economic and social success. The lucky ones have greater access to the rewards in society and therefore have more power. The remaining less lucky people understand that the differential treatment they experience in society is because of this hierarchical layering. They experience blocked access to opportunities and feel powerless. A sense of helplessness begins to permeate those in the lower ranks of society.

Labeling and Pathology

Rice (1996) wrote that the central characteristic shared by codependents is an excessive orientation to something or someone outside of oneself. Codependent behaviors appear to be a "positive impulse gone awry" (Krestan et al., 1990, p. 230). Van Wormer (1989) believed that females tend to become codependent more often than males because codependent behaviors represent an exaggeration of the female prescribed cultural role. These behaviors reflect what is expected of females. When comparing desired and undesired characteristics, both genders generally evaluate traditional feminine characteristics more negatively than those behaviors associated with masculine characteristics.

Gender related behaviors have been framed in such a way that to be more male-like is to be more normal. This is important when trying to understand how labeling creates the reality we perceive. If characteristics generally ascribed to masculinity are perceived as better (e.g., to be strong is better than to be seen as weak) then a false hierarchy is created that frames the way in which we view behaviors.

This is evidenced in the types of behaviors that are assumed as normal versus abnormal. It is seen as more normal for females to behave in more traditionally masculine ways than for males to behave in more traditionally feminine ways. As children it is okay for females to be "tomboys" but not okay for boys to be "sissies." Even the words we use to describe this reverse role assumption carries a stigma. Generally, girls are proud to be called tomboys, but most boys will feel degraded being called a sissy.

Society continues to value masculinity above femininity. Even when females behave in more masculine ways, they are not given equal value to a male performing the same task or reaching the same goal. Interestingly females are prone to attribute their success to luck while males take more personal responsibility for their achievements. Being a female in society creates results in differential treatment from both males and females. We all tend to prefer the descriptors that describe masculinity.

Although the definitions of femininity are compartmentalized to describe that female behaviors differ from male behaviors it also creates a separation of how we treat females. The dichotomy goes further than to simply describe the differences between males and females. If one side of the coin describes one gender, then the other side represents the other gender. Male/female. Strong/weak. Independent/dependent. Active/passive. Good/bad. Healthy/mental illness. The list could go on and on. The point here is that labels create division and restrict how we view others.

It also creates problems when clinicians apply these perceptions to understanding and treating individuals (Frank & Bland, 1992). We are in danger of creating a self-fulfilling prophecy that limits our choices when we blame or criticize behaviors by focusing on the behaviors of people without considering how our definitions have shaped our perceptions. Once behavior is labeled we generally dismiss other valid viewpoints and behaviors that could produce more positive change. Labeling behaviors in effect creates a perceptual lens that feminists fear distorts current understanding of the female psyche. Given current definitions of codependence, one does not merely act codependently; one *is* a codependent.

The limitations of language create a propensity to divide and differentiate in order to understand. While the dualities of language are descriptive in nature, they also serve to create boundaries around our perceptions (Wilber, 1979a). People and ideas that fit into our boundaries are considered acceptable but anything outside those parameters is seen as foreign or unacceptable. When language serves to dichotomize, the tendency to create good and bad categories arise as well. One polar end is described as healthy and normal and the opposite is viewed as unhealthy and abnormal.

Society expects us to conform to gender standards and parents follow these standards so that we can *fit in* when we become adults. Girls are taught that to be a woman she must learn to be caring and nurturing. Boys are taught to be strong and independent. As adults this often translates into women focusing more on empowering others, helping them build their inner strength, and resources while males tend to focus more on establishing independence from others and moving up the corporate ladder.

Learning the expected qualities of being female--nurturance, interdependence, caring, sensitivity, and emotionality--condition women to be care takers. What we usually consider as normal and appropriate behaviors for females may turn into *too much* nurturing and care taking in the case of codependence. These behaviors then become labeled as "enmeshment, enabling, controlling, and dependent with feelings of extreme responsibility for others."

> It might be better to conceptual codependency as dysfunctional behaviors to identify, rather than a disorder to diagnose. A person might exhibit codependent behaviors, rather than suffer from codependency per se. Such an individual might have a diagnosable mental disorder, but codependency itself would be subsumed under a larger rubric. Also, any given individual might exhibit codependent behaviors in one or more relationships, but not in others (Mc Grath et al, 2011, p. 53).

Familial Structures

Another concept that needs scrutiny is the idea that there is some inherent difference between a functional family and a dysfunctional one. We all claim to have been reared in one type or the other but when we examine the nature of these two types of families an interesting thing happens. We find that our assumptions about what is functional or dysfunctional are culture bound and that they reflect predominantly white, middle or upper class values (Krestan et al., 1990). What is seen as indicative of the normal family structure in heterosexual relationships is actually a codependent structure. In other words, a **functional** family is largely mythical and presumes a family power arrangement that…was never functional. The roles, rules and communication that exist within a larger context of gross power imbalance between men and women are in itself dysfunctional. The mythology about what constitutes a normal family gives rise to the notion that not living in one causes codependence (Krestan et al, 1990, pp. 221-222).

This may explain why many family researchers have noted that an unusually high percentage of people (estimates are about 97%) came from dysfunctional families. Statistically speaking, the dysfunctional family is the norm while a "functional" family would therefore represent a deviation from what is "normal."

When problems arise in families it is generally the female who assumes responsibility for the emotional aspects of resolving issues. Taken to the extreme in difficult circumstances this female role can be called "enabling" or "care taking," terms associated with codependence. Women's power is more covert in the family unit where

women are socialized to be emotionally central in the family, codependent, and responsible for relationships….(T)hey automatically take the emotional responsibility for explaining and interpreting the men to the children, thus maintaining the men's inability to deal with emotional relationships (Krestan et al., 1990, pp. 223-224).

According to some writers, codependence describes the emotional condition of an oppressed group and is an adaptation to subservience more so than representing a pathological condition. Women have struggled to gain the rights and privileges that males have been afforded. The Woman's Movement began much earlier than the 1960's. To better understand why codependence may be more of a social and political problem than it is an individual one comes from an historical examination of woman's place in society.

Much of history recounts women's dependence upon males for economic security and social standing. The right to vote was a crucial step in helping women achieve a voice in society. To live in a society where women were not allowed to vote meant that the laws that governed their lives were made without their input. Changes had to be made that helped females out of their economic plight.

The hierarchical nature of male and female roles has resulted in power inequities on many levels. These inequities have led to adaptation, compromise, appeasement and often, covert manipulation on the part of females (Haaken, 1990). Women have had to do what they needed to do in order to survive in a society that did not give then equal status. When it came to love, their choices were predicated heavily upon economic security.

Women have learned that their power must be used in indirect and subtle ways (O'Neil & Egan, 1993). As in the animal kingdom submissive behaviors denote subservience to a more dominant animal. As lower status citizens, females have learned to be hyper-vigilant to the cues of others so that they can determine the emotional climate of a situation. They can then choose the appropriate feminine response to the circumstances. "Males do codependent things; women are codependent" (Krestan et al., 1990, p. 225).

Ironically, women have readily used the term of codependence to describe the interpersonal pressures they feel in relationships. Women are supposed to care for others, aren't they? Feeling emotionally overwhelmed in relationships, the description of codependence provided relief for many people who didn't understand why their relationships weren't working, but the price of taking on this label results in self-criticism and self-blame (Frank & Bland, 1992). Women blame themselves for being the caretaker (it looks like they are being too controlling). So for women the exact behaviors that are expected of them by society reaches a point where it is now "too much." Women become unsure of what society expects of them.

The standard for mental health in the United States has long been associated with the masculine stereotype of an autonomous, individuated, separate self—quite the opposite of the typical feminine role. "The frustrations of non-reciprocity in a relationship may make it easier to assign a codependency label to one's self rather than to recognize inequality in a relationship" (Loring et al., 1997, p. 122).

It seems imperative that the underlying social and cultural dynamics regarding definitions of normality need to be scrutinized more carefully. The popularization and evolution of the term of codependence may be nothing more than a diversion away from social inequities that arise from traditional attitudes towards females (Mastronardi, 1995; Jimenez, 1997; O'Gorman, 1993; Van Den Bergh, 1991).

Some writers propose that it would be more useful to see codependence as a problem between two people where one person is **under-functioning** while the other partner is **over-functioning**. This perspective could lead to a partnership wherein both people are accountable for the problems in their relationship and therefore in the resolution.

Gender and the DSM

The *Diagnostic and Statistical Manual of Mental Disorders* (DSM) was developed in 1952 to address some of the concerns that arose from using the earlier classification scheme found in the *International Statistical Classification of Diseases (ICD)*. The criteria were established by the American Psychiatric Association and outlined the behaviors considered pathological. Subsequent editions of the DSM, DSM-II (APA, 1968),

DSM-III (APA, 1980), DSM-III-R (APA, 1987), and DSM-IV (1994) were attempts to establish more consistent diagnoses for treatment and research purposes. Most recently, in May 2013 the DSM-V was released with a new organizational structure that will align the manual so that it is more in harmony with the ICD, which is the manual used by physicians. Developers of the DSM-V felt that most people first seek help with their physician rather than with a psychiatrist and by aligning the DSM-V with the current ICD, it would facilitate diagnoses and follow-up care. Controversy roils over this alignment, however, and time will tell if this new organization of the DSM will facilitate or hamper clinicians to effectively reach and help others.

Up until the latest edition of the DSM, dysfunctional behaviors were categorized into two major axis categories with three additional axes, or categories, to help psychologists diagnose and prepare treatment plans. These diagnostic categories allowed the medical profession to classify disordered behavior into a standardized "language" understood by those involved in the mental health profession and simultaneously established diagnostic categories to assist insurance companies stipulate conditions of reimbursement or coverage for medical claims. Each diagnostic category specified the duration, symptoms, etiology and treatment protocols to consider when determining pathology.

Gender Bias

Through its historical use and establishment, the DSM has provided clinicians with a valuable diagnostic tool, but at the same time has implied an element of pathology to those behaviors described. Szasz (1978) proposed that mental illness is a fabrication developed to establish and perpetuate a hierarchical position between those being diagnosed and those doing the diagnosing.

Endemic with problems of sociocultural and psychological significance, established categories in the DSM provide a functional value to the mental health profession while concurrently perpetuating some myths about mental illness.

Wetzel (1991) pointed out that the DSM has historically discriminated against women and ignores the possibility of social change. Wetzel (1991) also stated that the development of these manuals had

> more to do with power and money than with altruism and the pursuit of knowledge...by linking third-party insurance payments to diagnostic categories found only in the DSM, psychiatry, a profession that has the smallest membership with the highest rate of pay, has ensured its power. All symptoms must be categorized as diseases of some sort to meet the criteria of insurance companies and the right to establish such categories is bestowed solely on the medical profession. Although psychiatrists, on average, have the least educational training in psychosocial diagnosis and treatment, they retain the sole power to diagnose (p. 14).

In the earlier classification system with five axes used to diagnose mental disorders, *Personality Disorders* were listed under Axis II along with *Intellectual Disabilities*. This has changed with the publication of the DSM-V. *Personality Disorders* are now grouped on an equal level with other diagnostic categories such as schizophrenia, depressive disorders and anxiety disorders to name a few and the axes system has been eliminated.

Of the ten *personality disorders* listed in the DSM-V, most of the diagnostic categories are descriptive of expected feminine behaviors carried out to the extreme. Only one personality disorder, *antisocial personality disorder* is generally assigned to males. For females, the very behaviors instilled in them as children will be considered to be pathological if codependency is listed as a *Personality Disorder*. It has not reached this status, however. In fact, great debate continues whether codependence should be regarded as a bona fide disorder although efforts are being made to measure the construct (Dear, 2002; Dear, 2004; Dear & Roberts, 2000). Is it more than simply a set of behaviors acted out in trying circumstances? No scientific validation for the construct of codependence has been attained therefore caution must be taken when we talk about codependence as if it is a real "syndrome," "disease," "personality disorder" or whatever term you have heard applied to these types of behaviors in relationships. Researchers are concerned that this line of thinking perpetuates an unfair bias towards females by diverting attention away from the social circumstances that encourage and sustain these behaviors in females (Burris, 1999; Favorini, 1995; Roehling, Koelbel, & Rutgers, 1996).

The DSM categories have been established within the historical context of the changing nature of acceptable standards of behavior for each gender group. The evolving norms concerning which behaviors are appropriate for women can be determined by looking at the trends of psychiatric thought. The social relations of power are reproduced through this avenue of inquiry.

> Normative values about gender roles are linked to ideas about mental disorders in women…(T)he work of feminist theorists since the early seventies…(cite)…that one reason women have higher treatment rates for mental illness is that masculine-biased assumption about healthy (male) and 'crazy' (female) behaviors continue to be codified in diagnostic criteria. Behaving in feminine stereotyped manner alone will earn a…diagnosis, such as Dependent Personality Disorder or Histrionic Personality Disorder (Wetzel, 1991, p. 12).

The word *hysteria* was an early gender biased term that meant, "the disease of the wandering womb" (Jimenez, 1997, p. 12). Hysteria is and has been an exclusively female disorder used to label undesirable personality characteristics especially when they were seen as exaggerated feminine responses. Another personality disorder, *Histrionic Personality Disorder*, was originally called hysteria. The term was relatively ignored from the 1930's-mid 1960's. Since the 1940's, the term *borderline* was used to describe persons who are thought to be on the borderline between psychosis and neurosis. *Borderline Personality Disorder* (BPD) replaced the classification of hysteria in the DSM-III (1980). BPD became an Axis II category classification at that time and captured "contemporary values about appropriate behavior for women." Seventy-six percent of borderline diagnoses are women.

Renewed interest in the use of the term of *hysteria* arose in the 1960's. It emerged in the midst of the beginnings of the feminist movement and the fight for changes in gender roles and expectations. "The reintroduction of hysteria signaled an effort to return to a more traditional conception of women's roles" (Jimenez, 1997, p. 156). Modern hysteria of the 60's-70's was characterized by the old 19th century descriptions of hysteria with "excitability, emotional instability, over-reactivity and self dramatization" as key features (Jimenez, 1997, p. 156). *Dependent Personality Disorder* depicted behaviors such as "attention seeking, seductive, immature, self-centered, vain...and dependent on others" (Jimenez, 1997, p. 157). Some argued that hysteria was the female manifestation of the male sociopath.

Jimenez (1997) wrote that the DSM classifications served to blame women for their failure to gain equality in society. One such classification, Self-Defeating Personality Disorder, known earlier as Masochistic Personality Disorder

> describes what feminist have documented as the transient effects of battering or sexual assault on women's functioning...(which)...conveys the implicit belief that women's failures are due to an inherent masochistic characterological defect that prevents them from using the power that this 'egalitarian' society...provides them (Jimenez, 1997, p. 16).

There is no agreement as to which DSM category should be applied to codependence (Wells, Glickauf-Hughes, & Bruss, 1998; Wells, Glickauf-Hughes, & Jones, 1999). Problems and weaknesses of personality disorder classifications continue to exist. Diagnostic categories in the DSM not only describe symptoms of various disorders but propose treatment protocols as well. Because personality disorders are notoriously difficult to treat successfully, including codependence as a personality disorder does nothing to direct clinicians about how to successfully treat the condition and instead, perpetuates the bias against females and femininity.

In the second edition of this book I wrote that this bias was being perpetuated once again with the push to include premenstrual syndrome (PMS) as a new diagnostic category in that 1994 revision to the DSM-IV-TR. PMS is also known as *late luteal dysphoric disorder* and *premenstrual dysphoric disorder* (PMDD). Feminists fought to stop the inclusion in that revision of the DSM while proponents argued that including it would help women who are seeking treatment although no effective psychiatric treatment has yet been identified for PMS (Jimenez, 1997).

> The fragmentation of symptoms into an array of labels has rendered the reality of women's shared experience invisible long before the DSM was published. It is interesting, if not appalling, to recognize that yesteryear's neurasthenia, hysteria, melancholia, and even schizophrenia share common symptoms with today's depression, anxiety disorder, borderline and narcissistic personality disorders, agoraphobia, eating disorders (anorexia and bulimia), posttraumatic stress disorder, psychosomatic behavior, burnout from care giving, teenage pregnancy, alcoholism and codependency (Wetzel, 1991, p. 18).

Although it was not included in the DSM-IV it was added to the appendix of that revision for "conditions for further study." It was elevated to a new diagnostic category in the DSM-V and is now listed as ***Premenstrual Dysphoric Disorder***. This raises more concern that what is a medical condition for most women will now be presented and treated as a mental disorder if a woman experiences 5 of the 11 symptoms of impairment one week prior to her menstruation. No doubt this will impact the number of women who want to seek relief from premenstrual symptoms but fear that they may receive a psychological diagnosis at the same time! Diagnosis and treatment from a patriarchal perspective do not address concerns about gender bias. By using criteria that unfairly target one group (females in this case) without substantial evidence that it is a behavioral anomaly is to ignore that the female experience differs greatly from the male experience in society.

Perhaps the biggest concern of the expansion of categories in the DSM is its alignment with the International Classification of Diseases (ICD-11) used by the World Health Organization (WHO). This creates compatibility between the two systems, but many are concerned that this push is not in the interest of those who suffer from mental challenges but more in the interest of the pharmaceutical companies that develop expensive drugs to treat these disorders. Ironically, there are disorders listed in the DSM that used to be seen as simply behaviors that are a part of being human--part of being a child--part of growing up. Now we see behaviors that we don't want to deal with as behaviors that we can control through chemistry. Scary.

♥

Chapter Five

12-Step Program and Recovery

The primary model guiding codependence treatment is fashioned after the 12-Step model for alcohol recovery. The 12-Steps is a spiritual program of recovery. It is not a religious program because it has no religious affiliation. It is "...a program that helps us to discover the spiritual part of ourselves and recognize its importance in our lives" (Friends in Recovery, 1987). Originally formed to assist alcoholics in recovery, the 12-Steps have been used to assist other groups affected by alcohol or dysfunction, such as Alanon or Alateen. Recovery begins by working the steps of the program one by one in a self-paced program that is loosely structured. Groups that follow the 12-Step model are not led by professional therapists, but are conducted by the members of the group who are experienced 'recovering' addicts, or family members, who have worked through the 12-Step program themselves.

The 12-Step Model is presented below with some annotation and discussion, but keep in mind that this is only one model of addressing codependence and is not the model that is emphasized for healing in this book. It is not within the scope of this book to present the entire process within the 12-Steps, but to simply describe the steps. The thesis of this book is to provide a model that moves one beyond recovery and into healing from codependent relating. Although the 12-Steps program has been very helpful for many people in recovery, it promotes just that—recovery and not necessarily healing. Healing entails a complete understanding and awakening to our full potential without giving ourselves up to another "power." Neither does it perpetuate the notion that codependence is a disease that one "has," thus shattering the idea that a person suffering from codependence is responsible for the problems experienced in relationships. As we will learn, the road to healing is to heal the relationship that we have with ourselves. Learning how this condition of codependency comes about empowers us to understand and effect the changes in perception, attitude, and behavior that will lead to changing the ways in which one relates to others while also facilitating an integrative process in the brain.

12-Steps Model of Recovery

Following are the twelve steps of the recovery model for codependence, based upon the 12-steps for recovery from alcoholism. Unlike most therapy groups, 12-Step groups are not led by professionals, but instead are led by members, usually with a long-term member leading the meeting. The 12-Step groups have been very useful for many working with codependence, giving them the first steps towards healing, but this model believes that one is never fully recovered, but always *in recovery*. The steps are presented first followed by a discussion about the appropriateness of these groups for both genders.

Step One

We admitted we were powerless over the effects of alcoholism—that our lives had become unmanageable.

> The road to recovery beings with surrender...Step One consists of two distinct parts: (1) The admission that we have an obsessive desire to control and that we are experiencing the effects of an addictive process that has rendered us powerless over our own behavior; and (2) The admission that our lives have been, are now, and will continue to be unmanageable by us alone (Friends in Recovery, 1987, p. 2).

This step involves total surrender of the belief that you can successfully manage your own life. It is difficult for many to take this first step because in American society we are taught to be responsible adults in full control of everything (Friends in Recovery, 1987). When the first step is achieved, self-described "codependents" learn to be more objective about their own behaviors, dropping the disguises that have been assumed over the years, and becoming more honest with themselves.

Step Two

Came to realize that a power greater than ourselves could restore us to sanity. This has been called the Hope Step and provides a foundation for the spiritual growth necessary to attain recovery. There are two problems generally associated with this step. First of all, you must believe that there is a power greater than you. Some people find it difficult to let go of the control that has ruled the way they have lived their lives.

> Letting go of one's will allows for the unconscious to take over...assisting, empowering, and doing things for us that we could not possibly manage ourselves... In order to make changes in our lives, we must be willing to look at ourselves honestly and recognize our own degree of insanity (Friends in Recovery, 1987, pp. 7-8).

The second problem associated with this second step is that you have to admit to having been *insane*...out of your mind. Without this admission sanity cannot be "restored." This step presumes that the behaviors of codependence stem from your own character defects and "insane" way of being in the world. It doesn't account for the circumstances in which you have been reared or for the blocked opportunities encountered on the road to independence. Step two does not account for having lived in a dysfunctional family environment or for not having learned to identify our own needs so that we could make good choices, assuring that our needs were met.

Step Three

Made a decision to turn our will and our lives over to the care of God as we understood him. The slogan, "Let Go and Let God" expresses this tenet of the 12-Steps. This act of total surrender is believed to allow a person to stop feeling so responsible for everything and everyone. To let go implies that we must surrender our power (but did we ever have it so we could let it go?).

Step Four

Made a searching and fearless moral inventory of ourselves. This inventory is not a history but "relates to what is on hand at the moment...a list of things in stock now and does not concern what was there in the past (Friends in Recovery, 1987, p. 18). Judgment is not a part of this list but is a process wherein you discover the underlying ideas, beliefs and attitudes that determine your behaviors. The list consists of both our strengths and weaknesses. Because denial is a primary factor in codependence, this inventory helps penetrate the denial system that has kept a person from discovering the real underlying personal feelings within.

Step Five

Admitted to God, to ourselves and to another human being the exact nature of our wrongs. This step helps codependents to "move out of isolation and loneliness... (and)...towards wholeness, happiness, and a real sense of gratitude. It questions our humility" (Friends in Recovery, 1987, p. 38). Through sharing with another what we are learning to admit about ourselves, recovery progresses. The core issue of the fifth step is to determine the person's willingness to change.

Step Six

Were entirely ready to have God remove all these defects of character. Throughout the first five steps, codependents "inadvertently (have) begun to experience confidence in the ongoing process of working and living the Steps one day at a time" (Friends in Recovery, 1987, p. 42). The sixth step teaches a person to "let go, and let God" take care of the character defects that have caused the unhappiness of being codependent. By expressing our humility we can allow our character defects to be removed by a higher power (assuming these were character defects to begin with).

Step Seven

Humbly asked him to remove our shortcomings. Humility is seen as the foundation principle of the 12-Steps and allows a movement away from being self-centered to being self-less. Through humility, one can become peaceful, serene and happy according to this literature. This is achieved through "accept(ing) things as they are when we cannot change them and to ask God for the courage to change the things we can" (Friends in Recovery, 1987, p. 46). When character defects have been removed, the remaining traits are believed to be an essential part of our personality that will be changed into positive traits by our higher power.

A problem with this step is that it again assumes personal culpability for the problems you experience. It assumes that one is self-centered, which is not an accurate reflection of the problem of codependence. Most codependents have never been able to discover their own feelings but have been more concerned and focused on others' feelings. Perhaps it would be more useful to describe the movement from "self-centered to being self-less" differently. To be more in line with codependence research would require a statement such as *learning to be more self-loving and being less concerned with pleasing others.*

Step Eight

Made a list of all persons we had harmed, and became willing to make amends to them all. In this step, as a codependent, we must list past misdeeds, the dates and names of those involved. This step is aimed at helping us forgive ourselves. Secondarily, it teaches forgivenesss. Forgiveness allows a person to overcome any guilt, resentment, shame, low self-worth, or fear of others.

These feelings have kept people suffering from codependent behaviors locked into a cycle of self-loathing and a fear of authority figures. It teaches us to be more relaxed with our self expectations. Resentments and grudges are acknowledged and released helping us to learn tolerance and flexibility, especially towards ourselves.

Step Nine

Made direct amends to such people wherever possible, except when to do so would injure them or others. This is an action step. The willingness to make amends captures the readiness to accept the consequences of our past (Friends in Recovery, 1987). By naming and making amends we learn to let go of the past so we can begin to live in the present.

Step Ten

Continued to take personal inventory and, when we were wrong, promptly admitted it. Step ten is considered as the beginning of the growth stages of the program. Where the first nine steps represented a cleansing process, the last three steps address maintenance, sustenance and growth. As progression in recovery continues, we may be tempted to believe that a cure has been actualized. People in recovery are likely to begin missing recovery meetings or may feel that they no longer need to work the 12-Steps. Step 10 reminds us that the work is never done in recovery but must become a daily part of our spiritual development.

Step Eleven

Sought through prayer and meditation to improve our conscious contact with God as we understood him, praying only for knowledge of his will for us and for the power to carry that out. Having the courage and strength for doing the work required of the 12-Steps comes from developing a stronger relationship with your own higher power. The eleventh step focuses "on the daily process that is necessary for...spiritual awakening...(that)... comes when we know there is a Higher Power that has been taking care of our wills and our lives when we know and we can depend on that Higher Power to run the show from now on" (Friends in Recovery, 1987, p. 72). It suggests the ways we can improve conscious contact with God as we understand this higher power. This step outlines those things that can help in our spiritual awakening such as "Ask(ing) God to direct our thoughts and actions...for inspiration and guidance...for clear, intuitive answers, for freedom from self will...(W)e pray for nothing else except His will and the courage to go forward and do what He makes us want to do" (Friends in Recovery, 1987, pp. 74-75). This step implies that the issue underlying codependence has been our rampant will and that to let it go and be free of our inner drives, we can progress upon the path of recovery.

Step Twelve

Having a spiritual awakening as the result of these steps, we tried to carry this message to others, and to practice these principles in all our affairs. When a person reaches this step in the program consciousness has changed sufficiently to allow for changes to happen. By carrying on the work of the 12-Steps to others, the work that was done in the first eleven steps is facilitated and strengthened. The spiritual awakening process helps a person to "become more lovable, make friends more easily, and feel more comfortable with people.... (R)elationships with...families improve. We no longer have unrealistic expectations of ourselves, and we accept ourselves for who we are" (Friends in Recovery, 1987, p. 80). Telling our story to others and sharing how the 12-Steps have helped to transform our lives encourages others who also seek help to recover from codependence.

The 12-Steps help those who want to recover from codependence by providing an ongoing workable format to maintain recovery. The work of recovery is never done but is a lifelong process.

Applauding the 12-Steps

Writers have applauded the 12-Steps for the spiritual nature of the program (Miller, 1998; O'Gorman, 1993b; Shockley, 1994; Van Den Bergh, 1991). Recovery from codependence requires that we each address the deeper spiritual issues that underlie our codependence. A spiritual focus represents an important route to recovery by honing in on the broader issues of meaning and character.

Being spiritual is not the same as being religious. "Spirituality focuses on transcendence and defies customary conceptual boundaries" (Miller, 1998, p. 980). Private practices of prayer, scripture reading, or having a more generic spiritual dimension provides a sense of meaning in life and is associated with a lower risk for substance abuse. Although both spiritual and religious involvement may be an important protective factor against alcohol or drug abuse, more punitive forms of religion are likely to produce a higher risk for substance abuse (Miller, 1998).

Uhle (1994) wrote that the self-help programs and the literature outlining codependence have helped people to feel better about themselves. By listening to others' stories, a person entering recovery begins to feel more normal and that one's experiences with codependence is a story told by many. With the changes that occur in the consciousness of a person who enters recovery, the 12-Steps have helped many, especially women, to leave abusive relationships and change destructive patterns of behavior.

Through the 12-Steps a new language is learned that helps us describe the common experiences that have characterized our codependence (Uhle, 1994). These groups teach about self-care and what that entails. Caring and nurturing ourselves, learning to feel and identifying those feelings, expressing those emotions, and taking less responsibility for others have all had a positive effect on recovery. I think Messner (1996) sums it up rather nicely. "Recovery involves learning one new behavior: taking care of ourselves...learning self-responsibility, instead of feeling excessively responsible for others" (p. 116). Another important change that occurs through actively working the steps is that the person now has a "family" that understands the nature of the problems experienced. These people constitute a supportive social network for formerly isolated people struggling with codependence (Uhle, 1994).

♥

Chapter Six

Moving Beyond Recovery

In this book, I am proposing that recovery is not enough and that what we really need and want is to be healed from the conditions that have culminated in codependent relating. Healing differs from recovery because the latter assumes that the condition is still lingering within but has simply been controlled and in remission. Additionally, recovery implies that one admits to character defects and insanity that require a person to "let go and let God." The feeling of personal responsibility can be overwhelming.

Healing implies that the roots of the problem have been discovered and addressed in such a way that the person is internally a different person who now sees the world through different eyes. At the cellular level of belief we know our own truths and can begin to make choices based upon those discovered truths. Real change must include a multifaceted approach if we are to heal. Just changing our thinking is not enough because much of the codependent patterns of behavior arise from neural nets that become activated when thoughts or environmental triggers these ingrained reactions. We have to change the patterns of firing by changing our reactions and applying therapeutic techniques that impact the neural pathways that we are attempting to change (Dispenza, 2012; Lipton, 2009). Trauma that is not completely processed keeps the amygdala vigilant and ready to respond to any situation that even resembles the past trauma. Even simply thinking about the past trauma is enough to activate the emotions again, activating the autonomic nervous system's sympathetic branch even though no real danger is present. In an upcoming chapter you will be introduced to transpersonal healing techniques that impact the energy systems of our body and physiology, allowing for the changes in the structure and physiology of the brain, leading to changes that result in more fulfilling social interactions and choices.

As outlined in earlier chapters, codependence affects us in ways that prevent us from being aware of our own emotions and desires. We think we know what others feel, want, or what they "might" desire and subsequently never learned to monitor and understand our own feelings. Being so busy caring for others, we never learned to care for ourselves. "Codependents cannot meet their own needs and live their own lives if they fail to detach from others and learn to take care of and love themselves" (Messner, 1996, p. 116).

Recovery requires that we experience a dramatic change in identity. Through the process of the 12-Steps we discover who we are and try to live "one day at a time." This means that we must relinquish our need for control, which is not to imply that we are control freaks, but that we have learned to moderate chaos in our lives through our attempts at controlling the environment and others around us. Codependence skews our focus so that we don't turn inward for answers, but that we turn outside of ourselves, believing that the answers are "out there." "If only others would do ____ or not do ____. Then I would be happy!" We have to catch ourselves in the act and let go of the urge to orchestrate others' behaviors. We need to turn inward to discover in calmness what has been hidden from us because we were too focused what we felt would make others happy or at least to keep them from blowing up! By letting go, we begin to look within for the answers to our questions, to our internal truths. These are the truths that arise from our unadulterated selves or the Self that would have emerged had we grown up in more functional environments. Looking within for answers, we overcome denial and learn to feel our emotions, perhaps for the first time. They are *our* emotions, it is what *we* want and not simply what we think we want because by wanting that, we might be able to ward off impending chaos or what might happen around us.

Healing requires us to be more self-nurturing, to understand how growing up in a dysfunctional environment has affected us. We have to learn to assert our rights (once we discover what they are!) and become less focused on controlling the world.

> Power also becomes reconceptualized as what one can do for oneself (enpowerment) rather than how one can control another. A bottom line of recovery is self-acceptance, authenticity and humility...To rename one's experience is to get back to the basics of being only who we are, rather than feigning to be something different...recovery is not finite; there is no specific end product one can achieve. Rather, recovery is an ongoing process in which the individual continues to practice dealing with 'life on life's terms' (Van Den Bergh, 1991, pp. 24-26).

One Size Fits All

Van Den Bergh (1991) wrote that the characteristics of treatment programs (e.g., staffing, types of services, and the confrontational model used in 12-Steps) may actually deter females from entering recovery. The 12-Steps model is a confrontational model. The female style of communication is geared more towards connecting with others rather than confronting others, which is considered to be a more masculine style of interacting (Tannen, 1990).

Another factor that prevents females from entering 12-Steps programs is that most females live in poverty. This condition often prevents them from getting treatment because they are not equipped to afford treatment and/or they fear losing their children by admitting that they have an addiction—relationship addiction in this case. Entering treatment is equal to admitting one has an addiction.

The term, codependency can be seen as dysfunctional in that the manner in which it has been popularized and conveyed to the public keeps its clients in a constant repair mode. While reinforcing the conditions that sustain interpersonal insecurity, it also promotes anxiety and fear of others and at the same time promises future deliverance. It confers a sense of identity for those who have been troubled by relationship difficulties, albeit it is a dysfunctional identification.

> People are not thought to "have" codependency, but are codependent... one is never deemed "recovered," but always in recovery....This serves to promote a culture of specialized therapeutic experts that struggle to maintain their elite status by continually coding what was once considered normal behavior as pathological, and thus in need of outside intervention (Gemin, 1997, p. 262).

Gemin's statement is similar to the argument made by Thomas Szasz (1978) wherein he argues that mental illness is but a ruse fabricated by experts to legitimize their professions. Szasz believed that mental illness represents an individual's lack of responsibility for right action and behaviors. When codependence is viewed as a disease, a person suffering from codependence must rely on outside intervention for help, just as one would do with another type of "disease." Self empowerment is not a goal from this perspective.

Walters (1990) wrote that our current ways of seeing codependence can be considered as a *deficit model*. He described that surrendering to a spiritual higher power indicates a deficiency in the individual. "Surrender is seen as preferable to encouraging peoples to join together to challenge and restructure power arrangements in the larger society" (Walters, 1990, p. 55). The irony of surrender to a higher power is that this does not empower a person. Wetzel (1991) wrote,

> One's belief in one's powerlessness and the necessity to relinquish the self to a 'higher power'... (is)...something most women have been doing all their lives in a secular sense. Women are at risk because they are asked to do what they are not yet ready to do: to surrender something they never had (p. 22).

In Wetzel's estimation, women have been surrendering to powerlessness throughout most of history and therefore criticized the appropriateness of this step of the 12-Steps for females. Some researchers argue that the weekly group meetings of the 12-Steps foster addiction to the group. The person focuses intently on working the program, but this may well represent a simple trading of one addiction for another (Shockley, 1994). Instead of being addicted to the addict, the person is now obsessed with the need to work the steps and cannot focus on other aspects of healing. Individual therapy remains a crucial element to heal from codependence, which is not a part of the 12-Steps program.

Arguments both for and against codependency's basic premises contribute to the manner in which codependence is understood (Faludi, 1991; Haaken, 1990; Gemin, 1997). It is seen as a disease-based pathology over which the individual has no control, or as a habitual behavior that the individual can control. If it is seen as a disease that is part of the person's personality, then the cause of the dysfunction is attributed to factors inside-the-individual. Either way, the problem resides within the person who is labeled as the codependent. A clear dichotomy is established between self and other with responsibility falling upon only one of the partners within the relationship.

The causes of codependence are formed from factors that are either inside a person or by factors coming from the situation according to these premises. This type of thinking has created either/or thinking and has discouraged more creative solutions to understanding the causes of codependence (Gemin, 1997). Little has been advanced in codependence research that regards it as a couple's problem or a problem that could be addressed through sociopolitical changes.

Even critics of the construct inadvertently locate the problem and solution for codependence within the individual by touting that a person with codependence must learn to control their thoughts and feelings (Katz et al., 1992). Greenberg (1994) stated that advocating the recovery of 'self' through denial of 'other' symbolizes a breakdown, deeply embedded in the culture. "Taking care of oneself is not 'self-absorption or neglect of one's social obligations...(but must be achieved through a)...balance between attending to oneself and attending to others" (Messner, 1997, p. 15).

The recovery movement calls for the reestablishment of secure "boundaries" between self and others. Women possess a talent for promoting the development of others and this rightfully needs to be seen more as an asset, rather than a liability. Relational issues that differ for males and females need to be addressed if women are to be successful in their recovery so that they can progress towards healing. The masculine ideal of independence may not apply to females because women are reared to establish and emphasize connection with others. To judge female behavior according to a male standard of "health" may not be fitting.

Growing Up Female

Gilligan (1982) argued that the socialized differences between males and females arise from the patriarchal emphasis on hierarchies, power and autonomy. Patriarchy teaches females to be dependent and for them to emphasize relationships and mutual support. In contrast, males are reared to be independent and autonomous. Given these patriarchal definitions assigned to gender roles, being dependent is devalued over being autonomous.

Ironically, healthy behaviors also tend to be associated with the male-mode, which in this case would be to develop greater independence over dependence. In the 12-Steps model a person must separate and recover outside the context of a relationship because to be independent of others is seen as a strength from this patriarchal perspective.

Miller (1986) argued that a woman's sense of self develops not as a result of moving away from others but rather develops within the context of being in relationships where she can establish and maintain interpersonal connection and interaction with others. Women's self is derived primarily from the experience of *self-in-relation* and identity is embedded in the nature and mutuality of those relationships (Dupuy, 1993). In other words, females do better when they are in relationships than when they are alone. This doesn't imply that women always need a partner in their lives to be happy (the classic erroneous definition of codependence!), but that their sense of well-being and a full sense of self is found in relating with others.

Females are taught to value having connection with others. This is demonstrated in their abilities to focus upon empowering others, building others' strengths, resources, and fostering personal empowerment in others. "Many feminine traits, such as receptivity, concern for others, emotional expressiveness, and a capacity for empathy allow women to look at situations from many perspectives and understand relational complexities" (Granello, D. et al., 1998, p. 354). These traits give women a certain strength in interrelationships, but as discussed earlier, if a female has never learned what is meaningful to her, these characteristics can result in codependent behaviors.

Psychosocial theory emphasizes that developing a healthy sense of autonomy, initiative, industry and identity in the earlier stages of development help us to develop a capacity for intimacy as a young adult. If women must disconnect from others or if they fail to participate in mutually responsive relationships, they tend to become depressed, angry, isolated and confused. When disconnection with others occurs women tend to strive even harder for a sense of connection and may end up feeling a diminished sense of well-being as a consequence. Ultimately, they try to act in ways that they believe will allow them back into a connecting relationship. Instead of viewing these attempts at reconnection as codependence, Zelvin (1999) asserts, *"Women's psychological development needs reframing as a struggle for connection rather than a difficulty achieving separation.*

Disparity exists between the *etiology*, or how the problem arises, and responsibility for cure in codependence. Codependence is a maladjustment that occurs in interpersonal relationships yet recovery focuses upon only one of the persons in a partnership who has to separate and claim responsibility for the problems of the relationship.

Am I Responsible?

As outlined in earlier chapters, there has been a trend to pathologize behaviors typically assigned to females. Characteristics that are generally associated with the feminine, such as softness, nurturance, weakness, dependence, compliance, or being the caretaker, are less desirable than being tough, invulnerable, strong, independent, assertive, or being the provider. Feminists argue that recovery models need to emphasize skill building that fosters self-empowerment. Rather than claiming that one is insane, as implied in Step Two of the 12-Steps, empowerment means that change can occur by providing information (i.e., education) about the biases that have evolved in our society and the social and political climate in which we have evolved. Empowerment also occurs through teaching a multicultural perspective that incorporates social and political factors that govern women's lives (Morrow & Hauxhurst, 1998). Although our notions of gender have been changing, societal constructions of gender continue to influence us unconsciously.

> A predominant belief for individuality in American culture has left the individual in a societal and cultural limb wherein the ideals, identities and institutions inherited from the past have been repudiated. However, there yet remains the formation of alternative ideals to engender a new basis for relationships, new institutional forms and practices, and social identities (Rice, 1996, p. 12).

When separation is emphasized as it is in the 12-Steps, it represents a model that is more fitting for males that is not gender-sensitive. Chodorow (1978) pointed out that in the process of forming a sense of gender identity and developing skills of relatedness and connection, females do not need to separate from their mothers to learn this. Their childhood and adult lives are centered around activities that emphasize connection and intimacy

105

with others. Separation is a sign of failure is some sense from this perspective (Tannen, 1990).

Males, however, must learn to separate from their mothers, who are generally the primary caretaker, to form their sense of gender identity. Separation thus becomes a powerful motivator from the male perspective and is also seen as representing more psychologically healthy behaviors than when a person wants to establish connection with others. This gender difference creates doubt regarding the validity of using a separation model (or "one size fits all") to help females with relationship problems.

Themes of division, exclusion and separation permeate codependency discourse. This promotes the impression that codependency can be observed as if separated from a relational context. The very context in which codependency emerges has been minimized. Codependence begins in our relationships to another person, yet recovery is a solitary endeavor. It is expected of the person with codependent behaviors to name the disease ("I am a codependent") as if the condition were a disease of one's character. Recovery is also an independent task because one must learn to focus on caring for oneself, as if that can only occur within the context of being alone.

We are social creatures by nature and we need others. Our relationships help bring out the best (or worst) within us, but without another person to reflect back to us our hidden potential, we might never know that part of ourselves. Instead, we are expected to "let go and let God" in the recovery model which implies that the inner work does not involve the active participation of another person within a relationship.

Whitfield (1993) wrote that codependence is a metaphor that helps to anchor identity. By calling ourselves "codependent" we allow the self to be conceptualized as "lost" which then motivates us towards a moral quest to be "found." Boundaries become seen as exclusionary borders to keep others out and that must be protected.

In recovery, we learn about the possession and containment of space in an effort to control whatever lies on the border's other side. Boundaries mark the place where my reality ends and where yours begins. The problem with an approach that excludes others is that it makes us so vigilant to perceived invasions of our boundaries that we don't allow others in. When we keep others out, we keep ourselves in and isolated. We blame ourselves for the problems of relating with others. It's our fault. The lonely venture becomes even more isolating. The 12-Steps encourages independence as the ideal as if interrelating can be damaging to the discovery or attainment of the self.

Zelvin (1999) wrote that reframing codependence as a "struggle for connection rather than difficulty achieving separation" is essential to understanding and working with female codependents. If we are to believe in the validity of such a construct as *codependence* it needs to be placed within a more familiar interpersonal context.

> This helps emphasize that people who never learned how to meet their needs for love and safety can acquire new interpersonal skills. Emotional health means balancing our needs for connectedness and autonomy throughout each stage of the life cycle (Hogg et al., 1992, p. 376).

By reframing codependence into a relational focus women are empowered to use their capacity for connection in the service of recovery and eventual healing. When a woman seeks connection with others, it represents strength, rather than weakness or as an attempt to resist the 12-Steps philosophy. Connection with others can be viewed as a means towards establishing psychological health. In this way we can feel a sense of maturity as we move toward healthy interdependence.

This maturity *includes* compassion and care, concepts that are seen as indicators of weakness and enmeshment in the old scheme of labeling. As Zelvin (1999) has written, as relationships progress towards maturity they naturally become more *interdependent*. After all, we are social creatures and we need one another for physical and emotional succorance.

On a positive note about the construct of codependence, Rice (1996) believed that the 12-Steps is similar to what is termed "liberation therapy." Seeing codependence from this perspective allows for a more complex explanation for the problems associated with codependent behavior and advocates for social/political change. Liberation therapy is a movement away from social and cultural conformity and towards individuality. He argued that in America the development of the *real self* is thwarted in the interests of social conformity and thus, one loses oneself.

> To get well...the self must get out from beneath the repressive thumb of culture and society...(Codependent recovery is similar to the)...ethic of self-actualization...which assigns ultimate moral priority to the self, over and against society. One must behave in accordance with inner directives, expressing autonomy from rather than subordination to conventional social expectations...To simply conform to social expectations is to be, in varying degrees, psychologically sick (Rice, 1996, p. 29).

However, attempts to discover our true self, to hear and act upon our inner directives is stymied by the lack of a guiding ideal that informs us of how to be in relationships and the world (Rice, 1996). Instead we are taught to feel responsible for the whole problem that has been conveniently labeled as *codependence*.

Names Will Never Hurt Me?

Essentially what we are saying is that we are sick, insane, and in need of letting go of our will if we are to buy into the myth of codependence and the recovery movement. To be sick implies that we need a cure. To admit to our insanity is to be culpable for our experiences. To let go of our will implies that we've known all along what we feel and want—that we have been able to find our will and assert it. According to the recovery movement, we use labels to describe codependent behavior and then apply those labels to ourselves as if they describe who we are. This is the opposite of empowerment. "Empowerment requires a reliance on the spiritual power within, understanding the impact that cultural factors and gender socialization have played in codependent relating, and seeing conflict not as something to avoid, but as an important process of developing intimacy" (Anderson, 1994, p. 682).

We need to see how our tendencies have become imbalanced. The structured identity provided by the 12-Steps program is initially helpful, but the rigid definitions of self as *diseased* do not solve the problems of codependence because they focus too much on self-blame. One criticism of the 12-Steps group format is that it "may foster addiction to the group" (Shockley, 1994, p. 105). This implies that codependents may simply trade one addiction for another without learning to feel their own feelings and know what they desire. Women with low self-esteem, weak personal boundaries, and an *external locus of control* (feeling that one is controlled by external circumstances in contrast to an *internal locus of control,* which implies that a person feels self empowered in life) tend to dwell on each other's external problems without deriving real therapeutic benefit (Petrie et al., 1992). The behaviors that arose within intimate relationships is transferred to the group setting.

Developing healthier interpersonal relationships and enhancing patterns of communication are necessary, but may be difficult to achieve in 12-Steps groups. These groups are usually led by "recovering codependents" without trained professionals guiding the process. Although the program is helpful to those who enter recovery, it should not replace professional counseling (Shockley, 1994). We must first have a healthy relationship to ourselves before we can have a healthy relationship with another person. Individual psychotherapy is necessary to help a person struggling with codependent behaviors to develop a stronger ego-structure and a greater sense of self-worth. Much inner work is needed to recover what was not allowed to grow and develop as a child. I wonder if the original intent of the word "recovery" was to "recover" what was not allowed to be "uncovered" or "discovered" when we were children?

Codependence is also known as *relationship addiction*. If we are to see the behaviors of codependence as actions that produce a release of particular neurochemicals in the brain to which we have become addicted, then the term does have some validity. The problem with associating codependence with the term *addiction* is that it implies a character defect that can be damaging.

When we act out the same behaviors over and over, even when they result in something that we do not want in our lives, we are being driven by an internal psychological state. This *repetition compulsion* of the behaviors of codependence can be explained as our need for another "fix" of the *neurochemical cocktail* that soothes our fears and anxiety. The good thing about viewing codependent behaviors as an addiction to this psychological state is that we are then empowered to break the cycle! By stepping back from our need to "act out" once again, we can become the observer of our behavior, and therefore, loosen the bonds of the neural nets that activate the chemical release in our brain. There is hope for breaking the neuronal connections that feed the compulsion to act out the behaviors!

In the ground breaking film about consciousness and reality, *What the Bleep Do We Know?!?!?* Dr. Candace Pert and Dr. Joe Dispenza tell us that neurons that fire together wire together. So when I am used to feeling a particular way in certain circumstances, I am compelled to repeat those behaviors (our repetition compulsion) that result in the same feelings I've become accustomed to. To break those neural nets, we have to step back from our reactions that fuel our behaviors. Neuroscientists have also discovered that neural connections that are not strengthened through repetition will weaken and may die (You know, "use it or lose it!"). This is similar to a muscle that we exercise. If we keep repeating the exercise, the memory is strengthened in the muscle group. But if we let it atrophy, it weakens.

From this viewpoint, when I feel compelled to act out because of emotions I'm *craving*, I can simply step back and be the observer. I can look at my emotions as something "out there" outside of myself. This is when I can become aware and say to myself, "Wow! I sure am scared (or hurt, or angry, or sad, etc)" and then, as the observer, I can ask myself if I choose to have that emotion or not. It becomes a conscious choice of the reality I want to experience. Most of the time, I will decide that I'd rather be happy or calm, rather than sad or scared. I choose in that moment to NOT buy into my emotional uprising, giving it a chance to fade away. I create a different reality. When I allow the emotion to fade away I am allowing for the neuronal connections to loosen and unbind, which will lessen my compulsion to act out those same dysfunctional emotions in the future!! Additionally I can be assured that I am creating changes in my brain that will help me regulate my emotions more easily because the areas of the brain associated with emotional regulation are being developed and strengthened that will result in less reactionary behaviors to those situations that used to set us off. Developing a meditation practice, stopping your emotions before they become too activated, stepping back and being the observer, and actively addressing moments of heightened emotions with healing techniques, real changes are occurring at the cellular level that lead to healing.

Learned Helplessness

Although the etiology of codependence is slowly being unraveled, if it is seen as a disease, there is no known cure. O'Gorman (1993b) wrote that relabeling codependence into **learned helplessness** would be more useful. Learned helplessness is a psychological condition wherein we do nothing to change what is happening. Our past has taught us that escape or avoidance of painful situations and chaos is not possible. We give up and just continue to take what comes our way. Relabeling codependence as learned helplessness is empowering because it teaches us that healing is about

> resolving the trauma by remembering it and understanding both one's own and another's role within the trauma, making peace with what happened and moving on... (O'Gorman, 1993b, p. 163).

Being able to let go of the past and learn from it is essential to healing. Codependence makes a person tend to focus upon the traumas experienced within the family of origin instead of moving on. This focus needs to be decentralized as the organizing principle around which we focus if we are to heal from codependence. Anderson (1994) believed that gaining emotional neutrality about our family of origin empowers us to maintain our autonomy in other relationships.

Developing Social Consciousness

Developing consciousness of how problems emerge from a lack of power is advocated in feminist principles. Seeing how patriarchy and its emphasis on hierarchy have created an unequal distribution of power, we can see that our powerlessness does not stem from *who we are,* but from *where we are.* Becoming aware that the problems of codependence have emerged from not having power in society encourages us to seek political change that will help alleviate the conditions in society that cause us to **over function** in relationships. These principles teach us that the personal is political (Van Den Bergh, 1991).

One useful model to help a person grow beyond codependence comes from a psychosocial spectrum model. Four major themes are emphasized in this model: (a) *connectedness,* (b) *aloneness*, (c) *action*, and (d) *perception* (Wetzel, 1991). Each of these dimensions describes a continuum of values that on one end are negative and positive on the other end. Wetzel's four criteria help us to focus on the balance within each of the themes she identified. For example, aloneness is not always negative, but too much aloneness negatively impacts our self-image. Being too connected to others, to the point of forgetting our own needs, is detrimental to our self-image, and no connection to others at all is also negative. We need to evaluate our sense of connection, aloneness, action, and perception within these parameters.

Healing involves the development of a solid and positive self-image that includes being able to identify what you want and need from the world, and then, acting on your own behalf, to fulfill these needs without feeling you are being selfish. Instead of using this term to imply that you are self-centered, and therefore *self-ish,* I like to substitute it with the term, *self-love*. It is more accurate because without self-love we cannot love others. If I do not love myself and treat myself in loving ways, then how could I believe that another person could find me loveable?

Most of us feel a sense of shame when our relationships are not working. This shame needs to be interrupted by learning to be more self-empathic. It is a natural antidote for shame. By learning to care for ourselves and to nurture our inner child, we can release the shame that has bound us to codependent relating (Whitfield, 1987). Self-esteem can be bolstered by learning to depend upon our own thoughts and feelings instead of acting out approval seeking behaviors (Springer, Britt, & Schlenker, 1998). It is a form of self-parenting or re-parenting.

Developing relationship resilience can also help us from withdrawing when we feel shame. Through using a mutual problem-focused perspective that includes our partner, we can oppose the tendency of self-focused internalized blame (Wells et al., 1999). Stressing self-nurturance and naming our own reality allows us to discover what we need for self-growth. It facilitates ending the drive for perfection. Messner (1996) added that being honest with ourselves and with others, setting boundaries, letting go of negative messages, being direct, and releasing anger and resentment, are all vital to recovery. By reconceptualizing power, anger can be redirected to motivate us to create change that helps us become more assertive and establish clearer boundaries (Van Den Bergh, 1991).

There are other dimensions of empowerment to consider as well (Morrow et al, 1998). First, there are the *personal factors* that enhance our sense of empowerment (e.g., being assertive, recognizing and expressing feelings, nurturing ourselves more than others). Secondly, the *interpersonal realm* includes an analysis of those people who either limit or enhance our personal power. Last of all, the *social/political realm* requires scrutiny of the laws, norms, values, rules, sanctions, taboos and prejudice within society that limit empowerment.

How To Heal

Self-esteem and boundaries need to be built. By nurturing ourselves we can give ourselves what we didn't receive as children. Learning to say "no" without feeling the other person will die, asserting our rights without feeling like we need to change the world, or simply setting limits for ourselves will help us heal from codependence. By realizing that the codependent identity includes the tendency to over-function in relationships, we can stop blaming ourselves for all the problems in our relationships. If one person is *over-function*ing it means that the other person in the relationship has room to *under-function*. Just seeing this dynamic alone allows us to let go of the responsibility for everything to go right in our relationships. There are two people involved.

Assessing the extent of codependent relating, going to group therapy, and using experiential techniques in therapy such as psychodrama, journalizing, and empty chair work, are helpful. Learning relaxation techniques and creating positive affirmations help us to think more positively and worry less about whether we are measuring up to others expectations. A psychoeducational approach--tending to our personal growth and becoming educated about how codependence develops--is necessary for recovery and essential for healing. By addressing the social, emotional, intellectual, occupational, physical, and spiritual functioning in therapeutic aftercare, we can begin to heal. We must value equally both product and goal...recovery is an ongoing process. It is not a condition that will finally be reached or achieved. Emphasis needs to be placed more upon the process and the steps taken towards a goal rather than fixating upon when that goal is completed. "There is no 'right way' to proceed...accept gradations" (Van Den Bergh, 1991. p. 25).

Although the group aspect of 12-Steps programs may not be appropriate for everyone, women need a sense of connection and intimacy with others and thus some writers have emphasized the value of a group setting for females because they are reared to emphasize intimacy, conversations, affection, and attachment (O'Gorman, 1993a). Same sex groups are helpful in this regard.

Part II

♥

Part I explored the nature of codependence, its measurement, characteristics and treatment in the 12-Steps format. We also examined how society has contributed to the development and perpetuation of this concept called *codependence,* a term that is more like blaming the victim than assisting the person who is traumatized. By understanding the nature and etiology of the behaviors that constitute this behavioral syndrome we are now prepared to embark upon the path to healing.

Part II is about the transpersonal, or evolving consciousness by becoming more aware of our reactionary patterns of behavior and perception so that we can live a more conscious life—one where we learn to *respond* to life instead of *reacting.* As we change our thoughts and behaviors, our brain and physiology accommodate our efforts and new neural nets are formed that will facilitate our flexibility in life and allow for more complex responses instead of habitual reactions. Simultaneously, as you stop the emotional reactions by becoming the observer, you loosen the older neural nets that have kept the codependent patterns alive. The information from Part I brought to your awareness the complex nature of how codependent behaviors become established. This essential information will help us in **breaking the code of codependence**. We begin to see the encrypted beliefs we hold that culminate in acting codependently. In turn, this knowledge enables us to change the reactionary patterns of behaving into conscious choices of action in our lives. We reach within and find an inner resource of strength, creativity, and compassion that helps us move beyond recovery and into the healing process.

In the chapters that follow you will learn about the emerging fourth force in psychology, the ***transpersonal***. We explore its placement within the development of the other major forces in psychology, namely, Behaviorism, Psychoanalytic, and Humanistic perspectives. We will also see how the transpersonal includes the perspectives and knowledge learned from the other three forces in psychology and that it relies heavily on the biological and the cognitive. It interfaces scientifically with quantum physics and what is known about the interaction within the body/mind connection and our health— *psychoneuroimmunology*. You will learn that the transpersonal approach to understanding human behavior is the only perspective in psychology that is *inclusive*. In other words, it integrates information coming from the many approaches in psychology as well as other disciplines to form the current body of knowledge in totality regarding the human condition. It is an approach that incorporates wisdom from spiritual traditions in the human search from meaning in life. Neurobiology, anthropology, quantum physics, and psychology are combined with Eastern wisdom and healing practices to advance our knowledge towards greater happiness and well being--deeper needs of the spirit and soul.

Through the transpersonal, you will be challenged to understand how you have formed your reality and how these interpretations of reality can be changed by consciously becoming aware of them. Knowing that our experiences of our emotions are the result of various chemicals released in the body and that our repetition of these emotional states is similar to addiction gives us valuable information about how to interrupt the process and break the neural nets that bind us to repeating these emotions. By understanding that our interpretations of reality create the attendant states of mind we experience, it becomes possible for each of us to take full control of our lives. As we learn to be co-creators of reality, we operate from a higher level of consciousness. Consciousness requires a moment to moment awareness so that our decision-making process forces us to reach down into our core to honor and value who we are—who we can become—through finding our own truths and living by them. Learning how to identify those truths and use them in our decisions is the content of Part II.

♥

Chapter Seven

A Primer of Transpersonal Psychology

The word **transpersonal** refers to those aspects of human experience that are *beyond* the personal. *Trans* can refer to *that which is beyond*, or it can also refer to *across*. Cortright (1997) explained that

> Transpersonal approaches move across the personal realm and take in...(and)...explore all aspects of the self and the unconscious that traditional psychology has discovered while also placing...personal psychology in a larger framework....(T)he self is very much the focus in transpersonal psychotherapy. But by moving across traditional personal psychology to the larger spiritual context, the individual self moves out of its existential vacuum into a wider dimension to which the world's spiritual teachings point (Cortright, 1997, p. 10).

The first three forces in psychology--behaviorism, psychodynamic thought, and the humanistic model, respectively—have formed the major influential forces that have guided psychological research. The first two forces, behavioral and psychodynamic thought ruled the discipline until about the 1960's, when humanistic thought emerged as a driving force in psychology. There have been other areas of investigation that have heavily influenced the direction of psychological investigation, such as the medical and cognitive models. In regards to therapy, the medical model appears to be the ruling model as more and more prescription medicines are being invented and used to treat every imaginable malady that human beings experience (Lipton, 2005). While the medical model has provided us with the biological knowledge necessary to understand the mechanisms of behavior, using the biological model as the sole approach to treatment neglects important information we know about the interrelatedness of the human organic system. Cognitive psychology, which was revived in the 1980's, has investigated the function and structure of consciousness (e.g., memory, intelligence, sleep) but has steered away from examining other consciousness states. This is perhaps due to the difficulty encountered when attempting to quantify consciousness.

With the advent of such technology as the MRI and PET scans, we are now able to peer into the physiology of consciousness states, but many questions remain regarding the more subtle energies of consciousness states. For example, how do we measure what is occurring when a person is able to use consciousness in order to help government intelligence efforts? I read an account about Paul Smith, who worked for a CIA funded research project called Center Lane as a remote viewer. In essence he was a psychic spy. So, even though we cannot explain why some people can "see" what is happening elsewhere in the world while they are somewhere else, even the government has employed the use of these subtle energies.

The western scientific model focuses on measurement and observation and has been the primary force in shaping what psychology investigates. Inch by inch, we progress and discover new technologies to help explain what is happening. Even in the face of our limited ability to measure and explain consciousness states, the transpersonal paradigm is providing the foundation and encouraging practitioners and researchers to examine what is difficult for us to measure—human consciousness. Whole organizations are supporting the efforts to research, advance, and share what we are learning about the human energy system. The Association for Comprehensive Energy Psychology (ACEP) gathers researchers and practitioners from around the world highlighting the latest advances in energy medicine and "are dedicated to exploring, developing, researching and applying energy psychology methods to alleviate human suffering, enhance human performance and access human potential." Even with the current limitations of our technological abilities to study human consciousness, the transpersonal paradigm has forged ahead to expand the ways in which we treat human mental illness. These approaches are more humane and less invasive than surgeries or drug treatments. Through the power of consciousness new therapeutic treatments, such as Energy Psychology, are being used with effective and impressing results (Feinstein, 2006).

Forces in Psychology

Mental illness, its descriptions, definitions and therapeutic interventions have always reflected the zeitgeist of the psychological cultural context in which these problems were defined. *Behaviorism* focused on observable behavior and limited its investigations to that realm. It helped psychologists answer questions about how we learn through conditioning and reinforcement.

This focus on observable behavior and its quantification fit neatly into scientific methodological schemes and gave the discipline of psychology more credibility in the scientific community. This narrow focus limited the realm in which psychological research could occur, however. Additionally, because animal models formed much of the knowledge gained in behaviorism, generalization to human behavior was often criticized and looked upon with skepticism. Humans are considered to be much more complex organisms than the animals being used in these behavioral studies. It represented a reduction of the total human experience into its component parts, but did provide explanations for simple human learning.

Psychodynamic thought focused more upon the instinctual nature of human behavior and the processes that governed psychological functioning. This force is primarily concerned with the unconscious and its impact upon behavior. Psychodynamic thought, as proposed by such early psychoanalysts as Sigmund Freud (Hall, 1954), explained behavior as the result of the clash between inner drives and cultural expectations. Carl Jung (Hall, 1973) also believed that we were instinctual creatures, but believed that we were driven more by our inherited human tendencies, predispositions and preferences of our ancestors (this is the concern of Evolutionary Psychologists today). Jung called this our *psychoid* inheritance, which stems from the influence of the collective unconscious.

Alfred Adler (1957) and Karen Horney (1966) were also both contemporaries of Freud and Jung. Adler advocated that the ego was the crucial factor in determining personality and that the internal sense of fragility—being a vulnerable, mortal human being—set the stage for our strivings in the world. Horney believed that we are all seeking safety in an insane world where love is difficult to find. We learn to relate to others by adapting our behaviors to bring ourselves a sense of safety. These psychodynamic approaches were early pathways to understanding the nature of the psyche and provided theories to explain personality development. If we see the psyche as a dynamic system where much of the action takes place below the level of consciousness, then we are better equipped to understand how we have become the person that we seem to be.

These two early driving forces in psychology, behaviorism and psychodynamic thought, provided valuable, but limited insight into human behavior. They helped us see how we learn our behaviors and why we react to certain stimuli or situations as we do. Behaviorism addressed averages and taught us how to change behavior without necessarily using consciousness as a tool to facilitate growth and individuality. That was not its concern. Behaviorism is more concerned with adjusting behavior.

Psychodynamic thought helped us understand the workings of the unconscious and how this impacts our perception and behavior. These forces provided limited understanding about human behavior, but failed to address more humanistic concerns, such as uniqueness and potential of the individual. Thus, out of these limitations, the Humanistic Movement was born.

The Humanistic Movement

Out of the 1960's, the human potential movement emerged as the next major force in psychology. Psychologists, such as Abraham Maslow (1971), embraced this task, leading the Humanistic Movement, or Third Force Psychology. With the emergence of the Humanistic Movement, psychologists were now able to go into a different realm of inquiry. They studied a different set of questions about human potential and its actualization.

Humanistic psychology didn't discard the knowledge gained by the earlier psychological perspectives, but used this information to help shed light on the nature of how we can achieve our best. What were the conditions and mechanisms involved that fostered or hindered the full blossoming of an individual? Fritz Perls (1972), Rollo May (1953), and Carl Rogers (1961) joined in the movement and devised other strategies for exploring the humanistic realm.

What was significant about Third Force psychology was the conceptual re-integration of the body/mind split. Prior to the work of the pioneers of this movement, the body and mind were essentially seen as separate. The body did not affect the mind, or vice versa. Third Force practitioners worked on bringing the physical body back in tune with consciousness, or the mind. Body-based therapies were emphasized to help people "get back into their bodies." Massage, acupressure, acupuncture, Rolfing, Lomi therapy, Feldenkraus method, and gestalt therapy all helped a person to understand how emotions get locked into the body.

These three paradigms served to form the basic foundations of the discipline of psychology up to about the 1980's. Confidence in psychology as a scientific discipline was augmented through its rigorous application of scientific method. Behaviorism's focus on structure, function and observable behavior helped establish psychology in the eyes of the scientific community while psychodynamic perspectives sought to provide insight into the mechanisms of the unconscious mind. Third force psychology, or the humanistic perspective, took psychology beyond instinctual reaction and learned behavior, focusing more upon individual uniqueness, human potential and its actualization. The body and mind were seen as interrelated facets of experience. One affected the other. Knowing the interaction of the body/mind connection paved the path to greater understanding of how thought, attitude, and belief affect an individual's mental and physical health. The humanistic movement expanded the realm of inquiry for psychology allowing for a more positive approach to understanding human desire, and the intrinsic mechanisms for self evolution.

Humanistic psychology valued studying *phenomenology*, or the study of how one experiences the world. Studying phenomenology provided a means by which happiness, meaning, fulfillment and self-actualization could be identified and nurtured in each person. There were no blanket prescriptions providing relief from anxiety, or *angst*. Instead, a private and personal search was required of each person who sought to actualize their inner potential. Will was now linked with choice and responsibility. Learning and childhood experiences held less power over an individual from this perspective. Choices confronting a person were in the present situation. Regardless of past influences, each person had the responsibility to make wise choices and discover meaning within the current context of living.

Thus, the Humanistic Movement expanded psychology's repertoire. Although a bridge was formed that linked the earlier two forces with the Third Force, issues that related to the soul were still not being addressed. The existence of a soul and the needs of a soul were seen as the province of theology or philosophy.

Carl Jung (1971a) played a critical role by proposing within his theory ideas that were to become the foundation of transpersonal thought. His writings regarding *synchronicity*, or déjà vu, were related to Einstein's ideas that space and time were not separate. Jung felt that humans had the capacity for greater consciousness, but were also influenced by a collective aspect to consciousness as well. By seeing the human need for interconnectedness to others and the cosmos, Jung reasoned that psychological health could only be achieved if humans found meaning through a sense of spirituality.

Having a sense of spirituality allows us to transcend the sense of being alone in the world. We learn that as we understand how the universe works, we understand how we work. Spirituality is the ability to live with our human emotions without destroying ourselves or others. By raising consciousness, we find out how we create our reality and therefore the problems we encounter. Are we so attached to our emotions that we cannot learn from them? We are connected to everyone else on earth by our humanness—our common experiences, similar needs, and potential for greatness. Seeking personal meaning within the collective endeavor, a person could find inner peace or a sense of interrelationship with everything.

The Fourth Force – Transpersonal Psychology

As a movement, humanistic psychology underwent a metamorphosis that included this neglected realm of human experience. What has emerged is the fourth force in psychology, dubbed Transpersonal Psychology (Cortright, 1997; Tart, 2000). A working definition of transpersonal psychology was published in the first issue of the Journal of Transpersonal Psychology in the spring of 1969. It stated that

> Transpersonal Psychology is the title given to an emerging force in the psychology field by a group of psychologists and professional men and women from other fields who are interested in those *ultimate* human capacities and potentialities that have no systematic place in positivistic or behavioristic theory ("first force"), classical psychoanalytic theory ("second force"), or humanistic psychology ("third force"). The emerging Transpersonal Psychology ("fourth force") is concerned specifically with the *empirical*, scientific study of, and responsible implementation of the findings relevant to, becoming, individual and species-wide meta-needs, ultimate values, unitive consciousness, peak experiences, B-values, ecstasy, mystical experience, awe, being, self-actualization, essence, bliss, wonder, ultimate meaning, transcendence of the self, spirit, oneness, cosmic awareness, individual and

128

species-wide synergy, maximal interpersonal encounter, sacralization of everyday life, transcendental phenomena, cosmic self-humor and playfulness, maximal sensory awareness, responsiveness and expression, and related concepts, experiences and activities. As a definition, this formulation is to be understood as subject to optional individual or group interpretations, either wholly or in part, with regard to the acceptance of its content as essentially naturalistic, theistic, super naturalistic, or any other designated classification (Tart, 1992, p. 1).

With the transpersonal movement, psychologists examined the common ground between the human need for individuality with a larger sense of being interconnected. Prior to the Humanistic Movement, psychology had not sufficiently addressed the questions that arose in our search for meaning. As Erich Fromm (1983) wrote,

(Patients')...complaints are only the conscious form in which our culture permits them to express something which lies much deeper....(T)he common suffering is the alienation from oneself, from one's fellow man, and from nature; the awareness that life runs out of one's hand like sand, and that one will die without having lived; that one lives in the midst of plenty and yet is joyless (p. 60).

Psychological health extends beyond our personal accomplishments and achievements. Fromm (1983) wrote,

Well being is the state of having arrived at the full development of reason: reason not in the sense of a merely intellectual judgment, but in that of grasping truth by "letting things be"...as they are. Well-being is possible only to the degree to which one has overcome one's narcissism; to the degree to which one is open, responsive, sensitive, awake, empty...to be fully related to man and nature affectively, to overcome separateness and alienation, to arrive at the experience of oneness with all that exists—and yet to experience *myself* at the same time as the separate entity *I* am...(p. 63).

By understanding the nature of consciousness through combining western knowledge with eastern wisdom, it is possible to understand how human consciousness can be evolved to a higher state.

Unity Consciousness

To classify more evolved states of consciousness from lesser ones, higher consciousness is described as inclusive of other forms of thinking, perceiving, and explaining situations. They are not limited by a set of rules that are exclusionary. More evolved states of consciousness allow us to be aware of the different levels of thinking that humans engage in, but doesn't eliminate the validity of less evolved states because it differs from the more inclusive states. To be inclusive is to have my opinions and beliefs, but simultaneously allows me to acknowledge and accept that others may see the world differently. It may not be like mine, but it is valid for them and I make attempts to understand their viewpoint. The difference between these two perspectives is that the higher form includes the validity of another's way of seeing the world, but the reverse is not true. An *exclusive* perspective is bounded and does not include the value of other ways of seeing the world. Their way seems to be the right and only way.

Transpersonal growth is a way of seeing and being in the world that allows us to transcend separation and encounter connection. It is a kind of consciousness that has been described as ***cosmic*** or ***unity consciousness*** and is believed to reflect the highest form of human consciousness (Bucke, 1961; Huxley, 1944; Wilber, 1979a). It is a form of consciousness that is available to all, but attained by only a few people such as Mother Theresa, Jesus, the Dalai Lama, Ghandi, or Buddha (Bucke, 1961). Yet all humans are capable of developing consciousness to these higher forms of awareness and through inner work and meditative practices that develop the capacities of the mind and spirit, we can hear the voice of our soul. The usual motivators of behavior are transcended in this state of consciousness and we operate more from a sense of unity with others and the universe. By examining the nature of consciousness and how we each form our notions of reality, better understanding of what prevents us from achieving unity consciousness can be determined.

Transpersonal Intervention

Traditional psychological intervention has been geared towards assisting people adjust through drugs or psychosurgery, insight, and behavioral change. Examining thinking patterns, understanding the power of reinforcement and conditioning, unraveling the effects of early experiences, and through drug treatment, a stronger sense of ego, or "I", can be effected in therapy. A transpersonal approach doesn't eliminate the wisdom gained from these perspectives in psychology, but takes us into another early area of interest in the discipline—consciousness.

Through examination and exploration of the nature of consciousness, the transpersonal augments what we know about human behavior. We explore aspects of behavior that cannot be seen or touched, yet are characteristics of what distinguishes us from other animals. We see humans as the highest form of life on earth because we are conscious, thinking, wondering, and evolving animals. The transpersonal explores questions of consciousness with the rigorous methodology of science—extra sensory perception, out-of-body experiences, premonition, telepathy, kundalini experiences, clairvoyance, channeling, shamanic journeying, unitive states, and near-death experiences, to name a few. You can learn more about how these phenomena are studied scientifically in a book by Dean Radin (2006), *Entangled Minds: Extrasensory Experiences in a Quantum Reality*.

Radin discusses the prejudice against the scientific study of psi phenomena and then presents study after study that verifies the existence of human psi abilities. Add to this the information coming from the field of Energy Psychology, which is gaining more credibility with the scientific community and creating inroads into faster, more effective means of healing from trauma, anxiety, guilt, shame, and other toxic emotions.

Some forms of energy techniques are approved for insurance reimbursement. Although limited in scope insurance reimbursement does includes acupuncture and *Eye Movement Desensitization and Reprocessing* (EMDR) as medically approved forms of therapy at this point. The thing to keep in mind about the approval of various forms of therapy is that there is little incentive for pharmaceutical companies to fund research into self-help interventions, such as emotional freedom technique (EFT), and other energetic interventions that at least on the clinical level are appearing to be effective. Because the drug companies have the funds to grant to research efforts, it makes sense that they are only interested in interventions that would boost their sales and the development of new drugs. They have little interest in funding studies that boost a person's ability to prevent illness, both psychological and physical. Much of the research efforts in the Transpersonal realm are privately funded at this point. Efforts are being made to convince Congress to fund studies that support these interventions based upon our understanding of subtle energies but the progress is slow (Feinstein, March 2010).

Individual and interpersonal psychology, as it has been studied in the west, is blended with a path of awakening by studying the wisdom of eastern spiritual traditions. Spiritual traditions teach us how to gain access to deeper levels of consciousness and give us knowledge about the problems involved with being conscious beings. These approaches acknowledge the unity of nature and see the mind/body as an interconnected system wherein perception, attitudes, and behavior interact with our physical state of well-being.

From a medical viewpoint, eastern approaches to medicine have built their healing practices upon a foundation of understanding that all things in life are energetic in nature. We are beings of energy (think of the electrical/chemical nature of the 100 billion neurons that comprise our nervous system) whose life force comes from the flow of *chi*, or energy, through our bodies. Physical and psychological problems emerge from blockages to that free flow of energy throughout our bodies. From an eastern approach, there is a greater emphasis in the holistic nature of our organism, and treatments are geared towards balancing the imbalances among the major organ and energy systems of our bodies. These ideas will be explored in a later section of this book.

We learn about our negative emotions and how they can harm our health. This integrative approach acknowledges that we are biochemical organisms. If we use that knowledge, we can create better physical and emotional health and well-being. The transpersonal is a truly eclectic approach. By combining different therapeutic techniques to help us get out of behaviors that come from being "stuck" in our emotional past, we can facilitate the healing process and move beyond simple recovery. By actively engaging the body and mind, opening up consciousness through meditative practices, and actively intervening with energetic body/mind techniques, true healing at the source of our problems can be effected.

Examples of bodily interventions that help alter consciousness are acupressure, acupuncture, massage, and Energy Psychology techniques. Combined with meditative practices that change consciousness, brain structures and physiology--such as meditation, yoga, tai chi or chi kung--we become empowered to heal ourselves and learn how to become conscious creators of our own reality. We learn to heal and gain our wholeness, maybe for the first time in our lives.

Recovery is limited because a person is seen as *always in recovery*. More self-empowerment is required if we are to heal. "Letting go" of an emotionally challenging situation is not the same as no longer being affected by those same types of situations. In the first case our sympathetic response is still activated but we learn to *let go and let God.* The triggers still throw us into our dysfunctional behaviors and emotions, but in an act of conscious volition, we release it and this allows us calm down after some time. In the transpersonal healing model, we use active intervention techniques to calm the emotions and change the cognitions that lead to real neurological changes (Siegel, 2011). Through developing neural structures that integrate the social and emotional areas of the brain, we can better regulate our emotions and not become so easily activated to stimuli that used to set us off. This dampening occurs because the neural nets are loosened or broken and we actively engage in perceptions that keep us calm and in the present moment. Thus in the former case, there is no end to that process from which we can emerge as whole beings. The transpersonal allows us to go beyond cure and into healing. To be cured means to be rid of a condition, but to be healed implies that we are made whole again.

"Spiritual systems study consciousness insofar as it transcends or encompasses more than the self" (Cortright, 1997, p. 49). To transcend the self does not imply that we lose our *self.* What happens is that we learn to find where our boundaries became blurred in the process of growing up so that we address the cognitive aspect to change. Simultaneously, we desensitize ourselves to the circumstances that used to evoke our codependent behaviors. We discover the necessary ego boundaries that help us make choices that address our real needs and desires.

Much unhappiness is caused by our sense of separation and alienation from others, but total enmeshment is not the answer for happiness either. What we will learn from studying consciousness, reality formation, and practicing some form of meditative healing practice (e.g., yoga, tai chi, chi kung or martial arts), we can dissolve our ego boundaries that separate us from others by learning how to be in the *here and now*. To be in the present moment is to facilitate our feelings of interconnectedness and harmony with others and our experiences. When we are *mindful* of the present, not being distracted by past or future anxiety, consciousness is expanded and helps us to fully appreciate and hear our own truth.

Mindfulness

Mindfulness is a meditative technique that results in a suspension of our preformed notions or expectations of experience. Full consciousness is channeled towards the present moment instead of focusing on the past or future.

> Mindfulness is currently defined in psychological terms as being characterized by paying total attention to the present moment with a non-judgmental awareness of the inner and/or outer experiences…It refers to the cultivation of a conscious attention on a moment-to moment basis and is characterized by an open and receptive aptitude (Chiesa & Serretti, 2010).

From this perspective, the definitions of reality that we carry are suspended, allowing for our inner truth to emerge. Truth in this sense is *that which is,* (as opposed to *that's what I fear*, or *that's what I expected*, or *that's the way it always is…*). This can be facilitated by psychological interventions that help to relieve us from emotional trauma, anxiety, guilt and shame that have accumulated in our lifetime.

Evolving consciousness means that we are expanding the way we use our consciousness so that we are able to more fully use the powers of consciousness. By loosening the restrictions to consciousness that we usually operate from, we tap into our abilities to discern a different level of awareness. We become aware, or mindful, of our automatic reactions to experiences and instead open up to take in the situation with a receptive consciousness. This helps us awaken from our **waking sleep**. *Waking sleep* is a term used by Charles Tart, emeritus UC Davis faculty. He described how most of us are unaware of much of our experience because we have learned to tune out and prejudge much of what happens therefore, we miss out on what is happening in the moment. Awakening expands consciousness so that we see the interconnectedness of all things. When we understand this, we begin to see how perception is fueled by our thoughts and past programming, making it imperative that we address the entire perceptual environment if we are to heal. Awakening must include all realms of human existence— the physical (body), the intellectual (mind), and the spiritual (soul) (Welwood, 2002).

Dropping Our Ego

Much of human suffering, or *samsara*, is the result of how we view the world. Suffering according to this Eastern term is that it arises because we cling to our expectations. We desire certain outcomes and things in our lives and when it does not unfold, we suffer. The remedy for this is to be in the *Here and Now* at all times. If we are in the moment, then we won't be worrying about the past or be anxious about what is to come. The next moment will come and if we are "in that moment" we have no room for worry or anxiety.

When we understand the nature of consciousness, the causes of anxiety are seen for what they are—thoughts, memories or expectations that we cling to and bring into the present moment, coloring our experience. These memories or experiences condition us, in a *classical conditioning* sense, to meet the environment in predetermined ways. Together these insights help us see that much of what we experience as reality is in truth is an application of our preexisting conditioning coupled with our predetermined definitions and expectations about the way life is.

Spiritual practices as emphasized in transpersonal approaches help us to dissolve these ego boundaries. This allows us to live life less from the storylines we hold in our heads so that we can participate more fully in the moment as it is (Welwood, 1983). Although spiritual systems emphasize the loosening of ego boundaries and being less identification with the ego, this strategy does not negate the importance of having a strong ego. As we allow consciousness to emerge and expand through meditative practices, the loosening of unconscious material may overwhelm us if we don't have a firm ground on which to stand.

This process may be so intense that it leads to what Grof et al (1989c) described as a ***spiritual emergency***. He describes cases where people experience their bodies vibrating or shaking as well as consciousness states resembling a psychosis as they wrestle with changing their former viewpoint into a new expanded consciousness. From a psychodynamic viewpoint, we would describe that ego is overwhelmed with the changing nature of one's consciousness. As one belief system is loosened to make way for a new way of thinking, disruptions to our known ways of seeing the world can cause psychological distress. From a transpersonal perspective, it is not seen as a mental illness, but is approached with compassion, helping the individual make sense of the conflicting material that may emerge when spiritual expansion occurs. This healing happens because it is a *caring* approach, contrasted to a *treatment* approach.

We need to discover, and therefore become familiar with who *we* are so that we don't get lost in the transformation process. By discovering what has been added to our basic Self by our family, cultures and society, we can separate the chaff from the grain. We get in touch with our true form underneath. With this strength we can begin to take active steps towards growth and the evolution of our own consciousness.

Psychology has not been the only scientific discipline concerned with human consciousness. Other scientific disciplines are proposing controversial theories that are requiring scientists to rethink how we believe the world and the universe works. As the theoretical foundations of ***quantum mechanics*** expand and notions of ***string theory*** continue to be developed, reality, as it has been understood, must evolve (Greene, 1999). Quantum mechanics explains the micro aspect of reality (atomic level) in contrast to Newton's Laws that explain the macro (or very large).

Using the theoretical model of quantum mechanics, effective energy interventions are being utilized more and more to help people heal quickly from a variety of traumas (Feinstein, 2006; Dispenza, 2012; Lipton & Bhaerman, 2010). Quantum physics is informing us of the healing potential of the human mind. We are able to positively (and negatively) effect our physiology and neural landscape in the brain through our thoughts. We generally look outside of ourselves for causes because we have grown up in a Newtonian framework of understanding the world. This is the "cause and effect" world where we determine that things happen because a physical force is exerted upon an object to "cause" it to change.

Consciousness can only be understood by examining the subtle energies that are believed to "cause" changes in an organism. One of the fascinating areas of scientific interest that has emerged from this paradigm is *psychoneuroimmunology,* or the study of how the mind affects the nervous and immune systems. By changing the ways we think and feel, and our reactions to experiences, we can change our physical health. Studying brain changes in physiology and structure simply inform us of the corresponding changes in the brain as we engage in these meditative practices, but we still ponder whether the brain causes our experiences or if consciousness causes the brain changes detected by modern machines. Research is verifying the neurological changes that occur through meditation, or the *contemplative practices* (Davidson, 2008; Davidson, Kabat-Zinn, et al 2003; Dispenza, 2012). Research informs us that the brains of those who have engaged in many, many hours of meditative practice differ from non-meditators or those who have not meditated for years (Davidson et al, 2003). These changes allow for better integration of the left and right hemispheres in the prefrontal cortex, the executive area of our brain that results in better attunement with others, more balanced emotions, improved stress response, and enhanced social skill ability (Siegel, 2006 Apr).

The body and mind are not separate, thus our thoughts and perception physically affect our bodies and brain. Western approaches are being blended with knowledge from eastern approaches to increase our understanding of how health is impacted through consciousness, providing a scientific, yet esoteric approach to understanding what makes us tick. Spiritual traditions have advocated roadmaps for living such as the

Four Noble Truths:

- *Life is suffering;*
- *Suffering is due to attachment;*
- *Attachment can be overcome; and,*
- *There is a path for accomplishing this.* This path is called *The Eightfold Path.*

The ***Eightfold Path*** consists of:

1) *Right View* – Understanding the wisdom of the Four Noble Truths and seeing ourselves and the world without greed, delusion, hatred, etc.

2) *Right Intention* – What are our intentions with others and ourselves?

3) *Right Action* – Do our actions bring suffering or harm to ourselves or others?

4) *Right Speech* – Being mindful that what we say matches Right Intention. Our words should not harm.

5) *Right Livelihood* – What we do in the world for our livelihood does not cause suffering or bring harm to others.

6) *Right Effort* – Our efforts have the motivation of lessening suffering.

7) *Right Mindfulness* – To be present in all that we do, being in the moment and open to seeing things in new ways.

8) *Right Concentration* – Quieting the mind through focused concentration, such as meditation. Training "to empty our natures of attachments, avoidances, and ignorance, so that we may accept the imperfection,

impermanence, and insubstantiality of life"
(Boeree, n.d.).

The first two segments refer to *wisdom* or *prajña*, seeing the world as it is without attachment or clinging to desires or materialism. The next three segments guide us regarding our words and efforts in the world and relate to *moral precepts* called *silas*. These help us align our acts and intentions, guiding us towards choices that lead to a happier life. The last three segments relate to meditation or *Samadhi*. With this ancient knowledge we are able to form lives that serve us on many levels and provides a practice that helps us to develop a more calm awareness and keeps us "true north."

♥

Chapter Eight

How Consciousness Works

Being human is an interesting journey. We are intelligent creatures who are only just beginning to tap into the hidden potential of the mind. Researchers and scientists are beginning to see that reality is not necessarily *out there* waiting to be discovered but that reality is a part of our own creation. We focus on particular aspects of the world around us and as a result, that reality forms. Think about a time when you perceived a situation to be a certain way. You saw what you thought was the truth of what happened. Upon further examination you realize that your perspective was skewed by the emotions you were attaching to the situation—your fears, doubts, memories—and so you *saw* what you believed was the truth of that reality. After you realized that it was your **reaction** that fueled the situation, you *saw* that you were mistaken. How many times has that happened to us all? We are co-creators of our own realities.

At this point it is necessary for us to understand that being human means we will be prone to act in typically human ways. Carl Jung called these predispositions **archetypes** and proposed that they are the **psychoid** inheritance of every human being. Archetypes are simply templates for human behavior that influence how we see the world and act in particular situations. It is our psychological (thus psychoid) genetic inheritance from our ancestral roots stemming from the time humans first walked the earth. Humans that behaved in particular ways were more likely to survive in their environments and thus increased the chances of procreating and passing on their genes.

Like all animals we are recognized as belonging to the human species because we all have similar physical characteristics, instinctual reactions, preferences and emotions that make us human, even though we are all different within our species. Humans are genetically influenced to look and act like humans. This is the same as with a duck. We know a duck is a duck because it looks and acts like a duck. There are variations in the kind of duckness that animal possesses in both physical and behavioral aspects, but we know a duck when we see one.

The variations of physical human characteristics are infinite, but we recognize a member of our species when we encounter one. There are never-ending ways to express our humanness, but we arise from the same template. That basic template is then filled with our family experiences, cultural influences, and societal images flashed before us in the modes of the mass media. We are programmed into habitual response patterns during the first six years of our lives and become programmed. These programs are simply taken in without censor and thus, we can learn dysfunctional ways of behaving in the world without our conscious intervention (Lipton, 2005).

Although our behaviors are all subject to the same basic genetic influence of humanness we can each take active steps to become more individual and less like the collective when we become adults and begin the process of evolving our consciousness. Jung called this awakening process, *individuation*—to emerge from the collective preprogramming of the archetypes and our early childhood to become a unique individual. To understand this ancestral influence is to understand how our culture, ethnicity and gender all interact to form the characteristic temperament, traits and personality we are born with. Our environment, parenting and experiences all influence this inherent nature. Nurture augments or stifles nature.

Much of our behavior is already predetermined in a species-specific way. Those instinctual patterns are hard-wired into our psyche. The rest comes from learning. When we realize that much of our individuality must be formed and discovered as it emerges from the archetypal influences, then we are empowered to heal from the wounds that have shaped our psyche, as in codependence, and make different choices. This is the conscious aspect of healing. There is another subconscious layer of consciousness that needs to be worked with in order to effect the changes that we desire. This will be discussed in the next chapter when we explore body/mind approaches to healing.

Consciousness takes on a higher level of awareness so that we transcend our preprogramming and can begin to make positive changes in our lives by making choices that allow us to experience a different reality. We become co-creators of our lives. What this implies is that if we are unhappy with the way we see things, we can change our perspective. This requires for us to stop feeding into our emotional reactions, however, so that the neural networks that keep the emotional addiction going can be broken (Dispenza, 2005; Pert, 2005). Like any physiological process, our emotions produce a flood of chemicals in the brain and body, similar to when a drug user gets high from a drug fix. As the effects of the *chemical cocktail* wears off, the craving for another fix comes on. The drug user in this case would seek out more of the drug of choice while "emotional addicts" seek out a repetition of the situations that result in getting another chemical flooding from our emotional "state of choice" (e.g., anger, sadness, victimization, impatience, etc.).

The late Candace Pert (2005), co-discover of the opiate receptor site, believes that dysfunctional behavioral patterns are repeated over and over again because each time we experience an emotional state, we are strengthening those neural pathways in the brain. These networks stand at readiness for the next similar situation that will fire off the same neural pathways so that we experience that emotional state again. Like a drug addict, we get caught up in emotional reactions and act out from the feelings that are evoked. Stimulus/response. We encounter a trigger, a surge of emotions are elicited, we act out in reaction to these emotions, and then we somehow "feel" better (Wegscheider-Cruse & Cruse, (2012). Each time this happens, we strengthen the neural connection that produces the chemical combination released in our brain. In order to change this addictive cycle, we need to recognize that it is happening to us. In a repetition/compulsion cycle, our perceptions, and the resultant behavior have a grip on us! We are addicted to our emotions in the same way a drug addict needs his or her drug. Candace Pert explained this process in the ground-breaking film, ***What The Bleep Do We Know!?!?!?!***

To break this cycle of emotional addiction is rather a simple process actually. Joe Dispenza (2005; 2012) described that we must stop, take a breath and step back from ourselves. We have to stop *being* the emotion and simply observe the emotion arising. We can say to ourselves, "Wow! I am really angry!" or "Wow! That really pushed a button in me!" Emotions are a physiological process and not necessarily *who* we are. I can ride the emotion out and defuse it, thus loosening the neural nets that have formed in my brain that mimic addiction. I now have the opportunity to make another choice in my perception and behavior. Why do I want to continue to feel upset? Why not let it go and focus my awareness on what I want rather than stew over something I probably cannot change anyway? This sounds easy, but as you might suspect the neural pathways may not be entirely eliminated and even though you have worked to loosen the neuronal connection that accompanies heightened emotional states, the potential is still primed from the past experience. The important thing to remember is that with conscious monitoring of our *reactions* we can stop the process and intervene so as to not engage in the dysfunctional emotion or behavior in that moment.

To actively and consciously choose which elements are impacting our perception, we can then embark upon a conscious path to intimacy and heal from codependence. But we first have to know how consciousness works and understand the limitlessness of the capabilities of our consciousness. We are much more powerful than we have been led to believe. Each person is conscious to a different degree, which means that some people seem to have a greater awareness of themselves and others. Knowing the inner forces that govern our behaviors allows us to choose *not* to act on them, but to form new choices of behavior and perception. I liken this process to the difference between **reacting** to a situation, or **responding** to what is happening. In the first scenario we are simply repeating the cycle of our emotions without conscious intervention. It's like a reflex. In the second case, when we respond we are using the power of our consciousness to intervene in the emotional reflex and move towards greater awareness.

The key to healing is to grow and expand the limited ways in which we use consciousness, knowing that it can either set us free or keep us locked in a prison that is bleak and demoralizing. It means we have to understand how these limitations have been ingrained in us by our society, families, cultures and ourselves so that we can begin to hear our inner truth. This doesn't imply that our parents have deliberately instilled in us a limited way of being in the world, but that much of humanity is unaware of the unlimited potential of the mind. According to Gayol (2004), codependence is a *transgenerational script* that is passed down from grandparents to parent to children. As outlined in Part I, some ethnic cultures, such as in the Latino, East Indian, and other Asian cultures instill more traditional gender scripts than what we ascribe to modern U.S. culture and these values and behaviors continue through the generations until someone in the family recognizes and makes efforts to stop the transmission of these patterns to their children.

Once we change old patterns of reaction for new ways of being in the world, these changes become more ingrained through repetition and we are on the healing path. We must stop reacting to our emotional baggage, step back and imagine different choices we can make— ones that feel better. If we are constrained by our biology to be addictive creatures, then why not choose what you will be addicted to? How about being addicted to happiness, love, peace, compassion, joy, spirit or soul? With each pause we take when our emotions clamor for attention, we move a step closer towards healing from behaviors that characterize codependence. We can see how our perceptions in situations do create our behaviors and actions. As Joe Dispenza stated in ***What the Bleep Do We Know!?!?!?*** each morning before we arise, consciously spend the time to actively create in your mind what you want to experience that day. We let go of the emotional hunger to recreate the pain and suffering in our lives and throw off our victim mentality.

Is Truth or Reality Fixed?

Our concepts of reality and the knowledge we apply to ascertain these truths are subject to what we know as a species. The truths discovered in one era must withstand revision in our attempts to better understand the world around us (Welwood, 2000). The great thinkers of our time--Galileo, Kepler, Copernicus, Schroedinger, Newton, Einstein, Bohm and Bohr--have all contributed to the changing conceptions of "truth" and reality. Each of these scientists contributed new knowledge to the human pool of truths that had to be revised when the discoveries of each were finally accepted.

Reality is determined by a set of perceptual beliefs or lenses applied to interpret that reality. In accordance with Heisenberg's *uncertainty principle*, one can never be certain of more than one aspect of an event at any given point in time (In Talbot, 1991; Zukav, 1979). When the elements of a situation coalesce into a pattern, that *reality* becomes true to the perceiver. By focusing on only one interpretation of a situation, all other possible interpretations are ignored. He also wrote, "What is observed is dependent upon the *measuring device* or unit of measurement being utilized" (in Talbot, 1991). Heisenberg believed that all things in the universe are potentials waiting to be observed, and it is not until we focus our attention that reality comes to the forefront. The chooser determines the nature of the chosen in this instance.

This is similar to the truths that have been gained through research. Every truth must in fact be viewed as a tentative truth, a *good enough* explanation for now. It is the best explanation that can be given considering the limitations of human knowledge at that time. We apply what is known to a situation until more information steers us in a different direction. We rely upon these truths in lieu of greater understanding that may be forthcoming as we advance our abilities to measure and observe. For example, it was not until the inventions of magnetic resonance imaging [MRI], positron emission tomography [PET], or laser technology that enabled us to advance in neuroscience. As has been true for any generation of thinkers, we ascribe meaning to experience through the lens of the time in which we live. History is explained and understood according to the perspective from which we view the situation.

Thinking can be seen as a system that is self-perpetuating. Once we see things in a particular way, it becomes a *known* about our world. Each time we apply this perceptual lens, it brings order to the chaos of life. We then habitually apply these known factors about life without conscious appraisal of the situation. This results in a reduction of tension because we don't have to figure it out all over again, but we may be applying erroneous or outdated concepts to understand our world. Sound familiar? Our thoughts create physiological changes in the brain and we become conditioned to react to the world in the same way over and over again until we intervene consciously (Bohm, 1994).

We attach meaning to situations based upon our definitions and expectations that we apply to the experience, even if those definitions are wrong. Old paradigms are applied to new situations because they have worked in the past. Like a habit, we do the same repetitive things again and again in our lives. These thoughts, or words and their definitions continue to be applied to all situations because they bring order out to the chaos of living in a modern world.

Chaos generates anxiety because humans don't do well with the unknown. We like order and predictability. When we are anxious, we call upon strategies to reduce the tension and get things under control again. Many of these strategies are reactions, or a knee-jerk reflex. Unless we become aware of how reality is formed, we are likely to continue the automatic, habitual programming we have learned so well. We are like Pavlov's dogs and Skinner's pigeons. We learn a connection between two things, either through classical conditioning or through reinforcement; we react, then behave in a particular way. Certain circumstances evoke particular emotional reactions and physiological responses that become hardwired into our brains. We hear the bell and then salivate like Pavlov's dogs. Or, we learn that if we behave in a particular fashion, it prevents chaos from breaking out or anxiety from getting out of hand. In this repetitive cycle we unwittingly strengthen the likelihood of our repeating the same reaction patterns over and over again because we have repeatedly been conditioned and reinforced. We learn these behaviors.

Another way to see the dysfunction of using old outdated experience to live today's life is to imagine that the preprogrammed behaviors are similar to what Glasser (1984) called our *old pictures*. We access the old pictures that have worked in similar situations in the past and to shape outcomes. These strategies had survival value then and at least produced a temporary reduction in tension as they were resorted to again and again. But these behaviors have become over learned in codependence. They are habitual reactions that are applied indiscriminately to similar circumstances. New strategies must be formed that update the old ways of reducing anxiety. Behavior change requires reflection to understand the nature of our reactionary mechanisms. This reflection is accomplished by examining how language and its usage affect our consciousness.

What's That?

All little children reach a point where their favorite phrase seems to be, "What's that?" So we tell them what it is. What we tell them can be our truth or the truth that our parents told us or the truth that society wants us to believe. It can even be something we make up. The result is the same. That child applies the definition learned to everything and anything that resembles it without regard to the accuracy of the information.

Words make up the primary form of communication between two beings and are a symbolic system used to represent experience (Bruner, 1990; Fromm, 1951; Fordham, 1966; Glaser, 1984). At best, words approximate our meanings and help us describe the *reality* we are experiencing, but words are not the same as the actual experience (Wilber, 1979b). Experience is a total picture of what happens on all levels. It's impossible for any of us to convey it all in words. But it's generally the best form of communication that we have. Together, they form a narrative of what we saw or felt, but even then, we are limited because words cannot mimic experience. The names and labels we use help us categorize and define the world, but they are tools and are not the same as what we encounter in the world.

This is something to consider when we examine how consciousness is formed by the reality applied by the person doing the thinking. I can tell you that the sunset in Monterey is so unbelievable that you must see it, but that does not describe the totality of the experiences I've had while viewing those sunsets. Words are like a map. They are useful to describe experience but they cannot convey the experience itself. On a map, there are markings to help me locate places of interest, and the map helps me to find those places. However, those map markings cannot do justice to the experience I will have once I am there. I have to be there and experience the place to really *know* it.

Wilber (1979b) quotes Schoedinger, the founder of quantum physics:

> Subject and object are only one. The barrier between them cannot be said to have broken down as a result of recent experience in the psychical sciences, for this barrier does not exist...There is not a fact and an observer, but a joining of the two in an observation...that event and observer are not separable...All sensations of "matter" exist nowhere but in somebody's mind—doesn't that demonstrate that matter is really nothing but an idea? (p. 38).

Our consciousness is a subjective state and consists of all aspects occurring in a particular moment. To translate that consciousness into a form others can understand we have to use language. It has allowed humans a symbolic way to exchange information and experience.

Symbols are constructions of the mind, and are not the phenomena, object or behavior itself. Like all reductionistic pursuits, *the whole is greater than the sum of its parts.* Listen to a symphony in its fullness with all instruments playing their respective parts. Now break down the parts to the different sections of instruments— the woodwinds, brass, percussion, strings or voices. By themselves, the different sections sound one way. Put them all together and you have a masterpiece of creativity that surpasses the individual instruments and players themselves. When we apply this concept to human behavior, we realize that although we may understand the mechanics of how human beings work, it is not the same as the experience of being human.

The nature of consciousness and our use of language create the schemas or cognitive structures that help us organize our world. This categorization creates our initial sense of separateness at the same time. We use words and descriptions to describe ourselves. There are those things that believe are a part of us, and, those things that we believe *are not* who we are (Wilber, 1979b).

We form boundaries and separation from people and things that we see as either different from our self-ideal or simply as external to us. We forget that the naming of *me* and *not me* categories was simply a way to describe things. We create separation where there really is none (as in those aspects of ourselves that we reject) and then go about defending our artificial boundaries. "I'm this kind of a person, but not THAT kind!" We see only the positive aspects of ourselves but remain blind to the shadow we've created. In other words, this makes is easy to identify with those things that are familiar to us so we repeat the patterns again and again. We have pre-formed ideas about "the way it is," and then simply fit experience into our definitions. We create good/bad categories, but find it more difficult to think out of the box and imagine that perhaps what we are experiencing can be seen from a different perspective. We think that what we interpret is what is really *out there*.

> The Mind appears as a subject and an object. The creation of two worlds from one is like when you place an object in front of a mirror—you get "two" objects where there is in fact but one...we reflect upon the world and get "two" images, a seer and a seen, but actually the Mind is one (p. 59).

Because there are so many definitions and gradations to meaning that we can apply to any thing or situation, when we try to communicate using language, we are bound to have problems. This is when we learn to be better listeners. We must meet the other person in the middle where we can come to some agreement as to the definitions we are each applying to the words we are using.

The point here is that what we have learned about the world may be false or erroneous. When we are told that we are "worthless," this concept may become a truth for us, but in fact, it is simply a label someone applied to describe us. It has no basis in reality. It is not who we are. So by examining our assumptions we begin to see how the assumptions may have given us erroneous information about the world outside (and inside) of us. These aspects of consciousness formation make it difficult for us to see that we may be our own worst enemy at times. The good news is that we can revise and update our notions of reality. Updating implies that we begin to use words based upon *our own definitions, or meaning* to those words. We take our expanded awareness and begin to experience each new encounter as if we see the world through the eyes of a baby. We strive for what Ken Wilber calls, *No Boundary* thinking.

In "Acts of Meaning," Jerome Bruner (1990) stated that the original intent of the cognitive movement in psychology was to incorporate and reestablish the lost status of the *mind* in psychological research. Behavior and meaning cannot be understood without understanding how the mind determines reality. A person explains reality through the assumptions or implicit "truths" held about the world and those in it. These "truths" may be incomplete or outdated, however; thus feelings, thoughts and behaviors based upon these personal truths reflect those biases. Reality is the result of assigning meaning and value to internal processes. Transpersonal approaches propose that reality is a more complicated process than simply discovering what is "out there" or external to ourselves.

The Spectrum of Consciousness

In order for us to determine more evolved states of consciousness from lesser ones, Wilber (1979b) proposed a *Spectrum of Consciousness* model. He wrote,

The unconscious is stratified. Each level of the Spectrum has intrinsically different characteristics—different needs, different symbols, different modes of awareness, different motivations, different compensations, etc. The 'total' unconscious content is the sum of all the characteristics and aspects of the universe with which we are not identified in dualistic thinking (151).

This model represents a useful description of consciousness with levels. Think of a triangle or pyramid with the highest level of consciousness actually occupying the bottom portion of the pyramid. It is the widest part of this triangular shape and therefore represents the most inclusive type of consciousness.

As we ascend up the triangle or pyramid, the levels begin to narrow. "Each level of the Spectrum is marked by a narrowing of identity...a characteristic set of potential dys-eases" (Wilber, 1979b, p. 200). The narrowest forms of thinking are found at the tip of the pyramid shape of the Spectrum (see Figure 1). We therefore begin our journey as humans at the top of the pyramid, with the narrowest form of consciousness according to Wilber. As we age, we learn things that restrict our consciousness, but when we embark upon a path of greater consciousness, we descend down the pyramid and the levels of consciousness expand from the one above it. Any level below the tip is inclusive of all those above it.

So as we review the nature of each of these levels of mind, remember that we are first describing the most evolved form of consciousness (starting at the foundation, or base) at the *Level of Mind*. We will then progress up the pyramid that will reveal how consciousness is more restricted at the beginning of our lives and that through efforts to evolve one's consciousness, the levels of mind expand.

The bottom of the pyramid, *the Level of Mind* is considered to be the most evolved state of consciousness that humans are believed to be capable of attaining. At this level there is no separation of self from others. The mind, body and the rest of the universe exist in unity at this level. Next, above the *Level of Mind,* is the *Transpersonal Level.* This second level includes consciousness experiences that Jung felt were a part of the collective unconscious—"extrasensory perception, the transpersonal witness, astral projection, out-of body experiences…and other such occurrences" (Wilber, 1979b, p. 120). The *Transpersonal Level* is a more awakened consciousness than the level above it, but is not as awakened as when we are at the *Level of Mind.*

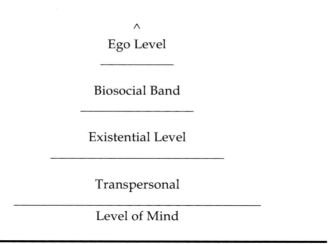

∧

Ego Level

Biosocial Band

Existential Level

Transpersonal

Level of Mind

Figure 1. Spectrum of consciousness (Wilber, 1979b).

The next level after the *Transpersonal Level* is the *Existential Level.* It is the level where we grapple with our lives as it pertains to the existential questions of life. We form our ideas at this level about meaning and purpose in life. We ask, "Why was I born? Why must I die? When will I die? What is my purpose? Do I have a purpose?" The mind and body are seen in opposition. We have a body, but we are not our body. We have a mind, but we are not our mind. In fact, the mind and body are separate at this level. We don't realize just how much our thinking affects our body and health. Wilber (1979b) referred to this as the

> Primary Dualism-Repression-Projection: Mind is severed... and it is then projected as organism vs. environment, with man centering his identity in his organism as existing in space and time (p. 120).

Dualism creates a consciousness that sees itself as distinct and separate from everything that is *not I*. It is a level of separation from others. This dualism creates the split that forces us to confront our mortality and spurs on our flight from death.

Above that, the *Biosocial Band* reinforces the dualism created in the Existential Level. The tip of the pyramid is the *Ego Level* and "...is in essence, nothing but a bag of edited memories" (Wilber, 1979b, p.136). One identifies predominantly with things that one has done in the past.

> The ego is happy today only if promised a happy tomorrow...(and can)...endure incredible misery in the present if it believes that there lies ahead a joyful future—but that future will never be enjoyed, for it doesn't exist now, and when it does arrive, by definition the ego will then be content only if promised yet another happy future (Wilber, 1979b, p. 137).

Consciousness as a spectrum is thus pure metaphor or analogy telling us what consciousness is like, but, not what it is. What it is goes beyond words and symbols "to the inwardness of one's spiritual experience, which cannot be analyzed intellectually without somehow involving logical contradictions" (Wilber, 1979b, p. 26).

Briefly stated, this model involves the development of consciousness as a descent into levels that are progressively less bounded by cerebral activity and thinking. Experience takes on a deeper quality when we don't feel compelled to apply the usual labels that predefine the quality of our experiences. As we descend into the higher forms of consciousness in the Spectrum of Consciousness, the quality of consciousness from prior levels is incorporated and integrated.

Without pre-formed ideas of how things *should* be, or what we expect them to be, we are open in the moment of the experience to see it with what Buddhists refer to as *beginner's mind.* "In the beginner's mind there are many possibilities, in the expert's there are few" (Suzuki Roshi in Welwood, 2000, p. 141). Like a beginner, we enter new experiences with no pre-formed ideas of how things ought to be. This makes room for more possibilities. From this level, we realize that reality is a perception formed by the fictitious character of our "normal" consciousness (Bohm, 1994; Fromm, 1983; Wilber, 1979b). More expanded consciousness demonstrates our ability to live in the moment, letting go of preconceived notions of meaning to objects or people, thereby allowing consciousness to remain more receptive and open to the experiences at hand.

Transcendence

According to transpersonal psychology, each individual can transcend the existential sense of separateness and alienation that is inherent in human experience (Tart, 1992a; Wilber, 2000). Rejecting qualities and characteristics of *self* denies individuality and creates a sense of alienation. When we reject various aspects of ourselves because they conflict with the self-image we hold, repression occurs. What we hate about ourselves becomes submerged into our unconscious and stays hidden from us until we project it onto others. We cast outside of ourselves the fears, dislikes, and qualities that we don't want to believe are a part of us. We tailgate others on the road, but hate tailgaters. We dislike deception yet we engage in it ourselves. We fear we will be betrayed, so we look for it in every word or action of others.

Projection is a Freudian defense mechanism that we utilize to reduce anxiety. Anxiety arises because we must control our inner drives that conflict with societal expectations or our own self-image. *Repression* helps us deny what is happening and projection casts it outside of us. This process results in a useful tool for the projector, however. By casting outside what lies within, we can see our true inner nature. This allows us to re-own what we have split from ourselves.

To transcend this splitting doesn't imply that we have to get rid of parts of ourselves, but that we must embrace what is within us so we cannot be ruled by it. If I know that I have a tendency to blame others, it won't help for me to take responsibility for everything all the time. When I am projecting and blaming others, it will serve as a red flag to check in with myself to see if I am shirking responsibility for myself onto others. When incorporated into personality in a conscious fashion, we can become more aware of how reality is created by our perceptions.

Acknowledging the disowned parts of self and integrating them takes self-understanding and self-compassion. De-repression is necessary if one is to become fully awake (Fromm, 1983). When repressions are lifted and we confront these issues, we no longer have to find strategies for numbing and can thus live a fuller life. Being fully alive to the totality of experience without clinging to the labels applied to conditions formerly seen as good or bad leads to greater well being (Welwood, 1990).

Understanding is directly related to the habitual thought system in place that culminates in the perception we have (Bohm, 1994).

> Being out of step with the context of the moment, drifting off into worrying about the future, or having a tendency to

divert attention from what is to "what was" characterizes this approach to interrelating. Existence is a process. Self-understanding is not a finite process. It is only from moment to moment that we can live. Knowing oneself is not the same as knowing about oneself. Transformation and healing can only occur through man's knowing himself (Hora, 1962, p. 35).

This type of consciousness nullifies experience into being what we believe it "ought" to be, rather than what it actually is.

Broadening the range of our consciousness is an evolution of our human capacity (Wilber, 1979a). Reality becomes revealed as the unfolding of an inner perception, or *enfolded reality*, as it unfolds into the reality we see and experience (Zukav, 1979; Hitchcock, 1991; Cortright, 1997; Wilber, 2000). Our experiences become shaped by the perceptions we apply in the moment. There are countless possible perceptions to choose. The possible meanings inherent in any situation represent the *enfolded reality*, while the reality perceived is the *unfolded reality*.

Evolving Consciousness

The evolution of the human mind was examined by Julian Jaynes (1990) in his book, *The Origins of Consciousness in the Breakdown of the Bicameral Mind*. Jaynes (1990) described the bicameral mind in which humans appeared to not be aware of themselves as individuals, but that they were part of a collective state of consciousness. These people were guided by visions and voices from above. Each individual still acted individually, but there didn't seem to be any indications or references to *I* or *me*—a sense of self. As the bicameral mind gave way to our present right/left brain, conscious/unconscious arrangement, humans attained greater consciousness, especially of the self. According to Jaynes (1976), humanity had not yet developed the self-reflecting ego that characterized modern consciousness prior to the second millennium B.C. (Feinstein, 1990b, p. 170). The dawning of the Mythical Epoch, roughly 10,000 B.C., was when language sophistication reached its full influence.

> With language, the verbal mind could differentiate itself more definitively from the physical body. People began to understand that the word is not the object for which it stands. Language was the major psychological vehicle for...consciousness.(With-out
> it)...humankind...was...incap-able of projecting into the future or of organizing itself in large membership communities...Because language embodies mental goals and futures, the new self could delay and channel its bodily desires...Language and mythmaking have replaced genetic mutation as the primary mechanisms by which awareness and innovation are carried forward ...As consciousness evolved, so did the ability to reflect, to step out of the myth and consider the way the myth structures experience...Stepping out of a particular myth is neither easy nor instinctive. The capacity to do so marks the birth of psychological freedom...mak(ing) it conceivable that a people can speed the process by which they free themselves from the inadequacies of their mythic inheritance, a particularly critical matter in a rapidly changing world...The mind becomes capable of turning back upon itself and reflecting on what it perceives (Feinstein, 1990b, pp 165-171).

Ironically, greater self-awareness meant less awareness of the collective, or our link to the universe. Visions and voices of guidance ceased and each person was left to find his or her own answers. Jaynes referred to this as a step in the evolution of the human mind, but at the same time separated consciousness from access to other sources of information that were common in the bicameral mind (e.g., auditory and visual hallucinations). Having visions and being led from "voices above" were considered blessings from a universal spiritual source. They were not signs of pathology as they are now perceived. Modern, traditional psychology has seen hallucinations as symptomatic of a psychosis, and therefore, as something to be rid of through medication. In the bicameral mind, however, these same voices and hallucinations were seen as a form of divine guidance from a higher source that collectively led societies towards a common purpose (Jaynes, 1990).

But the mind evolved, and with the advent of our sense of individuality, humans ceased to have hallucinations unless they were on drugs, in the middle of a psychotic break, or suffering from a high fever. When a child has a high temperature, it is not unusual for him to hallucinate. This regression in consciousness is similar to the regression in behavior we experience when we are under great stress. We return to earlier ways of coping with the world. How many of you have experienced hallucinations when you were ill? An even better example of regression is to recall what happens each night when we go to sleep--we hallucinate, or are psychotic. We hear voices that are not there, see and interact with people who are dead, and some of us even fly unaided by mechanical contraptions!

Using Jaynes' ideas, Wilber (1986) traced the development of human consciousness through four epochs and compared them to the stages of cognitive development as proposed by Jean Piaget. Piaget's theory describes the cognitive limitations we experience at different ages. The two year old does not see the world in the same manner as a ten year old. His theory provides us with a developmental scheme to the development of consciousness.

Thinking expressed in the *Archaic Stage* is likened to Piaget's Sensorimotor Stage and is limited to the way an infant is able to think. The *Magical Period* is related to Piaget's Preoperational Stage, or ages 2-6 where children demonstrate magical thinking and are fooled by appearances. The third period, the *Mythical Period* describes consciousness as similar to Piaget's Concrete Operations stage, approximately ages 6-12. This kind of thinking is bound by rules and the child is able to operate within those rules of thinking. The last period is the *Rational Period* and relates to Piaget's Formal Operations Stage, which begins at age twelve. This kind of thinking allows us to understand abstract concepts, form hypotheses, and imagine what can be rather than simply what is.

Wilber believes that consciousness evolution necessitates an additional stage to Piaget's theory. Cosmic or unity consciousness represents a movement of human consciousness into a more transpersonal form. He calls this the *Post-Cartesian Mythology* or post-personal or trans-personal character. In this paradigm, individuality remains a prominent feature in the guiding myths of the culture that reincorporates community values and transcends the personal ego. Consciousness is evolving towards a re-attunement with nature and the spirit (Feinstein, 1990b).

By understanding that the modern brain emerged from bicameral origins indicates that human consciousness must continue to evolve. Writers and researchers such as Deepak Chopra (1993), Larry Dossey (1997a), John Hitchcock (1991), Paul Pearsall (1998), Roger Walsh (1983), Ken Wilber (1979b), Colin Wilson (1987), Fred Alan Wolf (1992), Gary Zukav (1989), and others are continuing research into transpersonal dimensions attempting to define and describe the characteristics of transpersonal awareness. In the spirit of Darwin's theory of natural selection, researchers seek to know the history, evolution and implications of evolved consciousness.

Consciousness evolution may well represent the evolution of the human spirit (Wilber, 2000). This evolution can become a collective endeavor if each person takes personal responsibility for his or her consciousness progression. Wilson (1987) stated that, "if man is really to evolve, then he must develop depth, and power over his own depths" (p. 125). This evolution of consciousness requires that humans must learn to perceive the true nature of *reality*, actively participating in uncovering the guiding myths that are guiding behavior. Only by knowing what we know, can we change. What also arises in the process of uncovering our personal mythology is that an opposing myth emerges that counters the way we currently see the world. This is the antithesis (and just as unworkable). Feinstein refers to the antithesis as the opposite to what we currently believe. Thus, if I have concluded that I have been *too dependent* all my life, when I attempt to break out of this pattern I will tend to go to the extreme opposite. I will be *ultra independent*. It represents an extreme reaction to the older "map" we had been using to guide our lives. When former strategies fail to work, humans tend to believe that the opposite is better, although it is not. Each extreme position holds a gem of wisdom for the present and needs to be discovered and synthesized into a modern personal mythology that works for the individual (Feinstein, 1990a; Wilber, 1979a; Whitmont, 1991). This synthesis is addressed more fully in the next chapter.

With these ideas about reality, consciousness and the transpersonal in mind, it is now possible to form a framework for understanding codependence. The nature of that framework must be inclusive enough to include all that has been discovered regarding codependence to date. Codependence is a complex behavioral pattern that appears to emerge from the interaction of the many shaping forces in our lives. Our families teach us their particular interpretations of appropriate behaviors for each gender, our cultures reinforce those beliefs and add to it, and then society puts the finishing touches to those roles. They tend to limit and define the appropriate roles we are to assume in relationships. It also creates a belief that we must follow a particular scripted role about who we are and who we can become. It restricts the manner in which we can consciously create a warm and loving intimate relationship with another person.

♥

Chapter Nine

What Is My Mythology?

Socrates wrote, *"Know thyself."* To know ourselves is to be able to understand how our beliefs and emotional landscape have impacted the reality we see and experience. Greater inner awareness provides a strong foundation for choice-making that reflects our individuality. This intelligence of the self is what Goleman (1995) refers to as ***emotional intelligence***. Only through identifying internal truths, and applying them, can we live an authentic life. Knowing our preferences we are better able to be in relationships and represent our true self—our hopes, dreams, desires, and needs.

When we understand that the belief systems we hold are essentially guiding myths about how to live life, symbolic understanding is evoked because myths provide metaphorical meaning about what lies ahead. It tells us what we can expect and also how others before us have either met or have been defeated by those circumstances. Discovering how life has been lived by others provides us with a template for developing an individual response to life's circumstances.

As symbolic creatures, we humans seek meaning through the stories or myths that have guided the peoples of the generations before us (Feinstein, 1998; Feinstein & Krippner, 1988; Feinstein & Krippner, 1994; Fromm, 1951; May, 1991; Whitmont, 1991). Myths are not falsehoods, but are useful guideposts that inform us about the challenges we will meet in the process of living. They represent the wisdom gained from those who have traversed those passages of life before us, giving us some indication of which strategies may or may not work when we are confronted with those same passages. Although we can never know if these myths will actually take us to where we want to go or bring us what we expect, they serve as a map, a compass that guides us through along our paths.

Myths are described as "large controlling images that organize experience and direct action" (Feinstein, 1990b, p. 163). Examining what others have encountered in life and how they adapted is instructional for us when we are just entering a new phase. The myths are helpful so that we know what to expect, but they cannot replace individual experience. It is through experience that we learn whether these myths work for us or not. "Myth-making...is the primary, though often unperceived, psychological mechanism by which human beings order reality and navigate their way through life" (Feinstein & Krippner, 1994, p. 206).

The many myths that make up our belief system and guide us on our journey have been called a ***personal mythology*** (Feinstein & Krippner, 1988). This personal mythology is initially shaped by the influence of the archetypes. There is the archetype of birth. We have each completed that physical process which is a human related event. But, we each come through the birth process differently. Some are born head first, some feet first, some have to share the womb with another sibling, and then some come into the world through cesarean section. Birth is the archetypal situation, but the experience is colored by our individual passage into life.

As cognitive adaptations, we form schemas that we use to understand experience. They provide us with a form to follow, a template of how to navigate the terrain we are traveling. In the case of codependence, our myth tells us how we are to be in relationships--how to relate to others and to ourselves. We live by those stories that we have learned about life, which in turn shapes the way we see the world. They also influence the choices we make within those experiences. Our personal mythology consists of the many guiding beliefs used to interpret the world and have been described as *storylines* (Fromm, 1983), *stories* (Welwood, 2002), *boundaries* (Wilber, 1979a), or *pictures in our head* (Glasser, 1984).

Working on our personal mythology differs from traditional therapeutic cognitive/behavioral approaches because the transpersonal utilizes mythical thinking in the therapeutic process. This type of thinking embraces the intuitive and spiritual dimensions of consciousness and the means to achieve these states (Feinstein, 1990b). In eastern fashion, illness is viewed as an imbalance within the energy system of the body, and thus, it is believed that if the blockages are released and chi is allowed to flow, health will be restored. Acupuncture facilitates this process.

Traditional methods of therapy are aimed towards addressing symptoms and are more treatment oriented. Treatment does not imply that a cure is possible, but focuses to alleviate symptoms. Transpersonal methods are geared to help a person *heal* from a condition. *Healing* is different from treatment because to be healed means to be cured. One is inherently different. Transpersonal approaches involve caring for the spirit and soul of the individual in therapy that requires getting to the root of the problem rather than just treating the symptoms. To be made whole again, the person's spirit and soul must become involved in the healing process. Healing the soul in complex and requires a multifaceted approach.

Gender roles are a good example of one type of personal mythology. We learn what is expected of us as males and females, and assume that following these guidelines will lead us to success and happiness. We live "as if" the myth is true. "If I get my college degree, I will be successful in life." "If I am a good wife, I will make my husband happy." "If I am a good man, I will make my wife happy." After statements as these, I would suggest that you delve deeper into those beliefs. What do we mean by "success?" Whose definition is it? Do I want my life to be like that? What does it mean to be a good wife or husband? Do I want to fit into the archetypal template of the "good wife" or the "good husband" and will it make a difference? The questioning process is enlightening and always leads to greater awareness.

Each culture and society has its own particular myth to guide their inhabitants, but the particulars of each myth differ. Each culture or society passes on different myths about being a man, being a woman, or being a good child. These myths are passed down from generation to generation and have helped the people of those cultures to adapt. Adaptation does not always lead to psychological health and happiness, however, but we get some idea of what we can expect in life, and perhaps, learn strategies for navigating through each passage. They provide us with a useful map of what we can expect from life and serve as guideposts for our behavior as well. Our personal mythology is built from these templates.

Death is an example of an archetypal situation. We each understand our mortality to a greater or lesser degree. We know that with life there is death, but until we are confronted in the moment with our own death, we can only imagine what will happen, how we will experience it, what will happen, etc. Some fear the worst, some hope for the best. At the thought of death we feel a mix of emotions ranging from fear, curiosity, hope and dread. This is an archetypal situation. Our tendency is to not think of death if we don't have to, so we avoid it and deny that it; especially, that it will happen to us. Inevitably we must cross that threshold at some point, however, thus if we have consciously explored what death means to us, or have actively prepared for the passage as Buddhist and Taoists do, we will be better prepared to face it when it comes. But what if we were to prepare for the inevitable? How could we do that? Would it make any difference?

An interesting example of this train of thought is to consider the near-death experience (NDE). NDEs are believed to be an out-of-body experience (OBE) that happens to some people when they have been pronounced clinically dead and have been resuscitated. Some people who have been in severe accidents have also reported the following phenomenon. Both OBE and NDE experiences have generated reports that the person's consciousness leaves the body. From this suspended position, they can observe what is happening to their physical body as they (or their consciousness) are suspended above the situation. Consciousness continues and these people report being entirely lucid and aware of what is happening.

When a person has been pronounced clinically dead, has a NDE, and is subsequently resuscitated, that person usually no longer fears death. They report having experienced a sense of peace and love, having knowledge that there is something peaceful and wonderful waiting for us after physical death. The collective fear of death is within us all, but evolving our consciousness to assist us in our transition from this lifetime certainly makes a person more at ease with the inevitability of our own mortality. Thus, we deepen our understanding of the meaning of death, updating and revising our old notions about it. With courage we are able to walk bravely into our futures because we have prepared for the battle.

Continuing with the prior example, when death arrives we are drawn into a fearful or peaceful sojourn into this unknown region, depending upon our preparation for the arrival of that moment. Those who prepare for death through a belief system that helps them recognize and cross over the bridge when the time comes will no doubt be better prepared for this archetypal situation than those who have avoided thinking about it. Each person is called to evolve the archetypes into a more personal version that fits one's individuality.

Consciousness evolution implies that the schemas used to understand our reality are identified and updated as needed to nurture the condition of our individual spirit. In the case of codependence, interrelating has taken on the form of the collective emphasis patterned for many generations. From an historical context, appropriate female and male roles have been assigned in a hierarchical fashion reflecting patriarchal values. Although archetypes cannot be destroyed, they can and need to be evolved to fit the unique circumstances of an individual. Codependence represents a myth of over responsibility for others, neglecting ourselves in the process. It is an imbalance, or one-sided expression that needs balancing and re-visioning.

Individuation

Individuation is an instinctual drive to emerge from the undivided, unconscious state in which humans are born (Jung, 1963). By recognizing the nature of the archetypal influences, we can each modify our reactionary behavior to respond in a way that fits our own individuality. The archetype is given a *modern dress*. It is human tendency to act out in typically human fashion, but *individuation* calls for awakening consciousness so that we see how the collective and social forms of expected behavior have influenced our individuality. This allows for *reacting* (unconscious habitual behaviors) to subside, making *responding* (conscious choices about behavior) more likely. We are able to assess how our emotions are influenced by earlier fears or experiences. This awareness empowers us. Through awakening consciousness, reactionary patterns can be stopped which facilitates our ability to consciously respond to situations in the moment.

When we *react*, it is a predetermined behavioral pattern and is under the influence of the past and the archetypes. *Respond*ing, however, allows for conscious living by seeing situations for what they are in the moment. We have no pre-formed notion of the meaning of the experience, and therefore, we are more awakened to the fullness of what is actually going on. Responding represents an updated guidance system for understanding life.

Archetypes can be likened to *action patterns* found in lower species forms (Stevens, 1995). Action patterns represent a series of behaviors that are evoked by situational factors that trigger behavior. When these archetypes, or action patterns, are evoked, the organism is compelled to complete the set of actions that constitute the pattern. Thus, until one encounters the elements that constellate an archetypal pattern, the behavior lies dormant. Once the pattern is activated, we generally find an overwhelming emergence of feelings that will govern our behavior. These feelings reflect the emotions of that archetypal pattern (such as the jilted lover, or the jealous spouse syndrome) and we act as if our personality has been taken over by the archetype (Bolen, 1984;1988). Bringing conscious awareness to the situation helps a person see the old patterns of reaction being acted out and gives that person a chance to revise behavior and respond consciously.

The power of the archetype's influence can be demonstrated with the following example. In 1939, a British ornithologist, David Lack, trapped 30 finches from the Galapagos Islands and sent them to Robert Orr, a researcher in California. When Orr cast a mock shadow of a predatory bird over the finches in his research, the finches cringed and emitted alarm calls. These finches had never seen a predatory bird, nor had their ancestors, for hundreds of thousands of years. Ironically, the pattern of reaction was still intact in this species (Feinstein, 1998). In other words, the pattern of behaviors lies as a potential within the unconscious of an individual until the situation is such that it activates the archetypal response or reaction.

With the help of the archetypes, we all develop supporting myths, or guiding principles about life that govern behavior and perception (Feinstein 1990b). Taken together, these myths constitute our personal mythology. By examining the contents of our personal mythology, especially as it relates to our interrelationships, we can update and revise our mythology into a healthier form and heal from codependent relating.

Our prevailing, or current mythology, can be described as our present perception about a situation. Does our perception take in the world with unclouded eyes, or are we seduced into seeing something familiar, a ghost from the past being repeated? We need to engage in a conscious process to determine how much of our perception is simply the result of our reaction that stems from our past? Only then can we rewrite the mythology we are living.

The transpersonal model beckons us to embark upon a journey of discovery, recovery, and evolution by understanding how these elements have combined to create the mythology being lived. It helps create the space where we can come to a fuller awareness by discovering the ways in which we have numbed and split consciousness.

What the Archetypes Tell Us

Consciousness research is synonymous with consciousness evolution. Both areas of research seek to understand how humans are predisposed to act out patterns of psychic origin. Evolutionary psychologists are involved in this pursuit as well. They attempt to describe how our contemporary human behaviors are influenced by the preferences and adaptations of our ancestral lineage. We have inherited the physical traits of human evolution and a unique human psychological component. These characteristics were passed down to us genetically, making it more likely that we would have the same genetic abilities to ensure the survival of our family gene pool. Those who adapted to the demands of the environment survived and procreated, passing on their genetic endowment to their offspring. This was perpetuated throughout generations, so that ultimately, we are born as the genetic totality of our ancestors. We are the product of the behaviors, predispositions, emotions, strengths and weaknesses of our forefathers and foremothers and will have similar behaviors, preferences, expectations, and appearance.

The mechanisms for this inheritance are usually sought for within the genetic coding of DNA, but where consciousness is concerned, it is possible that *archetypes* represent the evolutionary mechanism of psychoid inheritance. Stevens (1995) wrote, "Evidence in support of the archetypal hypothesis has been pouring in for decades…and it has come from the sciences of the body--from biology and neurology" (p. 355). It helps explain the persistence of human related patterns of behaving, and preferences we have for a particular type of person as a partner (Stevens, 1995; Wright, 1994).

As you will recall, archetypes were introduced in an earlier chapter. Although they influence collective human behavior, each generation is challenged to provide the archetype with a *modern dress* that fits with the times and circumstances of the individuals in that society. Each generation expresses its typical human behavior in its own fashion. The Baby Boomers had their brand of individuality and tried to establish a new order of value for their generation that was different from the generation before them. Baby-Boomers attempted to rear their children differently than they had been reared, hoping to instill values they felt were representative of the Baby Boomer mindset. But the offspring of Baby Boomers still found and created their own brand of individuality for their generation. Instead of males growing their hair long hair and females burning their bras, this next generation instead chose to pierce and tattoo their bodies as *their* unique form of collective individuality.

Archetypes lie dormant until we cross the threshold of the archetypal situation. When we are faced with an unfamiliar situation, the archetypal pattern is constellated within that circumstance. What this means is that we will not know how we might respond until we are in the heat of the moment. Each situation constellates particular aspects of experience together, evoking the archetype with its accompanying emotions, apprehension, and perceptions.

Although we tend to simply act out the archetypal pattern of human behavior, Jung believed that we each must prepare ourselves like warriors for the moment of entry into a new archetypal situation. Forewarned, is forearmed. We will be better prepared to meet the challenges that arise in the different situations of life. This is almost impossible for us to do as infants and children, however, because of the quality of consciousness during that stage of development. Lipton (2005) writes,

During early development, the child's consciousness has not evolved enough to critically assess that those parental pronouncements were only verbal barbs and not necessarily true characterizations of "self." Once programmed into the subconscious mind, however, these verbal abuses become defined as "truths" that unconsciously shape the behavior and potential of the child through life...As we get older, we become less susceptible to outside programming with the increasing appearance of higher frequency Alpha waves (8-12 HZ)...consciousness resembles a "sense organ" that behaves like a mirror reflecting back the inner workings of the body's own cellular community; it is an awareness of "self" (Lipton, 2005, p. 164).

The importance of this information comes to our attention when we look at what happens at around age twelve. According to Lipton,

At around twelve years of age, the child's EEG spectrum begins to show sustained periods of an even higher frequency defined as "active or focused consciousness," the kind of brain activity used in reading this book (p. 165).

Once we become conscious and aware, we are then capable of emerging from habitual and archetypal patterns of behaving because we have achieved the type of consciousness that is needed for this type of processing. We can begin to emerge from our habitual behaviors and shape ourselves in the person we can become.

Codependence As An Archetype

When viewed as an archetype, codependence and the recovery movement can be seen as the contemporary struggle to emerge from an older, traditional form of being in relationships. "Archetypes...seldom undergo significant revision on a larger societal and historical scale...but it is not unprecedented...Beattie's discourse may well signal the existence of a contemporary version of the 'new birth' archetype" (Messner, 1997, p. 12). The new birth in this case is the recovery movement, but it seems to represent mere coping rather than healing.

Individuality emerges when we embark upon our individual journey as the hero or heroine. A heroine or hero feels a higher calling, requiring us to tap into our inner strengths and resources so that we can meet the challenges ahead. It takes courage to delve into the past, to uncover the unconscious, and discover just what our personal mythology is made of. We must act as a hero or heroine to explore what we have disowned about ourselves, to identify and recover them, integrating them into our personality to make us whole. Re-owning what has been disowned, integrating and embracing the truth of our experience brings the inner self to life.

When life is seen as a story, metaphorical understanding enhances our ability to see the meaning and lessons within that story. A metaphor is defined as, "a figure of speech in which a name or quality is attributed to something to which it is not literally applicable, e.g. 'an icy glance, 'nerves of steel.'" (New Webster's Dictionary and Thesaurus, 1992). In the context of this book, uncovering our personal mythology gives us deeper understanding about how we have tried to translate the myths we have learned into actual experience in our relationships.

Knowing the power of archetypes provides insight into the nature of patterned behavior and tendencies. We can envision what changes are necessary for us to evolve our mythology. Eventually, we learn to dis-identify with the storylines we have used to explain reality and simply begin to see what is (Ng, 2012). As Welwood (2002) wrote, we learn that life's circumstances need not be either good or bad; they simply are. Lessening our compulsion to apply set definitions to our experiences is indicative of *unity consciousness*. Reality becomes more fluid and forgiving in this process.

Imbalance in the psyche occurs because of the suppression and repression that happens when numbing is required to adjust and survive. How the mythological structure was formed within the developmental process, replete with the attitudes and expectations of our families, culture, and society, reveals the story we are living out. It provides a map for us to follow in the healing process because we are forced to re-examine the stories we use and update that template for a more contemporary, useable one.

Breaking the Code

Being symbolic creatures, understanding is best achieved when metaphorical understanding is evoked because it lends color and emotion to language. As humans, the capacity for symbolism and narrative are rooted in the structure of the brain (Fromm, 1951). We understand best when we are able to evoke a "picture" of what is being said. For example, if I tell you I'm having a bad day, that statement evokes one type of understanding. But if I tell you that I feel as if I have been put out to sea on a stormy day in a leaky rowboat, with no oars, my hands and feet bound with leather bindings, and my mouth is gagged...well, you get the picture. Four interacting sources produce myths and provide clues to working with a person's mythology. These sources are *biology, culture, personal history* and *transcendent experiences* (Feinstein & Krippner, 1994).

Biologically, we are hard-wired in such as way that contributes to the development of a personal mythology. Our capacity for language allows us to communicate meaningfully, and simultaneously, forms the beliefs and perceptions we hold about the world. This is because we apply certain ideas, concepts, and definitions to the words that we use in our language. Other sources of biological influence that impact the development of our personal mythology are the information and attitudes that are neurochemically coded as well as our temperament, physique, and hormones.

Culture is another shaping force. It is represented by the idiosyncrasies of religion, ethnicity, gender, economic status, geographical location where one is reared, and other similar pockets of influence in one's country. Each of these cultural environments in our lives shapes the perceptions we have about normality and expectations for behavior of different age groups as well as each gender. Most cultures provide rules and mores that encourage or restrict personal tendencies and these need to be teased out in the process of discovering the content of our personal mythology to discover if these templates really fit our individuality and uniqueness or whether it is time for us to revise our maps.

Personal history describes the combined translations of experience and what is stored in our autobiographical memory. As mentioned earlier, a coherent narrative of one's live is essential to an integrated mental state that gives us flexibility of response and the capacity to attune to other's feelings (Siegel, 2010). The importance of attuned attachment experiences was emphasized of Part I of this book and the theories presented in earlier chapters provide a way to examine where the gaps might be in the case of codependence. Reviewing how one's personality coincides with the theoretical descriptions helps us understand how personal history impacts personality and clarifies how codependence develops.

The fourth source that contributes to the development of our personal mythology comes from *transcendent experiences*. Transcendent experiences can come from altered states achieved through natural or chemical means. Meditation and other forms of consciousness alteration help awaken and expand the ways in which we see and live in the world. Altered states have a mysterious quality of consciousness and challenge the established ways in which we have construed reality (Feinstein et al., 1994). We are able to access other ways of construing our realities and increase the likelihood that we will have more "ah-hah" moments. We transcend our limitations.

Consciousness evolution requires that the inner world is first understood. Becoming conscious of the beliefs we hold about ourselves reveals the nature of our relationship to ourselves, or our *intrarelationship*. To transcend the limited view of self that is characteristic of codependence, we have to learn compassion for ourselves. The harsh inner critic characteristic in codependence, prevents us from valuing and expressing ourselves. Having compassion for ourselves allows space for creativity and a deeper sense of inner knowing to arise.

When we delve deeper into our emotions, we usually have a reactionary response. We may reject what we "hear" from our inner voice or deny its existence. Nevertheless, this reaction opens up the possibility for us to learn the roots of our discomfort (Welwood, 2000). We examine the ways in which we were wounded and see how we have held onto these wounds. We feel as if we are somehow disfigured because of it. We bear it because it is a part of us. It is a part of our past. As we heal, our pain turns into wisdom.

Although the inner work needed to develop a healthier relationship to self is an introspective pursuit, the true test is discovered in interrelationships. Firman et al (1997) wrote,

> Archetypes, like self, do not act solely from within the person, but have an external, interpersonal dynamic associated with them....The evocation of human archetypes consists in the fact that their activation is dependent from the outset on the dimension of social relationship between human beings...(and)....operate through lived human relationships as well as within the individual psyche (pp. 41-42).

Codependence cannot be understood apart from relating with others. It is a condition that is evoked by the circumstances found within relationships. It may appear that a person who stays out of relationships has a healthy relationship to self because the buttons that generally trigger codependent tendencies don't get pushed. Avoidance of relationships therefore does not heal the person from the wounding that was created through relating with others.

Jung (1971a) believed interrelationships were necessary for the true self to emerge. Relationships challenge us in a way that cannot happen otherwise. Each person brings to a relationship a different personal mythology--about relationships and their role in it. We also have a mythology of how we see our partner's role in the relationship. The two mythologies may be similar in some areas but there are bound to be differences that will not come to the surface until the moment of interaction arises. These differences stem from the variations within and between their personal mythologies and will affect the perception, receptivity, creativity, and spontaneity of the relationship. This interrelationship dynamic is the proving ground wherein we can transform our former codependence. Both partners must engage in the process of evolving consciousness and uncovering their respective mythologies.

The elements of personality that we have disowned, or have not developed, are often cast outside ourselves and onto others. These **projections** are undeveloped, or incomplete, and represent what Jung referred to as **archaic** behaviors. This means that the behavior remains closer to its original archetypal form, as we see in small children. Little children must learn to control and moderate their expressions of anger, for example, so that they become socialized. Hitting and kicking must give way to constructive communication and problem-solving.

As another example of undeveloped aspects of our self, when we lack a quality in our own personality, we are usually attracted to someone who is strong in that characteristic, whether the characteristic is positive or negative. We want it; they have it, and we believe that by being with this person, we vicariously have it ourselves. We sometimes make horrible choices in mates simply because that person has something we don't. Rather than seeking our own balance through an external source such as a partner, transpersonal therapy forces us to focus upon developing that quality within ourselves.

What is primitive or undeveloped in our own personality needs to be developed and matured so that we can see past our projections and see the real person with whom we are relating (Ng, 1998). These projections need to be reowned. One positive function projection and other defense mechanisms have, however, is that they allow us to see in another what is really coming from within ourselves. The person projected upon serves as a mirror, reflecting back to us what we have disowned so we can take it back and assume responsibility for our perception and choices.

Awakening consciousness usually contains an element of vigilance and discomfort. This vigilance is not synonymous with scanning for boundary violations, but is a full awareness of self and our inner processes. The split between the body and the mind are mended and we pay closer attention to sensations and intuition, giving less credence to thinking and emotional reaction. Codependence makes it difficult to identify what is personally meaningful. Rather, it causes us to opt for greater control and predictability. Letting go of the familiar evokes anxiety, but by being compassionate with ourselves, we can work through the uneasiness by giving ourselves the space for these uneasy feelings to emerge (Welwood, 1990). When we give our feelings space to be, we open ourselves to deepening our understanding. We find that our anger includes our hurt, our fears, our sadness, or frustrations. But unless we can "dance on the razor's edge," we cannot see beyond the anger to find that there is much more complexity to our feelings (Welwood, 1990).

The rapid pace in society requires continual adjustment and adaptation to change. Personal mythologies quickly become outdated for many reasons. Experience, growth, and education contribute to our need for revision of the old templates of behavior. This means we need to continually update and revise our personal mythology so that it fits our current circumstances (Feinstein & Krippner, 1998).

The prevailing mythology must be discovered, uncovered, and analyzed. When the old myth no longer works, an antithesis or counter myth will arise that is the polar opposite of the tendencies that stem from the prevailing myth. Eventually, a synthesis must be formed from the two to create a new personal mythology.

The following section provides an additional aspect to the transpersonal framework proposed. The process of uncovering, discovering and updating our personal mythology is presented and can be used as an outline for taking steps in this process of healing.

Re-visioning Our Personal Mythology

Feinstein (1990a) outlined the principles that govern the evolution of personal myths as a set of testable propositions that can guide the therapeutic process. Each of these propositions frames codependence as a particular mythology that needs revisioning and outlines what can be expected in the process.

- To emerge from the mythic structure in which one has been psychologically embedded, and to move to another integrated set of guiding images and premises,

183

is a natural and periodic phase of individual development.

- Personal conflicts—both in one's inner life and external circumstance—are natural markers of these times of transition.
- On one side of the underlying mythic conflict will be a self-limiting myth, rooted in past experience that is best understood in terms of its constructive purposes in the individual's history.
- On the other side of the conflict will be an emerging counter-myth that serves as a force toward expanding the individual's perceptions, self-concept, worldview, and awareness of options in the very areas the old myth was limiting them.
- While this conflict may be painful and disruptive, a natural, though often unconscious, mobilization toward a resolution will also be occurring, ultimately yielding a new mythic image.
- During this process, previously unresolved mythic conflicts will tend to re-emerge—with the potential of either interfering with the resolution of the current developmental task or opening the way to deeper levels of resolution in the person's mythology.
- Reconciling newly conceived personal myths with existing beliefs, goals, and life-style becomes a vital task in the individual's on-going development (Feinstein, 1990a, pp. 390-391).

Feinstein's (1990a) model depicts change and balance within the psyche as a natural process that needs periodic attention. We need not feel bad about behaving in codependent ways, but need to have compassion for ourselves. By understanding the circumstances that fostered this type of interrelating and providing a framework for understanding how codependence developed, things can change.

As a structure to follow in the transpersonal setting, Feinstein et al's (1988) five-stage framework will be used for re-visioning and updating our personal mythology.

Stage 1: Framing Personal Concerns and Difficulties in Terms of Deeper Mythological Conflicts

Underlying the conflicts and concerns generated in codependence are the beliefs held about reality. These beliefs, or myths, capture the essence of the appropriate roles an individual is to assume and the corresponding roles for his or her partner. Discovering the prevailing mythology reveals the reasons we feel compelled to behave in particular ways. The contributing factors to codependence that were explored in Part I can provide a direction for the therapeutic process of unfolding the prevailing mythology. In this first stage, our personal history needs to be uncovered and understood within a framework of the shaping factors of family, culture, and society. Using traditional forms of psychodynamic or cognitive therapy, meditation, art therapy, journalizing, active imagination, dream work or empty chair work combined with non-traditional approaches, such as energy psychology, chi kung, yoga or tai chi, would all facilitate the uncovering process.

The areas of importance that need uncovering are the myths that have shaped how we view ourselves. The myths about gendered behaviors, the role of each gender in relationships, what relationships are like, the purpose of marriage, the meaning of intimacy—these all need conscious scrutiny. What we believe and why we came to those conclusions constitute the work to be done at this stage.

As this process unfolds, repressed and suppressed aspects of self will emerge making us uncomfortable. As mentioned in the last chapter, if you are helping another in this process, you must resist the temptation to explain things to the other person and instead simply allow the space for the answers and insights to emerge. Doing the work to identify any dis-owned aspects of self, or exaggerations that were created in order to adapt, provides enlightenment regarding our beliefs.

Stage 2: Bringing the Roots of Each Side of the Conflict into Focus

As old templates of behavior fail to bring about satisfactory outcomes in our lives, a counter-myth, or antithesis emerges. We will be tempted to simply discard the prevailing myth entirely, but Feinstein (1990b) warned that the prevailing mythology still holds truths that work for us and must be identified and retained in the development of the evolving mythology.

Generally, the antithesis is an extreme form of the opposing tendencies within the prevailing mythology and is also characterized by one-sided thinking (Feinstein et al., 1998). There is a general tendency to see only black/white, either/or solutions, thus what emerges as the antithesis is just as unworkable as the prevailing mythology. One might think that if relationships cause one to act codependently, not being in a relationship represents a good solution. This is more one-sided thinking that could be traded for expanded consciousness. As in any situation, truth lies somewhere in-between the extremes. Identifying the elements of the antithesis facilitates the direction to be taken in updating the current mythology. Integration, education, and courage mark the process of bringing our personal relationships up to date, giving the archetype a modern dress.

Stage 3: Conceiving a Unifying Mythic Vision

The prevailing mythology and the antithesis represent valuable end points on the continuum and reveal the nature of the middle ground. This middle ground is then explored for the workable aspects that can be applied to our lives and internal truths. Both the prevailing mythology and the antithesis contain workable components. We must glean and plant these seeds of wisdom so that they can be included in our revised mythology.

The synthesis is formed from the conscious creation of what has worked in the prevailing mythology combined with the more updated aspects from the antithesis. The purpose is to form an updated mythology that incorporates the newly discovered aspects of self within the context of relationships. It requires moving out of one's head and into the heart to find the truth lying within, paying closer attention to the wisdom of the body.

By bringing the strengths and weaknesses of each side into focus, we can discover the middle-ground upon which we can walk that incorporates the best of both myths. Solutions need to be examined to determine whether they are simply a reaction or a conscious ferreting out of the situation. When this has been done, then we can begin to conceive of a unification of the two myths that incorporates the strengths from both while adding new, updated knowledge.

Stage 4: Refining the Vision into a Commitment Toward a Renewed Mythology

The fourth stage of the model entails a commitment towards a renewed mythology developed through therapy. What emerges as the synthesis is refined by discovering more untapped regions of the psyche.

> The person is called upon to examine the new mythic vision that was synthesized from the processes...and to refine it to the point where a commitment to that vision may be maturely entered...A series of personal rituals is introduced in this stage which induce altered states of consciousness for accessing   deeper sources of awareness to examine and refashion the newly formed mythic image" (Feinstein, 1990a, p. 394).

The tools utilized in this refinement process are as varied as our comfort level. Meditation is highly recommended, but you must find a workable meditative method that fits you. Some practices are more ritualistic than others requiring repetition of words, mantras, or abstaining from particular practices or substances. In the last chapter of this book, I introduce Chi Kung as a practical way to awaken consciousness. It consists of imagery, breathing, massage, and movement, working with chi to produce long-lasting change in our energy and health. It does not require the austerity of some of the more traditional forms of meditation, to enhance spiritual development.

Through meditation and achieving altered states of consciousness, we not only change the structure and physiology of our brain, but we learn about things we might not realize in our normal state of consciousness (Ng, 2012; Siegel, 2012). Normal consciousness is full of rules and judgment. When we are on the healing path, we feel a need to think and feel in new ways. When consciousness is relaxed we become more tuned in to our inner lives and the world around us. We don't shut out the external world, but learn to be in it without needing it to be one way or the other. The new information can then be utilized to help us form a creative mythic vision of seeing ourselves differently and thus promote healthier interrelating. Balancing and refinement characterize the work of this step.

Stage 5: Weaving the Renewed Mythology Into Daily Life

The last step is to take the renewed vision into the world and begin living from that renewed mythology rather than the old one. Through the transpersonal setting, we will have gained some skill in identifying, asserting, and acting in congruence to this new approach to life. This is a living process and needs continual updating and revision in order to work.

In the final stage, we will come to a practical and vigilant sense of the commitment to achieve harmony between daily life and the renewed guiding mythology. This is where thought must turn into action. The elements of the new mythology must be awakened and lived within everyday actions, thoughts and feelings. When old patterns of thinking, feeling, and acting emerge, we must consciously override these tendencies and act upon our new vision.

The process of letting go of some of the old myths and forming new myths to replace or augment the old are done consciously. This revision of the myths we have applied to reality enables us to become more aware of the truth resonating within. We can begin to live a more authentic life.

♥

Chapter Ten

Work To Be Done

This chapter addresses transpersonal awakening in a therapeutic setting, but is also informative for those of you who are working on your own issues of codependent relating. This chapter elaborates upon the process of coming to consciousness by examining our own unique version of codependence as a personal mythology. It provides the essential ingredients that help us on the transpersonal path to healing from codependence. To heal, we need to be aware of how we got here. The earlier chapters in Part I outlined the characteristics and etiology of codependence so that as we enter into this part of the program, we are well aware of our own brand of codependent relating.

If you have called yourself a codependent, it is my hope that through this work you will no longer refer to yourself as a codependent but simply *a person who has learned to act in codependent ways*. There is quite a difference between the two ways of labeling. In the first case, labeling ourselves as *being a codependent* often sounds like something we are doomed to *be* forever. In the second case, you are empowered to change your behaviors because you have the power to do so—it's your choice to behave in one way or another. A person may act in codependent ways, but we are not our behaviors. Why is it that people say "*I am a codependent.*" but do not say the same thing when they have a different problem? As I wrote in an earlier chapter, the names used to describe a person's behavior is often damaging to the psyche. When it comes to behavioral problems we tend to take on the label, such as "*I am manic-depressive,*" "*I am schizophrenic,*" "*I am an alcoholic*" but you never hear anyone claim, "*I am cancer*" or "*I am multiple sclerosis.*" Again, labels can be damaging so I have made every effort to refer to codependence as something someone *does*, not *who* a person is.

Soul Work

If healing is to occur, soul work must be done. What is soul work and what does it have to do with psychology? Elkins (1995) wrote that psychology needed to return to its roots as "the study of the soul" (p. 78). The etymological development of the term, *psychology*, reveals the original intent of the discipline.

> The word...comes from two Greek words, *psyche* and *logos*. Psyche means soul, and logos, in this context, means study. Thus, the word psychology literally means "the study of the soul"...the word *therapist* originally meant servant or attendant. Thus, etymologically, a psychotherapist is a "servant or attendant of the soul...the word *psychopathology*...comes from the Greek words *psyche* and pathos and literally means "the suffering of the soul" (Elkins, 1995, p. 78).

Hillman (1989) wrote that the discipline of psychology needed to return to this foundation. "Where there is connection to the soul, there is psychology; where not, what is taking place is better called statistics, physical anthropology, cultural journalism, or animal breeding" (Hillman in Elkins, 1995, p. 79).

Developing the spiritual self and attending to the needs of the soul through focusing upon the journey instead of the goal "is the refinement of spirit-matter...that proceeds on many levels at once...Physicists define spirit-matter as the feeling for the oneness of all things in the cosmos which stems from the fundamental unity of spirit and matter" (Hitchcock, 1991, p 26-30).

The road to healing is a spiritual adventure. Spirituality is distinguished from religion because the latter generally denotes some relationship to organized, established structures associated with organized religion. "Spirituality is the soul's free quest for the divine" (Cortright, 1997, p 13). It is a conscious endeavor of ever-increasing clarity regarding our sense of self and interrelationship to others, life and the cosmos.

The importance of combining traditional psychotherapeutic methods with a spiritual approach has been advocated by a number of contemporary researchers (Cousins, 1989; Feinstein, 1984; Lukoff, Lu, & Turner, 1998; Miller, 1998; Tart, 2000; Walsh & Vaughn, 1980; Zukav, 1989). In order for consciousness to awaken, it is necessary to integrate what is known in psychology with spirituality. By doing this, we increase our insight about how the perceptual world, or our reality, is formed. By unlocking the "frozen" aspects of personality, we have the opportunity to expand consciousness towards what Bucke (1961) and Wilber (2000) referred to as *cosmic* or *unity consciousness*.

Because codependence has prevented us from finding the true spirit of our core self, therapy is needed to identify and sort through the elements of personality. Learning to *be* instead of doing what we think others desire is difficult, but well worth the effort needed to uncover the true self. Without first having a firm sense of individuality apart from the preconditioned programming we received, we cannot drop the ego defenses to awaken consciousness (Welwood, 2002). The ego first needs to be made strong because we have to have an ego in order to let it go. Awakening consciousness requires work to develop both the ego and the spirit. Avoidance of the work found on either path is to "bypass" what is needed to heal or awaken (Welwood, 2002).

In the last chapter you were introduced to the ideas of the collective unconscious and the effects of archetypes upon behavior. The archetypes influence behaviors that make us act in *typically human patterns* (Jung, 1959; Feinstein, Granger, & Krippner, 1988; Feinstein, & Krippner, 1988). Within each era, culture, society, and individual, these archetypes serve as guiding principles or templates for behavior. The potential is present to react or feel a particular way in a situation. One reacts and then reflects afterwards. With growing experience, the archetypes take on a more personal flavor, but still retain the basic instinctual human form. These predispositions can seemingly have a life of their own, as when you feel taken over by a mood or when you act in a way that is totally out of character for you. To outgrow these reactionary behaviors we have to *wake up* and consciously commit to uncovering *our* personal mythology.

These templates for behavior predispose us to action when the circumstances are constellated that evoke the archetypal pattern of reaction. In other words, we may be predisposed to act codependently through the influence of the archetype and our upbringing, but it is not until we are actually engaged with another person in interaction that the predisposed patterns emerge.

To illustrate the constellation of factors that evoke an archetypal reaction, think about how most humans act when they are afraid of being abandoned in a relationship.

If we stay out of relationships, we will probably not have our fears evoked. In fact, we often avoid relationships, or break away from one *before* the feared abandonment can happen. But, once we have allowed ourselves to be vulnerable in a relationship, we increase the chance that we might have to encounter our feared situation--abandonment. Thus, being in a relationship can constellate the factors that bring on an archetypal reaction of "running away" so that we won't be abandoned. Also, we are less prone to carry out our archetypal role of codependence if we are not in a relationship! We will play out other archetypal roles, however, such as *"no one wants to be in a relationship with me because I am damaged goods."* I believe that the archetypal tendencies of being female or male in a relationship have predisposed certain groups and individuals to relate more strongly to the codependent identity. I believe that viewing codependence as an archetypal pattern sets the stage for what we can do to heal.

Transpersonal therapy helps us to unfold the underlying belief system, or *personal mythology* that has created our codependence. We need to discover the stories and beliefs we have been using to explain the world and our experiences. Awakening consciousness brings awareness to our habitual reactionary behaviors and makes room for new behaviors, ideas, and action to occur. The various schemas that direct our beliefs can be seen as a story (Fromm, 1983; Welwood, 2002) or mythology (Feinstein & Krippner, 1988) that guides our thinking and behavior. Believing creates the reality experienced. If I believe something to be true, it is true for me. The beauty of this idea is that we each have the power to co-create our experiences. This is the transpersonal path. By recognizing how our thinking has limited us, we can change it.

When we make the mistake of believing that our cognitive schemas are reality, especially when those schemas bring us pain, we are creating what Buddhists call *samsara*, or "delusive appearance." We think that our perception is the truth, but our need to be right often creates our sorrow. We want validation for the beliefs we have about life and relationships. Even when I don't want to feel bad, I can make myself feel bad by simply *seeing* the circumstances around me as an oppressive or depressing situation, rather than a challenging one. Samsara creates human suffering because we expect or cling to what we want rather than seeing what *is* (Yeshe, 1987). Welwood (2002) described this as clinging to the stories in our head. We often perceive that the stories or myths we believe in are reality when in fact they are nothing more than guiding principles of how to live. In a transpersonal setting, these stories, or mythologies are identified, updated, and revised.

The transpersonal viewpoint sees mental health as inclusive of both psychological and spiritual dimensions (Cortright, 1997). In the therapeutic setting, a transpersonal approach is more the application of an attitude towards healing than it is a combination of techniques. The condition of the spirit is a primary focus and the means to elicit consciousness evolution are used (Jung, 1963). It is an integration of the work and contributions of the various perspectives in psychology, seeing them as different dimensions from which we can understand human experience.

The Road Not Taken

In a transpersonal clinical setting, the self-imposed limitations to thinking, perceiving, feeling, and sensing are examined. This helps us to discover how to facilitate consciousness expansion so that we can learn to trust the internal biological wisdom we were born with. This is called the *organismic valuing process* wherein we tune into our bodies in order to glean information our mind may be obscuring from us.

We learn to feel for the first time. They are *our* feelings, so they tell us valuable information about which choices will bring us happiness or unhappiness. Codependence requires that we must now learn to feel and become conscious of whatever is coming up from the unconscious, or from our gut, even if it makes us uncomfortable. Being experts at numbing, we must learn to penetrate through this invisible cushion we have erected around our bodies and feelings. By looking at the ways we have restricted our perceptions, we can form new ways of perceiving and living.

Jung's (1971b) typological scheme of the four functions of consciousness is helpful to tune a person inward because it focuses on the four ways of knowing the world--*feeling, thinking, sensation,* and *intuition.* Feeling is our emotional barometer. Thinking is our cognitive intellectual assessment of things. Sensation is the function that helps us learn through our five senses. Intuition is that sixth sense that helps us to see the possibility of things.

Generally, thinking is considered more valuable than the other ways of knowing because our society has reinforced this belief. Most of us use thinking as the primary means to problem solve, yet what would happen if we were to incorporate the other three ways of evaluating and taking in the world? Feeling my own emotions and giving them value, paying attention to the sensations in my body when I am in a given situation, or listening to my intuition about something or someone when I am in doubt, would all contribute positively to my ability to make better choices. What codependence has taught us is that thinking is the only way to make a rational or good decision. This is detrimental to a person who has learned faulty ways of seeing himself, or who has constantly numbed himself so that he doesn't *have* to feel. Yet, *feeling is the only road to the heart.*

As Jung (1971b) described it, we each have a preferred function that we tend to use more often than the others. Even if your primary function is feeling, thinking generally dominates the way we make decisions because society is in love with the thinking rational mind. More value is placed upon a decision that is arrived at through an unemotional, unbiased, and objective point of view.

In codependence, thinking has dominated every decision. Thinking has caused us to have an external focus, one that trains its attention on others and their feelings. So this is obviously *not* a good choice for someone who is wrestling with codependence. *Get out of your head and into your heart.* We have to tune into the other three ways of knowing the world before using the thinking function, reversing the process for codependent behaviors. *Sensing* (what our body tells through our visceral responses), *feeling* (whether we like or dislike something), and *intuition* (what we can imagine will be or the inherent possibilities of a situation) are processes that give us valuable information *before* we make a decision (*thinking*).

If we want to heal, we must learn to feel. This may be hard for some of us because we may not like what we are feeling. That's okay. To know how we feel about something is a gigantic step in the right direction. It allows us to use that information in our decision-making. If I ignore that I am angry at a person or situation, I will make choices based upon guilt or denial. No doubt I'll make a bad choice because I've not considered all the information at my disposal to make a good decision.

But what happens if I honor my anger? Does this mean I have to act like an angry person? Not really. By acknowledging my real feelings, I begin to see how numbing and denial have caused me to make choices that have locked me into situations I might not want to be in. Learning to acknowledge my feelings, I can now be honest and truthful with myself and others. I can say how I really feel because now I *know* how I feel! We can clear the air and get on with living instead of harboring feelings below the surface that affects the quality of our relationships.

If you are reading this book because you hope to help others who are wrestling with codependence, it is important to remember that the most significant factor that promotes healing is the attitude and approach of the therapist or clinician (Dossey, 1998; Feinstein, 1990b; Pearsall, 1998; Welwood, 2002). We are best able to help another by having gone through our own awakening process (Welwood, 2002). *"To the degree that I am aware of my own consciousness or reality, I can recognize and respond to that of others"* (Lee, Ornstein, Galin, Deikman, and Tart, 1976, p. 2). We cannot lead another upon a path we have not traveled ourselves. It is not the particular brand of therapy that is used that heals another, but the rapport and resonance between the two that heals. Uncovering the contents of the prevailing mythology, or belief systems that guide behavior helps us see the many possibilities of meaning that we have neglected to see in the past.

Awakening

To awaken consciousness implies that most often, we are not fully aware. Normal consciousness is similar to being in a trance state, or **waking sleep** (Tart, 1986). Tart believed that this happens because we unconsciously go about life reacting instead of responding. We are creatures of habit. As explored earlier in this book, we base our reality upon the ideas that we've learned, applying these "truths" indiscriminately without scrutiny. Our predefined ideas and notions about life, love, people and relationships shape our waking sleep. We used the descriptions and definitions learned during the developmental process regardless of their applicability to the current situation.

The labels we use and our preconceived ways of understanding the world, limit our consciousness to familiar and known forms of interpreting experience. They are the storylines we use to establish and maintain predictability, but which keep us stuck. This prevents our growth and access to our creativity and resources that allow us to deepen our experiences. To awaken, we need to become aware of the many forces that shaped our perceptual world, or ***personal mythology***.

This includes an understanding of how the soul and spirit have been imprisoned (Welwood, 2002). This captive state is a product of how, as infants, we came to consciousness through learning language, conditioning and reinforcement, applying those schemas to assimilate and adapt to the world. *Awakening* is a process wherein we become aware of the perceptions we've used to explain our reality, learning how this may be preventing us from tapping into the possibilities of a more creative formless state of awareness. As we awaken and change our reactions into functional responses, we change the structure and physiology of our brainscape that in turn, helps us to regulate our emotions in a healthier way and to stay more open and flexible in our social interactions (Davidson et al, 2003; Dispenza, 2012; Siegel, 2001).

No form awareness lets us take in the world without having preset notions about what is occurring. We discover the *soul cages,* or prisons of conditioned self-other concepts that we have learned (Welwood, 2002, p. 288). Welwood (2002) outlined the process of awakening that can be used in therapy. The four steps he described are *identification, conceptual reflection, phenomeno-*

logical reflection, mindfulness, and *unconditional presence.*

Identification

Identification marks the first step. These early identifications form our reality about who we are. We uncover how the true, authentic self may have been distorted through the hands of others. What learn that what we have reflected back to us through the eyes of others can either help or hinder our blossoming as a child.

Conceptual Reflection

The second step entails *conceptual reflection.* In conceptual reflection, or the active participation of increasing consciousness through therapy, we come to understand how the labels, definitions to experience, and the guiding principles we have lived by have coalesced to form the reality we experience and create. Perhaps for the first time, we process and relive the pain of any trauma, neglect, or abuse we suffered, feeling the experience in its fullness.

Phenomenological Reflection

The third step is called *phenomenological reflection* and marks an awakening of consciousness. We need to take this step, which is beyond mere conceptualization or being able to talk about what happened. Phenomenological reflection requires that we feel the fullness of whatever the memory or emotion holds. It is similar to Freud's idea of *catharsis.*

Mindfulness

The fourth step, *mindfulness* requires that we become aware of the labels we have been using to explain our memories and experiences. What is happening is simply observed and taken in without numbing ourselves. Mindfulness is a presence that is tuned into the moment without applying the labels habitually established to understand reality. As these skills become honed, *unconditional presence* leads to self-liberation. This last step is the ability to rest in being fully present with each experience. Nothing is good or bad, but simply *is*.

Welwood (2002) wrote, "Meaning, purpose, support, direction, stability, coherence—none of these are givens on which we can securely rely. Since our mind creates them, we can just as easily see through them, or suddenly find ourselves unable to depend on them" (p. 149). Existential angst occurs at *the moment of world collapse,* when the known structures, forms, expectations and beliefs that one holds, collapse and what is left is a void or emptiness in its place. This tends to create anxiety that existentialists refer to as a *loss of being*. We dread the sense of empty space because our mind wants to fill the silence. This type of chatter in the brain is what has been called *monkey mind* (Chia et al., 1993). The constant *roofbrain chatter* must be stilled in order for us to hear our inner self.

When we release our former ways of filling experience, a space is created that makes room for growth and expansion of consciousness. When our known boundaries of conditioned consciousness collapse, anxiety arises, but also allows for the wisdom inherent in problems to emerge. When emotions are allowed to emerge and to be experienced, the implicit felt meaning or the enfolded reality can emerge.

Have A Heart

Transpersonal approaches to understanding behavior are being advanced in the discipline of psychology and are providing insight into the advancement of consciousness and a more complex analysis towards the understanding and treatment of dysfunctional behaviors (Tart, 1992a, 1992d; Wilber, 2000; Wilkinson, 1999). What has commonly been defined as pathological behavior in need of a cure from the traditional perspective of psychotherapies is viewed differently from a transpersonal perspective. Instead, deviations from *normal* behavior are seen as expressions of emerging issues struggling for attention within the different realms of consciousness (Lukoff, 1997; Grof & Grof, 1989b; Wilber, 1999).

Instead of eliminating what we don't like about ourselves, we can transcend our conditioning, reactions, and molding. This means that we can take into account the many facets of our self and see situations from more expansive viewpoints. We can transcend trauma and pain by understanding the inherent lessons within every experience we have. We can rise above the confusion to see the bigger picture in the whole scheme of life. Through understanding and awareness, consciousness evolves to bring a sense of order and meaning to life, having the effect of healing us instead of simply providing relief from symptoms.

Healing occurs because of the ***resonance*** created between two people, rather than being due to the techniques used. "Love is more akin to a deep, inner desire to reestablish completeness in the patient…Love for the patient is this yearning to help him or her be whole, to be One. Without this love, healing simply does not occur" (Dossey, 1989, p. 71). Again, I must state that healing is not the same as treatment. Treatment is like a bandage while healing *is to be made whole again*. Healing requires that someone cares for us—our soul.

Effective transpersonal intervention doesn't mean that we have to have all the answers. If we are helping another person on the healing path, this is even more important to remember. Every effort needs to be made to help others find their own answers, even when they are begging you to give them an answer. By expanding their awareness they can begin to decipher the patterns of their own behavior. We have to resist trying to explain or interpret what the other person is experiencing. We don't have to have answers for everything. By allowing space for change to occur, healing can happen. Within this space, a person is able to discover what has heretofore been submerged.

Sometimes what a client says or does may push the buttons of the therapist. It is inappropriate for the therapist to react. Mindfulness when we are helping others facilitates the healing process and reminds us that there are still areas of work to be done in our own lives as well. We need to allow for what happens in the therapeutic setting without reacting to it. It needs to be put aside for later processing after the therapy session.

Presence in places that were formerly avoided facilitates real healing. With caring, intimacy, heart, and a sense of commitment to the process, a therapist can help a client awaken.

> Heart...is a direct presence that allows a complete attunement with reality...What shuts down the heart more than anything is not letting ourselves have our own experience, but instead judging it, criticizing it, or trying to make it different from what it is (Welwood, 2002, pp. 163-164).

Welwood (2002) referred to this process as *presence-centered counseling*. Presence-centered counseling is a process where both client and therapist are fully engaged upon a caring and concerned path. It means more than simply being present and hearing the client's words. Presence means being fully responsive and aware to all that is transpiring within the resonance set up between the client and the therapist. Both people must work towards continued awakening consciousness. Avoiding uncomfortable moments of silence or anxious feelings creates emotional black holes in the psyche that cause numbing or armoring of the personality.

"When loving-kindness does not circulate throughout our system, blockages and armoring build up and we get sick, psychologically or physically" (Welwood, 2002, p. 168). To break down the armoring, the dictates of the mind need to be shut down, allowing us to feel what the heart conveys. Our *unconditional presence* with another person expands the ground through which the other person can grow and evolve. To repeat myself, when each experience is entered into with a beginner's mind, the pre-formed notions of how things ought to be are released and space is created for more possibilities to emerge. *In the beginner's mind there are many possibilities, in the expert's there are few* (Suzuki Roshi in Welwood, 2002, p. 141). The more time spent in the gap between what is known and what is not known, the more comfortable we will become with gaps in our self-constructed identity.

> Unconditional presence promotes healing by allowing us to see the ways in which we are contracted and feel their impact on our body and on our relations with the world....We must both see and feel....When we have shut fear out of awareness, it remains frozen deep within the body, manifesting as background anxiety, tension, worry, insecurity. When we finally bring full attention to the fear, feeling and opening to it, our larger being makes contact with the fear, perhaps for the first time...the fear starts to loosen...we may also gain access to our compassion (for ourselves) (Welwood, 2002, p. 145).

The Heart Knows

Healing occurs in a nonlocal fashion that is in some sense fueled by the heart energy of a person. Nonlocality is a phenomenon explained by quantum physics wherein space and time are not considerations to an experience that occurs (Capra, 1990; Chia, 2001; Dossey, 1989;

Wolf, 1988). In the case of healing, this implies that although there is nothing tangible or material that is passing between the therapist and the client, some sort of *resonance* has been established between the two that facilitates the healing process.

In his book, ***The Heart's Code***, Paul Pearsall (1998), a psychoneuroimmunologist wrote that the heart's energy is much more powerful than the energy produced by the brain. He states that western psychology emphasizes that the intellect, or mind, is given a position of greater authority. The mind tends to give more credit to intellectual concepts than to heartfelt meaning. We are inclined to value logic and reasoning above feeling, sensation and intuition, which he believes, is often antithetical to what the heart conveys (Tart, 1992a; Pearsall, 1998). He tells of a psychiatrist who approached him at an international group meeting for psychologists, psychiatrists and social workers in Houston, Texas. She told the audience about one of her patients,

> an eight year old little girl who received the heart of a murdered ten-year-old girl. Her mother brought her to me when she started screaming at night about her dreams of the man who had murdered her donor. She said her daughter knew who it was. After several sessions...I finally called the police...using the descriptions from the little girl, they found the murderer. He was easily convicted with the evidence my patient provided. The time, the weapon, the place, the clothes he wore, what the little girl he killed had said to him...everything the little heart transplant recipient reported was completely accurate (Pearsall, 1998, p. 7).

The point of this story is that we need to trust what is in our hearts and listen. This also means that if we really want to help others or ourselves, it must be a *heartfelt* commitment. To contact the deeper aspects of Self requires more than cognitive activity.

How the Self Came Into Being

In traditional psychology, dysfunctional adjustment as an adult is believed to stem from the failure to individuate or separate from others (primarily the mother). This is reflected in the current 12-Steps recovery programs, which emphasize separation and autonomy from others as a sign of health. According to Firman et al (1997), however, dysfunction arises in a person because there have been violations in the relational bonds with others. Humans are social animals and need others (Aronson, 1972). Even the ability to be alone depends upon our relationship to another—we choose to be *a-part* from someone.

In *The Primal Wound: A Transpersonal View of Trauma, Addiction, and Growth* by Firman and Gila (1997), addiction and other psychopathology are explained as the result of disruptions in the *unifying centers* from which the sense of "I" emerges. Citing research done by Daniel Stern, author of *The Interpersonal World of the Infant,* Firman et al (1997) wrote, "...(I)nfants are not lost in a fantasy world distorted by instinctual drives, but are active and aware from the start, purposely engaged in the business of relating to the environment" (p. 31).

From this perspective, *self* does not necessarily emerge from an undifferentiated state to one of differentiation and separation from others. Instead, a *self* exists from the beginning of life. It emerges and is shaped within the environs of the three unifying centers of the infant's world and therefore affects consciousness development. When the proper ingredients for awakening consciousness within the infant's developing world are present, the true self can emerge and evolve.

When we are infants, other people provide a reflection of how they see us. This instills a sense of how we are seen and appreciated. When caregivers are responsive and present, an infant has reflected back an image of being unique and individual. The first unifying center that shapes our sense of self as an infant is called the *holding environment.* If we are in a loving environment, the holding environment nurtures our growth. It is our inherent state of awareness of self as infants, combined with neglect and abuse, however, that causes the primal wounding Firman described.

> The human being is one and the same event with two aspects or dimensions: body and soul.... The blossoming of human spirit seems to imply an intimate union between body and soul and, conversely, wounding to the spirit seems to disturb that union (Firman et al., 1997, pp. 66-67).

Without adequate and accurate mirroring, or *empathic understanding* from the primary caregiver, we don't receive a true reflection of our self as infants. What is mirrored instead is a distorted reflection which is usually "a projection of the mother's (or caregiver's) introjects onto the child...her own expectations, fears, and plans for the child...(What) the infant has reflected back...(is)...the mother's own predicaments" (Firman et al., 1997, p. 34). As infants, we need to see an empathic reflection through the eyes of others so that we do not end up splitting consciousness.

Addictive behaviors arise from this wounding because it creates a distortion between our *true self* and the self we have to represent to others in order to adapt (Firman et al., 1997). Additionally, our brain does not develop the left/right brain coherence that indicates integration (Siegel, 2012). Emotions, needs, feelings, and sensations are blunted and submerged and a *false self* develops. This *false self* represents what we have come to believe about ourselves in the developmental process. When we are reared without empathic understanding, self-compassion fails to develop. To heal, these rejected aspects of self must be reincorporated.

The second unifying center stems from the infant's relationships to empathic peers, teachers, mentors and others as *self-objects*. Again, the emerging "I" is shaped by the perceptual mirrors cast back to us as infants, helping us form a sense of *I-ness* that we then assume.

The last unifying center comes from the *archetypes or collective patterns of development* (Firman et al., 1997). "Archetypes, like self, in some way operate through lived human relationships as well as within the individual psyche...Self is distinct from the changing archetypes even though it is active through them" (Firman et al., 1997, p. 43). Certain situations evoke these characteristic human responses.

When the relational world is disrupted at any of these three levels,

> Human life is crippled...by the wound of nonbeing caused by neglect and abuse. This primal wound forces our lives to become dominated by the desperate unconscious avoidance of nonbeing, and the equally desperate search for a sense of being untouched by this wounding (Firman, et al., 1997, p. 24).

Consciousness splits because we learn that who we are is not acceptable. What doesn't fit into expected or approved behaviors is submerged and causes a pushing away of self. Anger, rage, disappointment, fear and rejection of experience sink into the *lower consciousness* (Firman, 1997). The other region is termed *higher consciousness* and contains the wiser self and inherent wisdom of the individual, including our biological wisdom (information from our bodily reactions). Transpersonal therapy is geared to heal this split by helping a person access the middle ground between the two regions of consciousness. Contact with this middle consciousness heals the split and integration of the subpersonalities occurs (Firman et al., 1997).

To work with consciousness in hopes of awakening awareness more fully, various transpersonal techniques can be used in conjunction with traditional methods of therapy. Depending on the person's level of consciousness, Wilber suggests different techniques to facilitate awakening. The details of his model are beyond the scope of this book; therefore, the reader is referred to read his book *The Spectrum of Consciousness* (Wilber, 1979b). Overall, a combination of traditional and spiritual methods is used in transpersonal therapy. It should be noted once again, however, that it is not so much the technique utilized that helps heal another, but the attitude from which the healer is working.

Body and Soul

Spiritual forms of awakening are useful to help expand awareness and evolve consciousness. Techniques that help us tap into different states of consciousness, such as meditation, tai chi, yoga, and chi kung combine body/mind approaches that can assist us to reach within for wisdom. We can move toward the embodiment and transformation of expanded consciousness, confronting the conditioned aspects of personality patterns that block integration.

Traditional techniques of psychotherapy are first used to help the client to begin the process. When these methods are combined with spiritual meditative traditions to awaken consciousness, the client learns how to be more present in everyday experience. Meditative techniques and psychotherapy both represent polar ends of therapy for awakening from our *waking sleep*. This includes therapeutic techniques such as chi kung, biofeedback, yoga, aikido, energy psychology, acupuncture or other methods of manipulating bodily tissue or skeletal alignment (e.g., chiropractic work, rolfing or massage). These methods of working with the energy of the body and the resulting effects on the mind "fit into the body-mind relationship….(A)ny process that organizes and patterns the nervous system and the body, whether by mantra, yoga, etc. is likely to affect the consciousness of man" (Lee, Ornstein, Galin, Deikman, & Tart, 1976, p. 10).

Although the transpersonal perspective emphasizes the use of meditative tools for awakening consciousness, it is not a negation of traditional psychotherapy but represents a joining of hands. "Each of the differing schools of psychotherapy—East and West—are primarily addressing different levels of the spectrum" (Wilber, 1979b, p. 119). Firman et al (1997) wrote,

> The psychoanalyst and depth psychologist expect us to be able to observe and report upon our inner flow of experience; the cognitive-behaviorist teaches us to study our behavior and uncover the cognitive and affective underpinnings of our actions; the existentialist-humanist invites us to experience the here-and-now of our personal existence, take responsibility for this, and make choices regarding this; and, the transpersonal therapist understands the human being as capable of moving among a stunning variety of states and levels of consciousness (p. 68).

Cognitive-behavioral approaches help explain the surface mind. Psychotherapy delves deeper into the psyche to help us unravel the dynamics of the psyche in action. Humanistic therapies go a step further to assist in the reconnection of the mind and the body. Meditation is used in the transpersonal setting to expand awareness and introduces a person to

> develop the sustained attention necessary…to stop being 'hijacked' by…thoughts. When…(one)…enters an emotion in this naked way, it cannot persist for long because it does not actually have any independent, solid existence of its own, apart from (one's) concepts or reactions (Welwood, 2002, p. 190).

We feed our emotional state by focusing on those aspects of "reality" that validate our perceptions. "Don't feed peanuts to your neuroses," is one of my favorite sayings in regards to this tendency. In meditation, we access a direct opening to our feelings without needing to find out the meaning of the feelings. Going within and deepening our meditative states allow us to have a greater sense of awareness and freedom, even when we get caught up in emotional reactions. Rather than following our compulsion to judge the feelings or invent a story to explain it, we simply experience *what is*. By releasing the "inner critic" one can open to pain, without stories. Meditation practice assists us to enter into the ground of *be-ing* that underlies thoughts and feelings.

Therapy addresses the need to reflect, while spiritual practices help us to be more present, or to have a greater sense of presence in the world. The combination of both approaches allows for the "...unpacking of a wider felt sense, which illuminates...(the)...larger relationship to the situation in question...dissolv(ing) the emotional entanglement" (Welwood, 2002, p. 186). Behavioral problems can be viewed more as opportunities for awakening the heart and deepening our connection to life instead of trying to rid ourselves of what we believe is pathological.

♥

Chapter Eleven

Healing the Body/Mind

Consciousness becomes bounded through psychological processes that culminate in somatic, or bodily, changes. This process is called ***armoring*** (Marrone, 1996). This armoring is the body's method of locking in the emotions that are unexpressed and held back. Numbing never works. We *push* down what we will then have to *keep down* through sheer force of will. Unfortunately, this stuff always comes to the surface when we least expect it. We have our rages, depression, sadness, impatience, worry and fears. When we shove our emotions down, they just get bigger. They become like ignored children who are trying to get our attention. It is better to let them rise to the surface, deal with the pain, and incorporate the resultant wisdom into our soul. This can be facilitated through the many transpersonal therapeutic interventions that combine traditional and nontraditional methods, such as "hatha yoga, bioenergetic analysis, structural integration, existential psychology, polarity therapy, humanistic psychology, logotherapy, and massage therapy...essential existential methods that can help one to move more permanently towards higher levels in the spectrum of consciousness" (Wilber, 1979b, p. 244). Combining these approaches with a meditation practice and using energy techniques such as EFT can further the healing process more quickly.

In brief, when consciousness has boundaries there is a tendency to interpret and perceive the world as static and unchanging because we use predetermined definitions of reality to understand the world. To loosen the constrictions to consciousness, we have to learn to stop the endless chatter that goes through our mind. Meditation can help change awareness by assisting us to access the realm of consciousness that knows *no form* (Chia, 1986a; Welwood, 2002; Wilber, 2000). *No form* consciousness is what Wilber (1979) called *no boundary consciousness*.

The Six Healing Sounds

Chi is an energy that is believed to exist everywhere. Although it cannot be detected directly, its effects have been measured through such instruments as Kirlian photography, galvanic skin response, heart rate, blood pressure, and other physiological instrumentation (Chia, 2001). The chi within our bodies is the same as the electromagnetic force of the universe. Science is beginning to find answers that are supporting what chi kung masters have known for over four thousand years. The human body is an energy producing and sustaining force and can be understood by using scientific knowledge.

Medical *chi kung,* or healing chi kung, is based on this esoteric Taoist philosophy that helps us achieve no boundary consciousness (Chia, 1986a). Greater health and happiness can be achieved through various meditations and exercises that utilize the abundant energy, or *chi,* from the universe and combine it with our own inner chi, or energizing force (Chia et al., 1993; Chia, 2001). What we all want is more energy. Working with chi kung helps us increase the energy in the cells of our bodies and spirit. We become healthier and happier.

One very effective meditation that can be done just about anywhere at anytime, is the chi kung method called *The Six Healing Sounds*. The Six Healing Sounds were discovered by Taoist Masters thousands of years ago (Chia, 1985). These sounds were believed to be

> the correct frequencies to keep the organs in optimal condition by preventing and alleviating illness...Chinese medicine teaches that each organ is surrounded by a sac or membrane, called fascia, which regulates its temperature. Ideally, the membrane releases excess heat out through the skin, where it is exchanged for cool life force energy from nature. An overload of physical or emotional tension causes the membrane, or fascia, to stick to the organ so that it cannot properly release heat to the skin nor absorb cool energy from the skin. The skin becomes clogged with toxins and the organ overheats. The Six Healing Sounds speed up the heat exchange through the digestive system and the mouth. (Chia, 1985, p. 67-76).

In Chinese medicine, the five major organs, or viscera, of the body are believed to store specific emotions. When we are experiencing any of the negative emotions, we are overheating the associated organ in our bodies. In like fashion, when the organs are overheated or imbalanced energetically, we will feel these negative emotions more often.

Referring to the chart below, you will find the major organs and their associated positive and negative emotions. When we feel any of the negative emotions, we can counter them by filling our organs with the positive emotions. For example, the lungs should be imaged as silver/white in color. While focusing on our lungs (you can place your hands over your lungs), detect any sadness or depression you may be feeling. Seek to identify the sources of your sadness or depression then transform these negative emotions into their positive counterpart, courage and righteous feelings. Do the Lung Healing Sound, "sssssssssssss."

Major Organ	Negative Emotion	Positive Emotion
Lungs	Sadness	Courage
Kidneys	Fear/Anxiety	Gentleness/Stillness
Liver	Anger/Cruelty	Kindness/Generosity
Heart	Impatience	Love, Joy, Happiness
Spleen/Pancreas	Worry, Pity	Compassion, Fairness

Table 1. Emotions and the major organ systems.

The next organ you would cleanse and cool would be the kidneys. If you are experiencing fear and anxiety, then the kidneys are believed to be weak and out of balance. The kidneys are associated with the color blue, like the sky or ocean. While lightly touching your kidneys, image them blue and proceed to identify any anxiety you might be feeling and transform that into stillness. Also, detect any fear you are experiencing and then transform it into gentleness. The Kidney Healing Sound is "choooooooo."

The liver follows the kidneys. When we are continually angry, we are hurting our liver. You would then want to identify what has been causing you to feel angry and then work to transform it into kindness. Also, we would examine the ways in which we may have been cruel, to ourselves or others, and then transform the cruelty into generosity. When you are detecting the anger or cruelty in your liver, imagine that you are consciously contacting your liver by focusing upon it (it is located on the right side under your lower ribcage) and seeing green, like the forests. You would then do the liver sound, which is "shhhhhhhh."

The heart is imaged as red while we detect any impatience and hastiness we have been feeling. What are the sources of these feelings? Transform them into the positive emotions or love, joy, happiness, radiance, light and spirit. Do the healing sound for the heart: "hawwwwww."

Organ	Healing Sound
Lungs (teeth together)	sssssssssssss
Kidneys (winter wind sound)	choooooooo
Liver (quieting a baby)	shhhhhhhhh
Heart	hawwwwww
Spleen/Pancreas (guttural sound)	whoooooooo
Head to Foot Zones	
Triple Warmer sound	heeeeeeeeeeeeeee

Table 2. Six Healing Sounds

Next, image the spleen/pancreas/stomach and the color yellow. Detect any worry or pity and then transform it into compassion and fairness after identifying the sources of your worry or pity. Do the healing sound, a guttural "whooooooooo."

We learn to train our energy and attention to the organs that create health. We shape intention by focusing on each major organ, examining if there is any of the negative emotion present, process it by identifying, one by one, the situations in our lives that are creating the sadness, fear, anger, impatience, or worry. This is the cognitive component that brings to consciousness your reasons for these emotions. You then use the corresponding Six Healing Sound to cool that particular organ (see Table 3 below). Note that the sixth sound is not associated with any particular organ, but reflects one of the major meridians in acupuncture theory.

When you do the Triple Warmer sound, imagine that heat from the upper energy centers are moving down into the cooler lower centers. Pretend as if you are pushing heat down through your torso. Exhale using the Triple Warmer sound, "heeeeeeeee" as you imagine the heat moving down through your body, going down into the earth. As you inhale, imagine that you are drawing the coolness of the earth up through your feet, cooling your body.

> The Triple Warmer refers to the three energy centers of the body. The upper level, which consists of the brain, heart, and lungs, is hot. The middle section, consisting of the liver, kidneys, stomach, pancreas, and spleen, is warm. The lower level containing the large and small intestines, the bladder, and the sexual organs, is cool. The Triple Warmer Sound balances the temperature of the three levels by bringing hot energy down to the lower center and cold energy up to the upper center, through the digestive tract. This induces a deep, relaxing sleep (Chia, 1985, p, 101).

It is important that as you do the Six Healing Sounds, that you rest for a couple of breaths in between each sound, breathing naturally.

In body-mind fashion, chi kung teaches us to appreciate and care for ourselves by using the chi available in the universe and combining it with our own chi to heal ourselves and others. We learn to rid ourselves of negative emotions by using imagery to compost the negative emotions, sending them into the earth, and combining them with the positive counter emotion.

Taoist methods of expanding consciousness include the idea that we have three minds. The brain, the heart, and the gut (*tan tien*). The **tan tien** (about 3 finger widths below the navel) is a much smarter brain that uses less energy and definitely less words! The tan tien is considered our center. As Master Chia teaches, "Make three minds into one mind." When you are caught up with thinking too much, move your center of awareness down into your heart. Once you are centered there, then move down into the tan tien. In Aikido, if we lead with our tan tien as we walk, we will seem strong and rooted to the earth. We are less likely to be a *pushover* because we can firmly stand our ground. Others sense this as well.

This has been an abbreviated version of the Six Healing Sounds. Some versions use different hand movements as you do the sounds. In an effort to streamline the practice, the hand movements can be eliminated without reducing the energy balancing that occurs when you do the Six Healing Sounds. I refer you to the book, *Transform Stress Into Vitality* by Mantak Chia (1985) for more details.

EMDR

Another eclectic procedure that is making an impact in therapeutic circles is Eye Movement Desensitization and Reprocessing (EMDR) (Shapiro & Forrest, 1997). This process combines cognitive psychology, psychodynamic therapy, visualization, imagery, active imagination, and eye movements to help identify and process the elements of unfinished emotional content.

At the heart of our behaviors are the beliefs that shape our perception. Trauma and pain that have not been fully processed emotionally become stuck and cause our discomfort, increasing the likelihood that we will resort, once again, to old patterns of behaviors. Recall the repetition/compulsion cycle of codependence and how repeating our codependent actions helps momentarily alleviate the anxiety we are experiencing. This provides temporary relief but we can be assured that the feelings will return. Traumatic experiences occurring in childhood years in particular are subject to memories being "frozen" without being fully processed and thus unable to connect with other information on a neurobiological level. Trauma memory appears to be localized in the right side of the brain and with bilateral stimulation, such as the left/right eye movements or tapping, allows communication between the hemispheres and integration of trauma material with speech and language areas. "With the effect of EMDR, the restoration of hemispheric laterality, memory integration, somato-sensorial-cognitive integration occur. During trauma, thalamocortical attachment is disrupted; EMDR activates the thalamus, which repairs this disruption" (Kavakci, O., Dogan, O., Kugu, N., & Adam, D., Sept. 2010).

When we experience trauma, we tend to create beliefs about the world and ourselves that result in our pain and suffering. These beliefs become the focus in EMDR. While the irrational belief we hold is targeted, eye movements are used to mimic the left/right movements that occur during rapid eye movement sleep, or REM. The EMDR process allows us to target emotions that have not been fully processed. These unprocessed emotions keep us stuck in turmoil, but through EMDR, it is believed that the emotions are processed to completion so that the impact of the memory is lessened. Similar stimuli to the traumatic situation will be less likely to activate the sympathetic arousal because the elements of that memory and its associative aspects will have been processed into a memory...one that is in the past that no longer activates emotions as if it is still here in the present. Additionally, by focusing on healthier beliefs we would rather have, while engaged in the EMDR process, new beliefs can replace the old in such a way that we now operate from the new, healthy beliefs instead of being haunted by the old cognitions. Theoretically, this method is based upon sleep research and REM deprivation studies. It has been hypothesized that one of the reasons for REM sleep is to clear the mind of extraneous information and to help complete the processing of emotional content (Shapiro & Forrest, 1997). It is unclear, however, whether the eye movements are essential to the healing process (Davidson & Parker, 2001).

Using imagery, cognitive techniques, body-mind awareness, and psychodynamic processing, EMDR is an eclectic approach to uncovering the stories that continue to affect our choices in life. The problems emerge because we have not been able to completely process the traumatic event or protracted trauma of dysfunctional environments. We live as if these circumstances are ever present and physiologically, we continue to react as if the trauma is stuck.

EMDR is becoming more widely used to assist those with PTSD, symptoms of which codependents manifest. It has helped those who suffer from flashbacks, nightmares, hypervigilance, and increased startle effect characteristic of those with PTSD. It is thus reasonable to believe that this technique would help in the process of healing from codependence. The more difficult memories that create our suffering could be processed through EMDR, helping an individual to get past it and on the road to healing.

From a transpersonal perspective, some serious mental health problems, such as psychotic breaks, are being approached with more compassionate understanding. As a person allows unconscious material to emerge into consciousness, feeling overwhelmed by these images and memories may lead to a breakdown. These symptoms are being approached as a form of Spiritual Emergence that requires attention (Lukoff et al., 1998). Spiritual Problems is a new DSM-IV category that is described and validated for treatment purposes in therapy. Pathological behavior can be interpreted as the soul's cry for attention. Exploring the transpersonal nature of the trauma, moving through it and finding the seeds of wisdom to be gleaned from that event or time in one's life, assist the individual to transcend the wounds. Reasoning guides the memories to be processed.

Energy Psychology

A new branch of transpersonal healing comes from what is called *Energy Psychology*. The therapeutic techniques are based upon changing the energy, or *chi*, of the body to facilitate healing. Energy psychology "utilizes techniques from acupressure, yoga, qi gong, and energy medicine that teach people simple steps for initiating changes in their inner lives" (Feinstein, 2005). Using simple tapping techniques on acupressure points while engaged in a cognitive/imagery process similar to EMDR, a person is able to desensitize to formerly disturbing situations or thoughts. Feinstein (2006) writes,

> Trauma is known to adversely change limbic system structures (involved in various emotions such as aggression, fear, pleasure, and also in the formation of memory) that are not easily corrected through talk or self-reflection.

It has been shown that relief is more than symptomatic using energy psychology techniques because brain physiology is changed in the process. When we are anxious, our brains respond accordingly, firing off neurons that match the over-activity in the different areas of the brain. If we are to treat various psychological states effectively, we would hope to change the anxious EEG patterns into that of a normal, non-anxious pattern. In Feinstein's report, the characteristic digitized brain EEG signature of an anxious person is changed in just 4-12 sessions to that of a normal non-anxious person using energy psychology.

There are a number of energy psychology techniques currently being used in therapeutic circles: Energy Psychology, Emotional Freedom Techniques, and PSYCH-K, to name a few. A quick internet search would result in a cadre of information about these methods. Briefly described, each session lasts about 30 minutes which has great implications for the time we have to spend in therapy to get better! Not all problems need 4-12 sessions as in my example above, but the study cited documented the increased normalization of digitized EEG patterns over the course of 4 to 12 sessions. Some problems have been successfully resolved in only one 30 minute session (Feinstein, 2006). Success is primarily measured by self report wherein those treated report that they are no longer emotionally affected by the thoughts or situations that had formerly thrown them into panic.

These techniques access the lower personality realm, or what Lipton (2005) calls the *subconscious*. Lipton is a cellular biologist, author, and former associate professor at University of Wisconsin's School of Medicine. He also pioneered research on cloned human cells at Wisconsin and Stanford University's School of Medicine. He believes that cognitive change may not be sufficient to erase the programming we received as children because much of it is stored outside of conscious awareness in the form of conditioned responses (remember Pavlov's dogs?). Self talk and affirmations fail to reach this inner realm of the subconscious, which he considers to be the central control of consciousness that overrides conscious efforts on our part to change.

In Lipton's book, *The Biology of Belief* (2005), he writes that our reactions begin to form while we are still in utero. The importance of this early nurturing period becomes apparent when we examine the biological changes that occur at the cellular level in response to environmental input. He illustrates his point by examining the human cell's response to environmental toxins or nutrients. In an experiment, he placed human cells in two Petri dishes. One dish had toxins placed in the same dish as the cells, and in the other dish he introduced nutrients. How did the cells respond in these environments? Do you think they moved towards or away from the toxins? Instinctively we know that the cells would naturally move away from toxins. They did exactly what most of us would do if we were placed in a similar environment. We would shift into a ***protective mode*** of action, and either move away or defend ourselves. In the other Petri dish with the nutrients, the cells actually moved towards the nutrients in what he calls a ***growth mode***.

> I first became aware of how important growth and protection behaviors are (while) in the laboratory where my observations of single cells have so often led me to insights about the multicellular human body. When I was cloning human endothelial cells, they *retreated* from toxins that I introduced into the culture dish, just as humans retreat from mountain lions and muggers in dark alleys. They also *gravitated* to nutrients, just as humans gravitate to breakfast, lunch, dinner and love. These opposing movements define the two basic cellular responses to environmental stimuli. Gravitating to a life-sustaining signal, such as nutrients, characterizes a growth response; moving *away* from threatening signals, such as toxins, characterizes a protection response...some environmental stimuli are neutral; they provoke neither a growth nor a protection response (p. 146).

I heard Lipton speak of this study at an Energy Psychology Conference I attended in 2006 in California. After hearing about this and then reading it in his book, I envisioned the cells as a little child, holding up its arms to be picked up. In the case of the nutrients, the child reaches out without reservation or fear. In the case of the toxins, I saw the child having reached out for comfort at an earlier time, being rejected either through verbal abuse, or worse, by being ignored. This time the urge is still there, but now the child is more reluctant to express her needs. Instead, with arms only half stretched out, she asks in a timid voice, "Mommy?" or "Daddy?" half expecting to be yelled at or rejected again. This causes her to contract the muscles that would normally allow her to extend her arms out in an open gesture. As you might imagine, it would only take a few trials of this type of conditioning for her to stop asking to be picked up. Ironically, the urge may still be there, but the behavior is now stifled. Holding back of inner impulses causes muscular armoring to build up, causing us various types of pain the areas that somatize the impulse or feeling.

When we are in nurturing, supportive, growth-enhancing environments, we feel free to reach out and expand ourselves, challenging our potential to grow. We are more confident to try something new and even if we don't reach the heights to which we aspire, we are still encouraged and heartened by our efforts towards those goals. With courage, we try again. In contrast to a positive environment, we feel blocked, oppressed, angry, and frustrated in negative environments. We generally will do what we have to do to survive, but growth and creativity are stunted. Like the cells that were put near a toxin in the Petri dish, we tend to pull back into a *protective mode* in order to survive. It is our form of adaptation.

Therefore, changing consciousness may require a more direct intervention in order to desensitize and counter-condition some aspects of a person's belief system. These beliefs fuel reactions and form the **habit** realm of behavior. These habitual reactions may be more difficult to change without energetic interventions, such as those techniques advocated by energy psychologists that reprogram our conditioning, and thus the brain.

With the documented effectiveness of Energy Psychology being reported among clinicians, these techniques may well provide a viable route to helping us heal emotionally by breaking the connection between the upsetting stimulus and our resulting emotional barrage.

This has strong implications for healing and our efforts to transcend codependent behaviors.

Emotional Freedom Technique (EFT)

Developed by Gary Craig, EFT, or Emotional Freedom Technique is a powerful method that is simple to learn and easy to carry out in a self-help format. You don't need a therapist to get some relief, although for work with deeper issues a therapist is highly recommended. It involves a process that incorporates different approaches: psychodynamic (unconscious processing), cognitive (thoughts), imagery (visualization), and energetic (tapping upon acupuncture points). When combined together, the elements of EFT help to desensitize you to the connection between the stimulus and the emotional reaction that you are having.

Later, I will briefly describe Gary Craig's technique and go into more detail with a variation of his protocol. This variation was developed by one of my mentors, Dr. David Feinstein. Feinstein's technique varies slightly from Gary Craig's technique, but the effect is the same. People who are suffering from anxiety, phobias, sadness, trauma, anger, and even physical pain are helped through this simple method of tapping on specific acupuncture points. It is believed that this technique helps to deactivate the neural connections between a thought or situation that evokes a particular neurochemical response and the emotion experienced. It defuses the connection so that a former thought or memory that caused you fear, anxiety or sadness can be "deactivated" so that it no longer arouses such an extreme response to the situation.

I have had my face-to-face classroom students use this technique prior to our exams. Many students have exam anxiety and if they go through a couple of rounds of this tapping technique, it deactivates their fight and flight response (sympathetic nervous system arousal) and allows them to think with their prefrontal cortex—the part of our mind that we need to recall answers for exams! When we are anxious, the blood is squeezed off to the thinking part of the brain (prefrontal cortex) and the blood flows to the large muscles and the cerebellum where we can use habitual reactionary behaviors to save ourselves from harm or to fight off impending danger, such as our fear of not remembering the answers to exam questions! Students have told me that doing a couple of rounds of this tapping (energetic intervention) accompanied by a short affirmation (this is the cognitive component), they feel more alert, calm and ready to learn or take an exam or give a speech. I describe this technique below.

How does tapping on specific acupuncture points work to defuse the connection between our thoughts or a situation that causes a particular unwanted emotional response? The acupuncture points have what are called *mechanoreceptor* sites. These cells are more sensitive to mechanical stimulation that calms the fight or flight response. The calming effect caused by the tapping combined with the upsetting thought or stimuli is a form of counter-conditioning. We reverse the original upsetting emotion that is attached to the memory or stimuli in the environment and now instead of fear, sadness, or anger, one feels calmness.

Feinstein's Tapping Technique

Energy Psychology uses "techniques from acupressure, yoga, qi gong, and energy medicine that teach people simple steps for initiating changes in their inner lives" (Feinstein, 2005). Using simple tapping techniques on acupressure points while engaged in a cognitive/imagery process similar to EMDR, a person is able to desensitize to formerly disturbing situations or thoughts.

Energy Psychology in Disaster Relief was the topic of a presentation I was privileged to attend with Dr. David Feinstein as the speaker. He recounted case after case of people who had been severely traumatized in Kosovo. Out of 150 patients with "249 specific memories of torture, rape, or witnessing the massacre of a loved one, 247 of those memories were "cleared" in the sense that the memory could be activated without the body going into a stress response" (Feinstein, 2006). Those numbers are phenomenal considering the difficulty of changing our limbic system reactions to trauma! Feinstein (2006) writes, "Trauma is known to adversely change limbic system structures (involved in various emotions such as aggression, fear, pleasure, and also in the formation of memory) that are not easily corrected through talk or self-reflection" (p. 21).

These techniques access the lower personality realm, or what Lipton (2005) calls the *subconscious*. He believes that cognitive change is not sufficient to erase the programming we received as children because much of it is stored outside of conscious awareness in the form of conditioned responses (remember Pavlov's dogs?). Self talk and affirmations fail to reach this inner realm of the subconscious, which he considers to be the central control of consciousness that overrides our conscious efforts to change.

It has been shown that relief is more than symptomatic using energy psychology techniques because brain physiology is changed in the process. The characteristic digitized brain EEG signature of an anxious person is changed in just 4-12 sessions to that of a normal non-anxious person. Each session lasts about 30 minutes which has great implications for the time we have to spend in therapy to get better! The changes in brain physiology are believed to be due to the counterconditioning that occurs while using EFT (Feinstein, 2011).

In unresolved trauma, it is believed that the memory has not been processed fully and becomes associated with the terror or anxiety that was experienced at the time of the trauma. This association between the stimulus (or generalized stimulus) and the resultant fear responses need to be counterconditioned. The EFT process combines a cognitive statement while the tapping on specific acupuncture points sends calming signals to the brain informing the amygdala that even while faced with the anxiety provoking stimulus, everything is okay. The new association is "learned" and the sympathetic arousal abates.

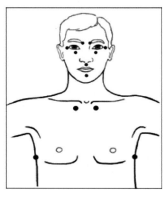

The Technique

When you are experiencing an overwhelming emotion, that is the time to identify what it is you are dealing with. You only have to create a setup word that will be the word that represents the memory or situation that evokes the overwhelming feeling. For example, if you are anxious about walking into your class to take your exam or going in for a job interview, your set up statement would go like this:

"Even though I have this anxiety (or fear), I deeply love and accept myself" or if you don't buy into the idea that you deeply love and accept yourself, use a statement such as, "Even though I have this "anxiety" or 'insecurity" I am ready to make a positive change" or "my intentions are pure."

This statement combines the negative self-evaluation that you are having with a positive cognition or recognition of an opportunity. The negative thought or situation will then become the trigger for positive choice.

228

The tapping sequence requires that you use your two or three fingers together to thump on the following acupuncture points on your body 7-9 times each as you say your set up statement, preferably out loud. So if you are working on anger, your statement would be something similar to, "Even though I have this anger with my mother, I deeply love and accept myself."

Craig uses the following tapping sequence:

- H – top of the head
- EB – inner edge of the eyebrow
- SE – side of the eyes
- UE – under the eyes
- UN – under the nose
- CH – center of chin
- CB – collarbone
- UA – under the arm

The following is based on Feinstein's technique as it is described in his book, *Energy Psychology Interactive: Self-Help Guide*. It is a condensed version of the detailed technique that he describes in his book. It is the basic format, but without all the details of the process. To learn more about the details, again, I refer you to his book.

Feinstein's technique uses the following sequence, 7-9 taps per location (this is the one that I use and teach my students):

- EB – inner edge of the eyebrow (above the bridge of your nose)
- SE – side of the eyes
- UE – under the eyes
- UN – under the nose
- CH – center of chin
- CB – collarbone (both sides simultaneously)
- Thymus (middle of the breast bone)
- UA – under the arm (4 inches below the armpit)
- Middle of the thighs on the outsides of the legs

- Karate Chop (hit the outer edges of both hands together)

Between the little finger and ring finger on the backside of your hands (called the *Triple Warmer* meridian in acupuncture medicine), use your three fingers to tap 7-9 times on this area while saying your affirmation.

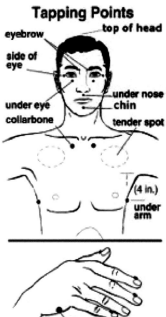

Tapping Points

Do this sequence at least 2-3 times. This is the short version that I teach in the classroom. Feinstein then adds what he calls the 9-Gamut method. While continuing to tap on the Triple Warmer area, you would do the following:

- Close your eyes
- Open your eyes
- Move your eyes to the lower left
- Move your eyes to the lower right
- Rotate your eyes in a clockwise circle (360°) or in a figure 8 pattern
- Rotate your eyes in a counterclockwise circle or figure 8 pattern
- Hum a tune for a few seconds (Feinstein uses "Happy Birthday to you")
- Count to 5
- Hum again

That's basically all you have to do, and as I mentioned I don't teach the 9 Gamut to my students. They simply do the affirmation and the tapping sequences 2-3 times and most report that they feel more alert, calmer, less anxious, headaches disappear, etc. Practice this tapping sequence so that you will remember what to do the next time you have an overwhelming emotion.

Remember to identify what you are feeling and you can just use a word (such as "Fear" or "Mom") to capture the situation or emotion that triggers the emotion combined with the affirmation of "deeply love and accept myself."

In my teaching of psychology, I have had some success stories for students who have used this technique. One student had taught her son, who has ADHD symptoms, this technique and she claimed that after he did it a few times he was calm. After he did the sequence, she stated that they were able to share one of the best hours they had had in a long time.

Another interesting case study involves a man who was in the Vietnam war working with the MediVac unit. Ron (his name has been changed to protect privacy) suffered from nightmares at least 2-3 times every week. After taking my course that introduced students to EFT and the Six Healing Sounds (see below), he creatively combined two of the energy techniques that I taught and was able to reduce the number of nightmares to about 3 per month. This is extraordinary! His last comment for the course after having used the technique for a few months was:

> The one psycho-physical thing that has changed about me is that I am now a great believer in the power of meditation. Using the E.F.T. (Emotional Freedom Technique) in combination with the 6 Cosmic Healing Sounds (from the Universal Healing Tao Center) I have been able to control over 30 years of physically debilitating nightmares, after 35 years I've been able to quit smoking, lost over 40 lbs., and in general I am much more physically fit and emotionally free of stress.

This chapter has introduced the basic work that must be done to heal from codependence and suggests a number of therapeutic techniques to help us to heal. The techniques introduced are by no means exhaustive. I encourage you to pursue greater detail of these techniques by referring to the appropriate citations listed in the reference section of this book. These are practical therapeutic tools that effectively work to help evolve stuck consciousness and create healthier minds and bodies.

♥

Chapter Twelve

Reframing the Construct of Codependence

Relationships are a powerful aspect of the human experience and are governed by the preferences our ancestors have chosen in mate selection. The qualities most valued in females, and those most valued in males have determined the types of relationships couples will experience. The social structures have shaped the characteristics we have preferred that enabled families to form and survive economically.

Biology, culture and society have all had a shaping hand in relationships. Biology has constrained females and males into particular behavioral patterns and preferences. It influences decisions regarding the roles each partner is best suited to perform to sustain the relationship and any offspring. Cultural and societal factors have contributed an additional shaping force upon this assignment of roles. Society, with its mass media influences, serves to disseminate and reinforce the patterns established.

Unfoldment occurs through discovering the mythology that fuels perception and behavior. "Women who have learned codependent behaviors can be seen as pursuing the archetypal Great Mother in their relationships with others. They seek to be everything to those they love; all nurturing, all powerful, all protective, bestowing blessings, tenderness and benevolence" (O'Gorman, 1993b). Females have been reared to assume this role and in the midst of a difficult relationship, these qualities tend to be overemphasized in order to establish equilibrium to the relationships again.

A transpersonal approach to understanding codependence requires that the many factors that shape codependent relating be revealed and understood in regards to their impact on what we each assume is acceptable behavior. Consciousness must evolve so that each individual in a partnership understands the impact that these forces have had on their respective needs, desires, expectations, and behaviors.

This book has outlined the myriad factors that constitute what is known about codependence and simultaneously indicates the problems associated with viewing interrelating in such a manner. Perceptually, therapy needs to focus upon these features to determine how they have impacted the development of a person's sense of self, or *intrarelationship*, that allows for a deeper expression of the one's inner nature.

Given the factors associated with the development of codependent relating, we need to explore how our consciousness has been limited because of these experiences. Through this process we can build a greater understanding of how this has created codependent patterns of relating with others.

The repressed aspects of self, the feelings associated with any neglect or abuse experienced, and how that has impacted self-esteem need to be revealed. Consciousness is restricted by the manner in which we frame the world. Krestan et al (1990) stated,

> On a metaphorical level (recovery) is the quest for painless relating. Current recovery models emphasize that one be perfectly fulfilled in relationship without ever focusing on the other person....Codependence recovery implies that if one is to recover perfectly then one has painless relationships. This perpetuates and maintains the errors and illusions of a patriarchal culture that promotes a false belief in the value of total independence and autonomy (a patriarchal value) and fails to recognize the need for healthy interdependence (p. 229).

How codependence has been framed in society, the labels and explanations for its development all need incorporation into consciousness so that we can begin to see how these perceptions have shaped how we judge behavior. Codependence is believed to be the result of not having been reared in a *normal* family environment. Krestan et al (1990) questioned whether the mythical *normal* family exists at all. Television promoted this ideal by reflecting predominantly white, middle-upper class values. The mythology of the normal family was depicted on television programs, such as *Father Knows Best, Leave It To Beaver,* and the *Ozzie and Harriet Show.* Although these are dated programs, they perpetuated the ideal within our parents' and grandparents' mythologies. These programs influenced societal values that gave rise to the notion that not living in such a family causes codependence. Krestan et al (1990) suggested that

> the 'normative' family of time honored tradition was perhaps never functional and thus definitions of deviance from the norm were flawed....The assumptions shared regarding the definition of functional families reflected the rules, roles, and communication existing within a larger context of gross power imbalance between males and

females. The power imbalance is dysfunctional (p. 221-222).

When normality is used as a reference point, it should be noted that approximately 97% of all people are reared in dysfunctional families, which makes dysfunction the norm. Reframing codependent relating into *overfunctioning* is a more useful term because it allows for us to change. It is describing behavior and not the person.

A Conscious Path To Intimacy

As a final aspect of this book, a commitment to a conscious path of intimacy is suggested. Welwood (1990) wrote,

> When we invite love to awaken us to the deeper powers of life, then working with its challenges becomes part of an ongoing adventure. Intimacy becomes a path—an unfolding process of discovery and revelation. And relationship becomes, for the first time, conscious (p. 4).

When relationships are conscious, we are called to develop greater consciousness to the hidden aspects of the unconscious parts of ourselves. It is a process, rather than a product that calls us to "mobilize inner resources—such as patience, generosity, kindness, and bravery—that give us a larger, deeper sense of who we are" (Welwood, 1997, p. 7). To be conscious implies that each person is committed to a singular path of becoming "more fully alive....Instead of looking to a relationship for shelter, we...welcome its power to wake us up in those areas where we are asleep and where we avoid naked, direct contact with life" (Welwood, 1997, p. 13). This process of intimacy challenges us to realize and express our humanness—humor, kindness, generosity, joy, gentleness, courage, patience, and compassion. In this context relationships can grow and thrive "because they inspire our heart to open while at the same time activating all the pain and confusion of our...entanglements" (Welwood, 1997, p. 19).

Gary Zukav (1989), author of the book, *Seat of the Soul*, stated that most couples now aspire to develop a **spiritual partnership**, rather than a marriage based upon traditional roles of husband and wife. A spiritual partnership is one where both partners engage in a conscious relationship. Welwood (1990) outlined the process for entering into a conscious path of love. It is a path we embark upon and commit to rather than seeking the fulfillment of a goal. This path is characterized by responsibility for our feelings, actions, and needs coupled with encouragement and support for each other.

The health of a relationship is measured by the spiritual health of each person. Both partners agree to continue to discover and evolve spiritually as individuals, tending to the needs of their individual souls and spirits. They in turn share the fullness of that evolving self with the other person. Simultaneously, each person encourages and supports the growth and evolution of his or her partner. The key may well lie in the fact that this is a path of conscious commitment that is entered into with mutuality.

Working out differences between our expectations and forming a reality that is nurturing to both of us entails conscious awareness. Each person assumes responsibility for any anger, disappointment, resentment, depression or disillusionment because both are committed to greater awakening. When we are angry, disappointed, resentful, or sad, we can best facilitate our mutual growth by opening up to allow space for the emotions. By not rejecting these emotions, or blaming our partner for "making" us have them, we can begin to question the nature of the emotion we are experiencing. What does it remind you of from your past? What are the circumstances that evoke these emotions? In what way are we projecting own fears or disappointment? These are the steps towards intimacy that you and I can take. We desire to have more conscious awareness of our reactions rather than blaming our partner.

We must each continually work towards opening consciousness by allowing space for our uncomfortable feelings to arise without blame. It may be tempting to invent or apply a storyline to what is happening, but we have to resist. Each moment is unique and is not a replication of some past experience. We enter each moment with a fresh awareness, seeing the relationship as a living process.

Conscious intimacy is a path that we choose in our relationships. Our roles and expectations are determined by the individuals in the relationship and is a growing flexible concept. By unraveling and updating the personal mythology we each bring to a partnership, we are better prepared to travel a united path that allows for individuality and evolution. We can heal from codependence.

References

Adler, A. (1957). *Understanding human nature.* New York: Fawcett.

Ainsworth, M., Blehar, M., Walters, E., & Wall, S. (1978). *Patterns of attachment: A psychological study of the strange situation.* Hillsdale, NJ: Erlbaum.

Alexander, W. (1997). *Cool water: Alcoholism, mindfulness, and ordinary recovery.* Boston: Shambhala.

Allen, J. (1995). *Coping with trauma.* Washington, DC: American Psychiatric Press.

American Psychiatric Association (1968). *Diagnostic and statistical manual of mental disorders (2nd ed.).* Washington, DC: American Psychiatric Association.

American Psychiatric Association (1980). *Diagnostic and statistical manual of mental disorders (3rd ed.).* Washington, DC: American Psychiatric Association.

American Psychiatric Association (1987). *Diagnostic and statistical manual of mental disorders (rev. 3rd ed.).* Washington, DC: American Psychiatric Association.

American Psychiatric Association (1994). *Diagnostic and statistical manual of mental disorders (4th ed.).* Washington, DC: American Psychiatric Association.

Anderson, S. (1994). A critical analysis of the concept of codependency. *Social Work, 39*(6), 677-685.

Aronson, E. (1972). *The social animal.* San Francisco: Freeman.

Ash, M. (1990). *The zen of recovery.* New York: Tarcher/Putnam.

Assagioli, R. (1989). Self-realization and psychological disturbances. In S. Grof, & C. Grof (Eds.). *Spiritual emergency: When personal transformation becomes a crisis* (pp. 27-48). New York: Tarcher/Putnum.

Baumeister, R. (1991). *Meanings of life.* New York: Guilford Press.

Beattie, M. (1987). *Codependent no more: How to stop controlling others and start caring for yourself.* New York: HarperCollins.

Beattie, M. (1989). *Beyond codependency and getting better all the time.* New York: HarperRow.

Beattie, M. (1997). *Stop being mean to yourself.* New York: HarperCollins.

Beauregard, M. (2012). Functional neuroimaging studies of emotional self-regulation and spiritual experiences. In A. Moreira-Almeida, & F. Santos (Eds.). *Exploring frontiers of the mind-brain relationship.* New York: Springer.

Biering, P. (1998). Codependency: A disease or the root of nursing excellence? *Journal of Holistic Nursing, 16*(3), 320-337.

Binswanger, L. (1962). Existential analysis and psychotherapy. In H. Ruitenbeek (Ed.) *Psychoanalysis and existential philosophy* (pp. 17-23). New York: Dutton.

Boeree, G. (n.d.) *The basics of Buddhist wisdom.* Retrieve from http://webspace.ship.edu/cgboer/buddhawise.html

Bohm, D. (1994). Thought as a system. New York: Routledge.

Black, C. (1981). *It will never happen to me.* Denver: MAC Printing & Publications Division.

Bolen, J. (1984). *Goddesses in every woman: A new psychology of women.* New York: Harper & Row.

Bolen, J. (1988). *Gods in every man: A new psychology of men's lives and loves.* San Francisco: Harper & Row.

Bowlby, J. (1969). *Attachment and loss: Vol. 1. Attachment.* London: Hogarth.

Bowlby, J. (1973). *Attachment and loss: Vol. 2. Separation.* New York: Basic Books.

Brazier, D. (1995). *Zen therapy: Transcending the sorrows of the human mind.* New York: Wiley & Sons.

Bruner, J. (1990). *Acts of meaning.* Cambridge, Mass: Harvard University Press.

Brefczynski-Lewis, J. A., Lutz, A., Schaefer, H. S., Levinson, D. B., and Davidson, R. J. (2007, July 3). *Neural correlates of attentional expertise in long-term meditation practitioners.* Retrieved from
http://www.pnas.org/content/104/27/11483.full

Bucke, R. (1961). *Cosmic consciousness: The study in the evolution of the human mind.* New York: University Books.

Burris, C. (1999). Stand by your (explotive) (sic) man: Codependency and responses to performance feedback. *Journal of Social and Clinical Psychology, 18*(3), 277-298.

Capra, F. (1980). Modern physics and eastern mysticism. In Walsh, V. & Vaughan, F. (Eds.). *Beyond ego: Transpersonal dimensions in psychology* (pp. 62-70). Los Angeles: Tarcher.

Capra, F. (1990). *The tao of physics.* Los Angeles: Audio Renaissance Tapes.

Capwell-Sowder, K. (1984). On being addicted to the addict: Co-dependent relationships. In Health Communications (Ed.), *Co-dependency: An emerging issue* (pp. 19-24). Pompano Beach, FL: Health Communications.

Carranza, L., & Kilmann, P. (2000). Links between perceived parent characteristics and attachment variables for young women from intact families. *Adolescence, 35,* 295-312.

Carson, A., & Baker, R. (1994). Psychological correlates of codependence in women. *The International Journal of Addictions, 29*, 395-407.

Cermak, T. (1984). Children of alcoholics and the case for a new diagnostic category of codependency. *Alcohol Health & Research World, 3*(4), 38-42.

Cermak, T. (1986a). *Diagnosing and treating co-dependence.* Minneapolis, MN: Johnson Institute Books.

Cermak, T. (1986b). Diagnostic criteria for codependency. *Journal of Psychoactive Drugs, 18*, 15-20.

Cermak, T. (1991). Co-addiction as a disease. *Psychiatric Annuals, 21*(5), 268-272.

Chia, M. (1986a). *Iron shirt Chi Kung I.* New York: Healing Tao Books.

Chia, M. (1986b). *Chi self-massage: The Taoist way of rejuvenation.* New York: Healing Tao Books.

Chia, M. (2001). *Cosmic healing I: Cosmic Chi Kung.* Chiang Mai, Thailand: Universal Tao Publications.

Chia, M. (2002). *Cosmic Fusion: Fusion of the eight forces.* Chiang Mai, Thailand: Universal Tao Publications.

Chia, M., & Chia, M. (1993). *Awaken healing light of the Tao.* New York: Healing Tao Books.

Chopra, D. (1989). *Quantum healing: Exploring the frontiers of mind/body medicine.* New York: Bantam.

Chopra, D. (1993). *Ageless body, timeless, mind: The quantum alternative to growing old.* New York: Harmony.

Coe, S. (1997). The magic of science and the science of magic: An essay on the process of healing. *Journal of Health and Social Behavior, 38*(1), 1-8.

Cohen, S., & Herbert, T. (1996). Health psychology, psychological factors and physical disease from the perspective of human psychoneuroimmunology, *Annual Review of Psychology, 47*, 113-120.

Collins, B. (1993). Reconstructing codependency using self-in-relation theory: A feminist perspective. *Social Work, 38*, 470-476.

Cook, E. (1993). *Women, relationships & power: Implications for counseling.* Alexandria, VA: American Counseling Association.

Cork, M. (1969). *The forgotten children.* Markham, Ontario: Paperjacks.

Cortright, B. (1997). *Psychotherapy and spirit: Theory and practice in transpersonal psychotherapy.* New York: SUNY.

Cousins, N. (1989). *Head first: The biology of hope and the healing power of the human spirit.* New York: Penguin.

Cowan, G. & Warren, L. (1994). Codependency and gender-stereotyped traits. *Sex Roles, 30*, 631-645.

Cowan, G., Bommersbach, M., & Curtis, S. (1995). Codependency loss of self and power. *Psychology of Women Quarterly, 19*(2), 221-236.

Crothers, M., & Warren, L. (1996). Parental antecedents of adult codependency. *Journal of Clinical Psychology, 52*(2), 231-239.

Csikszentmihalyi, M. (1990). *Flow: The psychology of optimal experience.* New York: Harper Perennial.

Csikszentmihalyi, M. (1993). *The evolving self.* New York: Harper Collins.

Cullen, J., & Carr, A. (1999). Codependency: An empirical analysis from a systems perspective. *Contemporary Family Therapy, 21*(4), 505-525.

Dass, R. (1989). Promises and pitfalls of the spiritual path. In S. Grof & C. Grof (Eds.). *Spiritual emergency: When personal transformation becomes a crisis* (pp. 45-51). New York: Tarcher/Putnum.

Davidson, P. & Parker, K. (2001). Eye movement desensitization and reprocessing (EMDR): A meta-analysis. Journal of Consulting and Clinical Psychology, Apr, 69(2), 305-316. doi: 10.1037/0022-006X.69.2.305

Davidson, R. (2008 January). Buddha's brain: Neuroplasticity and meditation. *IEEE Signal Process Magazine.* 25(1), 174-176.

Davidson, R., Kabat-Zinn, J., Schumacher, J., Rosenkranz, M., Muller, D., Santorelli, S. G. Urbanowski, F., Harrington, A., Bonus, K., and Sheridan, J. (2003). *Alterations in brain and immune function produced by mindfulness mediation.* Retrieved from http://www.mindingthebedside.com/wp-content/files_mf/alterationsinbrainandimmunefunc tionproducedbymindfulnessmeditation1.pdf

De Ropp, R. (1972). Self-transcendence and beyond. In J. White (Ed.). *The highest state of consciousness* (pp. 94-103). New York: Anchor.

Dear, G. (2002). The Holyoake codependency index: Further evidence of factorial validity. *Drug and Alcohol Review, 21*(1), 47-52. Retrieved from http://onlinelibrary.wiley.com/doi/10.1080/095952 30220119354

Dear, G. (2004). Test-retest reliability of the Holyoake codependency index with Australian students. *Psychological Reports, 94*(2), 482-484.

Dear, G. & Roberts, C. (2000). The Holyoake codependency index: Investigation of the factor structure and psychometric properties. *Psychological Reports, 87*(3), 991-1002. Retrieved from: http://www.ncbi.nlm.nih.gov/pubmed/11191419

Dear, G. & Roberts, C. (2005). Validation of the Holyoake codependency index. *Journal of Psychology, 139*(4), 293-313.

Dispenza, J. (2005). *Rewiring your brain to a new reality.* Symposium conducted at the conference of *What The Bleep Do We Know?!?!* Santa Monica, CA.

Dispenza, J. (2008). *Evolve your brain: The science of changing your mind.* Deerfield Beach, FL: Health Communications, Inc.

Dispenza, J. (2012). *Breaking the habit of being yourself: How to lose your mind and create a new one.* Carlsbad, CA: Hay House, Inc.

Donlevy, J. (1996). Jung's contribution to adult development: The difficult and misunderstood path of individuation. *Journal of Humanistic Psychology, 36*(2), 92-108.

Dossey, L. (1997a). Beyond nature and nurture: Twins and quantum physics, *Psychology Today,* July/Aug, 44.

Dossey, L. (1997b). Prayer is good medicine. *The Saturday Evening Post, 269*(6), 52-55.

Dossey, L. (1998). *Recovering the soul: A scientific and spiritual search.* New York: Bantam.

Dupuy, P. (1993). Women, relationships and Power. pp. 79-108.

Elkins, D. (1995). Psychotherapy and spirituality: Toward a theory of the soul. *Journal of Humanistic Psychology, 35*(2), 79-98.

Enns, C. (1994). Archetypes and gender: Goddesses, warriors, and psychological health. *Journal of Counseling & Development, 73,* 127-133.

Epstein, M. (1995). *Thoughts without a thinker: Psychotherapy from a Buddhist perspective.* New York: Basic Books.

Erikson, E. (1950). *Childhood and society.* New York: W. W. Norton.

Erikson, E. (1980). *Identity and the life cycle.* New York: W. W. Norton.

Fadiman, J. (1980). The transpersonal stance. In R. Walsh & F. Vaughan (Eds.). *Beyond ego: Transpersonal dimensions in psychology* (pp. 175-181). Los Angeles: Tarcher.

Fagan-Pryor, E., & Harber, L. (1992). Codependency: Another name for Bowen's undifferentiated self. *Perspectives in Psychiatric Care, 28*(4), 24-28.

Faludi, S. (1991). *Backlash: The undeclared war against American women.* New York: Anchor.

Farmer, S. (1999). Entitlement in codependency: Development and therapeutic considerations. *Journal of Addictive Diseases, 18*(3), 55-68.

Favorini, A. (1995). Concept of codependency: Blaming the victim or pathway to recovery? *Social Work, 40*(6), 827.

Feinstein, D. (1979). Personal mythology as a paradigm for a holistic public psychology. *American Journal of Orthopsychiatry, 49*, 198-217.

Feinstein, D. (1990a). Bringing a mythological perspective to clinical practice. *Psychotherapy, 27*(3), 389-396.

Feinstein, D. (1990b). How mythology got personal. *The Humanistic Psychologist, 18,* 162-175.

Feinstein, D. (1991). A mythological perspective on dreams in psychotherapy. *Psychotherapy in Private Practice, 9*(2), 85-105.

Feinstein, D. (1998). At play in the fields of the mind: Personal myths as fields of information. *Journal of Humanistic Psychology, 38*(3), 71-109.

Feinstein, D. (2005). Introduction to energy psychology [Film]. (Available from Innersource, www.innersource.net).

Feinstein, D. (2006, May). *Energy psychology in disaster relief.* Paper presented at the meeting of the 8th Annual International Energy Psychology Conference, Santa Clara, CA.

Feinstein, D. (2008). Energy Psychology: A Review of the Preliminary Evidence. *Psychotherapy: Theory, Research, Practice, Training. 45*(2), 199-213.

Feinstein, D. (2011). *Introduction to energy psychology.* [Video]. (Available from Innersource.net)

Feinstein, D. (2010, March). *Energy psychology's magical mystery tour of the U.S. Congress.* Retrieved from http://www.vitality-living.com/resources/Congressional+March+2010+report.pdf

Feinstein, D., & Krippner, S. (1988). *Personal mythology: The psychology of your evolving self.* New York: Tarcher.

Feinstein, D., & Krippner, S. (1994). Reconciling transcendent experiences with the individual's evolving mythology. *The Humanistic Psychologist, 22,* 203-227.

Feinstein, D., Granger, D., & Krippner, S. (1988). Mythmaking and human development. *Journal of Humanistic Psychology, 18,* 23-50.

Firman, J., & Gila, A. (1997). *The primal wound: A transpersonal view of trauma, addiction, and growth.* New York: SUNY.

Fischer, J., & Crawford, D. (1992). Codependency and parenting styles. *Journal of Adolescent Research, 7*(3), 352-363.

Fischer, J., Spann, L., & Crawford, D. (1991). Measuring codependency. *Alcoholism Treatment Quarterly, 8,* 87-100.

Fisher, D., & Beer, J. (1990). Codependency and self-esteem among high school students, *Psychological Reports, 66,* 1001-1002.

Fordham, F. (1966). *An introduction to Jung's psychology.* Maryland: Penguin.

Frank, L., & Bland, C. (1992). What's in a name? Considering the co-dependent label. *Journal of Strategic and Systemic Therapies, 11*(2), 1-14.

Frank, P., & Golden, G. (1992). Blaming by naming: Battered women and the epidemic of codependence. *Social Work, 37*(1), 5-6.

Freud, S. (1938a). *The basic writings of Sigmund Freud.* A.A. Brill (Ed. And Trans.) New York: Random House.

Freud, S. (1938b). The sexual abberations. In A. A. Brill (Ed. and Trans.). *The basic writings of Sigmund Freud* (pp.553-579). New York: Random House.

Friedman, H., & MacDonald, D. (1997). Toward a working definition of transpersonal assessment. *The Journal of Transpersonal Psychology, 29*(2), 105-122.

Friel, J., Subby, R., & Friel, L. (1984). *Co-dependence and the search for identity.* Pompano Beach, FL: Health Commuications, Inc.

Friends in Recovery (1987). *The 12-steps for adult children of alcoholic and other dysfunctional families.* San Diego, CA: Recovery Publication.

Fromm, E. (1951). *The forgotten language: An introduction to the understanding of dreams, fairy tales and myths.* New York: Grove Press.

Fromm, E. (1983). The nature of well-being. In J. Welwood (Ed.) *Awakening the Heart: East/West approaches to psychotherapy and the healing relationship* (pp.59-69). Boston: Shambhala.

Fuller, J., & Warner, R. (2000). Family stressors as predictors of codependency. *Genetic, Social, and General Psychology Monographs, 126.*

Gayol, G. (2004). Codependence: A transgenerational script. *Transactional Analysis Journal, 34*(4), pp. 312-322. Retrieved from http://www.imat.com.mx/pdf/codependence.pdf

Gemin, J. (1997). Manufacturing codependency: Self-help as discursive formation. *Critical Studies in Mass Communication, 14*(3), 249-266.

Gierymski, T., & Williams, T. (1986). Codependency. *Journal of Psychoactive Drugs, 18*(1), 7-13.

Glasser, W. (1984). *Control theory.* New York: Harper & Row.

Goble, F. (1970). *The third force: The psychology of Abraham Maslow.* New York: Washington Square Press.

Goleman, D. (1980). Mental health in classical Buddhist psychology. In R. Walsh & F. Vaughan. (Eds.). *Beyond ego: Transpersonal dimensions in psychology* (pp. 89-92). Los Angeles: Tarcher.

Goleman, D. (1992). The Buddha on meditation and states of consciousness. In C. Tart (Ed.) *Transpersonal psychologies: Perspectives on the mind from seven great spiritual traditions* (pp. 203-230). San Francisco: Harper.

Goleman, D. (1995). *Emotional intelligence.* New York: Bantam.

Gomberg, E. (1989). On terms used and abused: The concepts of codependency. *Drugs & Society, 3,* 113-132.

Gordon, J. (1997). Challenging codependency: Feminist critiques. *Journal of Studies on Alcohol, 58,* 221-222.

Gorski, T., & Miller, M. (1984). Co-alcoholic relapse: Family factors and warning signs. In Health Communications (Ed.), *Co-dependency: An emerging issue* (pp. 77-82). Pompano Beach, FL: Health Communications.

Gotham, H., & Sher, K. (1996). Do codependent traits involve more than basic dimensions of personality and psychopathology? *Journal of Studies on Alcohol, 57*(1), 34-39.

Granello, D., & Beamish, P. (1998). Reconceptualizing codependency in women: A sense of connectedness, not pathology. *Journal of Mental Health Counseling, 20*(4), 344-358.

Gravitz, H., & Bowden, J. (1985). *Guide to recovery.* Holmes Beach, FL: Learning publications.

Greene, B. (1999). *The elegant universe: Superstrings, hidden dimensions, and the quest for the ultimate theory.* New York: W.W. Norton.

Greenleaf, J. (1984). Co-alcoholic/Para-alcoholic: Who's who and what's the difference. In Health Communications (Ed.), *Co-dependency: An emerging issue* (pp. 5-18). Pompano Beach, FL: Health Communications.

Greenspan, M. (1983). *A new approach to women and therapy*. New York: McGraw-Hill.

Grof, S. (1980). Realms of the human unconscious: Observations from LSD research. In R. Walsh & F. Vaughan (Eds.) *Beyond ego: Transpersonal dimensions in psychology* (pp. 87-99). Los Angeles: Tarcher.

Grof, S., & Grof, C. (1989a) (Eds.). *Spiritual emergency: When personal Transformation becomes a crisis.* New York: Tarcher/Putnum.

Grof, S., & Grof, C. (1989b). Spiritual emergency: understanding evolutionary crisis. In S. Grof & C. Grof. (Eds). *Spiritual emergency: When personal transformation becomes a crisis* (pp. 1-26). New York: Tarcher/Putnum.

Grof, C., & Grof, S. (1989c). Assistance in spiritual emergency, In S. Grof & C. Grof. (Eds.). *Spiritual emergency: When personal transformation becomes a crisis* (pp. 191-198). New York: Tarcher/Putnum.

Haakam, J. (1990). A critical analysis of the codependence construct. *Psychiatry, 53,* 396-406.

Haakam, J. (1993). From Al-Anon to ACOA: Codependence and the reconstruction of caregiving. *Signs*, 321-345.

Hall, C. (1954). *A primer of Freudian psychology.* New York: Mentor Books.

Hall, C., & Nordby, V. (1973). *A primer of Jungian psychology.* New York: Mentor Books.

Harper, J., & Capdevila, C. (1990). Codependency: A critique. *Journal of Psychoactive Drugs, 22*(3), 285-292.

Health Communications (1984). *Co-dependency: An emerging issue.* Pompano Beach, FL: Health Communications.

Hemfelt, R., Minirth, F., & Meier, P. (1989). *Love is a choice: Recovery from codependent relationships.* Nashville, TN: Thomas Nelson Publishers.

Hitchcock, J. (1991). *The web of the universe: Jung, the "new physics" and human spirituality.* New Jersey: Paulist Press.

Hogg, J., & Frank, M. (1992). Toward an interpersonal model of codependence and contradependence. *Journal of Counseling and Development, 70*, 371-375.

Hora, T. (1962). Psychotherapy existence and religion. In H. Ruitenbeek (Ed.). *Psychoanalysis and existential philosophy* (pp. 70-89). New York: Dutton.

Hora, T. (1962). Existential psychiatry and group psychotherpy. In H. Ruitenbeek (Ed.). *Psychoanalysis and existential philosophy* (pp. 130-154). New York: Dutton.

Horgan, J. (June, 1994). Trends in neuroscience: Can science explain consciousness? *Scientific American, 271*(1), 88-94.

Horney, K. (1966). *Our inner conflicts.* New York: W. W. Norton & Co.

Horney, K. (1967). *Feminine psychology.* New York: W. W. Norton & Co.

Hughes-Hammer, C., Martsolf, D., & Zeller, R. (1998a). Development and testing of the codependency assessment tool. *Archives of Psychiatric Nursing, 12*(5), 264-272.

Hughes-Hammer, C., Martsolf, D., & Zeller, R. (1998b). Depression and codependency in women. *Archives of Psychiatric Nursing, 12*(6), 326-334.

Huxley, A. (1944). *The perennial philosophy.* New York: Harper & Row.

Huxley, A. (1956). *The doors of perception/heaven and hell.* New York: Harper Colophon.

Jacobi, J. (1959). *Complex, archetype, symbol in the psychology of C. G. Jung* (R. Manheim, Trans.).

Princeton, NJ: Princeton University Press. (Original work published 1957).

Jampolsky, L. (1991). *Healing the addictive mind.* Berkeley, CA: Celestial Arts.

Jaynes, J. (1990). *The origin of consciousness in the breakdown of the bicameral mind.* Boston: Houghton-Mifflin.

Jimenez, M. (1997). Gender and psychiatry: Psychiatric conceptions of mental disorders in women, 1960-1994. *Affilia, 12*(2), 154-175.

Jordan, K., & L'Abate, L. (1995). Programmed writing and therapy with symbiotically enmeshed patients. *The American Journal of Psychotherapy, 49*(2). 225-236.

Joy, W. (1979). *Joy's way: A map for the transformational journey.* Los Angeles: Tarcher.

Jung, C. (1959). Archetypes of the collective unconscious. In R. F. C. Hull (Ed. & Trans.) *The archetypes and the collective unconscious* (pp. 7-56). New York: Pantheon Books. (Original work published 1934).

Jung, C. (1963). *Memories, dreams, and reflections* (R. Winston & C. Winston, Trans.). New York: Pantheon. (Original work published 1961).

Jung, C. (1971a). Aion: Phenomenology of the self. In J. Campbell (Ed.) R.F.C. Hull (Trans). *The portable Jung* (pp. 13-162). New York: Viking.

Jung, C. (1971b). Psychological types. In J. Campbell (Ed.) R. F. C. Hull (Trans.) *The portable Jung* (pp. 178-269). New York: Viking.

Kaptchuk, T. (1983). *The web that has no weaver.* Chicago: Congden & Weed.

Kasprow, M., & Scotton, B. (1999). A review of transpersonal theory and its application to the practice of psychotherapy. *Journal of Psychotherapy & Practice Resources, 8*(1), 12-23.

Kavakci, O., Dogan, O., Kugu, N., & Adam, D., (Sept. 2010). EMDR (Eye movement desensitization and reprocessing): A different option in psychotherapy. *Istanbul, 23*(3), pp. 195-205.

Keen, S. (1991). *Fire in the belly: On being a man.* New York: Bantam.

Keen, S. (1994). *Hymns to an unknown god: Awakening the spirit in everyday life.* New York: Bantam Books.

Kepner, J. (1987). *Body process: A gestalt approach to working with the body in psychotherapy.* New York: Gardner Press.

Kornfield, J. (1989). Obstacles and vicissitudes in spiritual practice. In S. Grof & C. Grof, (Eds). *Spiritual emergency: When personal transformation becomes a crisis* (pp. 137-170). New York: Tarcher/Putnum.

Krestan, J., & Bepko, C. (1990). Codependency: The social reconstruction of female experience. *Smith College Studies in Social Work, 60,* 216-232.

Krippner, S. (1990). Personal mythology: An introduction to the concept. *The Humanistic Psychologist, 18,* 137-142.

Laing, R.D. (1962). Ontological insecurity. In H. Ruitenbeek (Ed.)._Psychoanalysis and existential philosophy* (pp. 41-69). New York: Dutton.

Laing, R.D. (1989). Transcendental experience in relation to religion and psychosis. In S. Grof. & C. Grof, C. (Eds.). *Spiritual emergency: When personal transformation becomes a crisis* (pp. 49-62). New York: Tarcher/Putnum.

Larsen, E. (1987). *Stage II relationships: Love beyond addiction.* San Francisco: Harper & Row.

Lee, J. (1990). *Recovery: Plain & simple.* Deerfield, FL: Health Communications.

Lee, P., Ornstein, R., Galin, D., Deikman, A., & Tart, C. (1976). *Symposium on consciousness.* New York: Viking.

Lerner, H. (1985). *The dance of anger.* New York: Harper & Row.

Lerner, H. (1988). *Women in therapy.* Northvale, New Jersey: Jason Aronson Inc.

Lerner, H. (1989). *The dance of intimacy.* New York: Harper & Row.

Linehan, M., Oldham, J., & Silk, K. (1995). Dx: Personality disorder...Now what? *Patient Care, 29*(11), 75.

Lipton, B. (2005). *The biology of belief: Unleashing the power of consciousness, matter, and miracles.* Santa Rosa, CA: Mountain of Love/Elite Books.

Lipton, B., & Bhaerman, S. (2009). *Spontaneous evolution: Our positive future (and a way to get there from here).* Carlsbad, CA: Hay House, Inc.

Loring, S., & Cowan, G. (1997). Codependency: An interpersonal phenomenon. *Sex Roles, 36,* 115-124.

Loughead, T. (1991). Addictions as a process: Commonalities or codependence. *Contemporary Family Therapy, 13*(5), 455-470.

Loughead, T., Spurlock, V., & Ting, Y. (1998). Diagnostic indicators of codependence: An investigation using the MCMI-II. *Journal of Mental Health Counseling, 20*(1), 64-76.

Lukoff, D., Lu, F., & Turner, R., (1998). From spiritual emergency to spiritual problem. The transpersonal role of the new DSM-IV category. *Journal of Humanistic Psychology, 38,* 21-50.

Lukoff, D. (1997). The psychologist as mythologist. *Journal of Humanistic Psychology, 37(3),* 34-58.

Lutz, A., Dunne, J. D., & Davidson, R. (2007). Meditation and the neuroscience of consciousness: An introduction. Retrieved from: http://www.sheermind.com/uploads/9/3/7/0/93704 22/meditation_and_the_neuroscience_of_consciou sness.pdf

Lutz, A., Slagter, H. A. Dunne, J., and Davidson, R. J. (2008, July). Retrieved from http://www.ncbi.nlm.nih.gov/pmc/articles/PMC26 93206/

Lyon, D., & Greenberg, J. (1991). Evidence of codependency in women with an alcoholic parent: Helping out Mr. Wrong. *Journal of Personality and Social Psychology, 61*, 435-439.

Mannion, L. (1991). Co-dependency: A case of inflation. *Employee Assistance Quarterly, 7*(2), 67-81.

Marrone, R. (1996). *Body of knowledge: An introduction to body/mind psychology.* New York: SUNY.

Martin, A., & Piazzo, N. (1995). Codependency in women: Personality disorder or popular descriptive term? *Journal of Mental Health Counseling, 17*(4), 428-440.

Maslow, A. (1971). *The farther reaches of human nature.* New York: Penguin.

Mason, M. (1984). Bodies & beings: Sexuality issues during recovery for the dependent and co-dependent. In Health Communications (Ed.), *Co-dependency: An emerging issue.* (pp. 61-66). Pompano Beach, FL: Health Communications.

Mastronardi, M. (1995). Codependence and the politics of inner resistance. *Women's Studies in Communication, 18*(2), 199-208.

May, R. (1953). *Man's search for himself.* New York: Dell.

May, R. (1991). *The cry for myth.* New York: Norton & Co.

McGrath, M. & Oakley, B. (2011). Codependency and pathological altruism. In B. Oakley, A. Knafo, G. Madhaven, and D. Wilson (Eds.) *Pathological Altruism,* (pp. 49-74). New York: Oxford University Press.

Mellody, P., Miller, P., & Miller, K. (1989). *Facing codependence.* San Francisco: Harper Collins.

Mellody, P., Miller, A., & Miller, K. (1992). *Facing love addiction.* San Francisco: Harper Collins.

Messner, B. (1996). "Sizing up" codependency recovery. *Western Journal of Communication, 60*(2), 101.

Messner, B. (1997). Archetypal evolution and "new birth" from codependency. *Communication Studies, 48*(1), 76-92.

Metzer, R. (1998). *The unfolding self.* Novato, CA: Origin Press.

Miller, A. (1981). *Drama of the gifted child and the search for the true self.* New York: Basic Books.

Miller, J. (1986). *Toward a new psychology of women.* Boston: Beacon.

Miller, R. (1998). Researching the spiritual dimensions of alcohol and other drug problems. *Addiction, 93*(7), 979-990.

Mishlove, J. (1993). *The roots of consciousness.* New York: Marlowe & Co.

Morrow, S., & Hauxhurst, D. (1998). Feminist therapy: Integrating political analysis in counseling and psychotherapy. *Women & Therapy, 21*(2), pp. 37-50.

Neher, A. (1996). Jung's theory of archetypes. A critique. *Journal of Humanistic Psychology, 36*(2), 61-91.

Ng, S. (1989). *Gender differences in personal mythologies.* Unpublished masters thesis. California State University, Sacramento.

Ng, S. (1998). *Metaphors of the feminine and masculine: Creating a personal mythology.* New York: McGraw-Hill.

Ng, S. (2005). *Towards a transpersonal framework for understanding codependence in women.* (Unpublished doctoral dissertation). California Coast University, Santa Ana, CA

Ng, S. (2013, April/May). (Review of the book *Exploring the frontiers of the body*-mind relationship). Retrieved from http://www.atpweb.org/jtparchive/pdfs/AHPPerspectiveApr2013.pdf

Ng, S. (2012). *Body, mind and psyche.* El Cajon, CA: Social Science Press.

Neumann, E. (1954). *The origins and history of consciousness.* New Jersey: Bollingen.

Norwood, R. (1985). *Women who love too much.* Los Angeles: Jeremy Tarcher.

O'Gorman, P. (1993a). Codependency explored: A social movement in search of definition and treatment. *Psychiatric Quarterly, 64*(2), 199-212.

O'Gorman, P. (1993b). Codpendency and women: Unraveling the power behind learned helplessness. In E. Cook, (Ed.) *Women Relationships, and Power: Implications for Counseling,* (pp. 153-166). Alexandria, VA: American Counseling Association.

O'Neil, J. & Egan, J. (1993). Abuses of power against women: Sexism, gender role conflict, and psychological violence. In E. Cook, (Ed.) *Women, relationships, and power: Implications for counseling,* (pp. 49-78). Alexandria, VA: American Counseling Association.

Ornstein, R. (Ed.). (1973). *The nature of consciousness.* San Francisco, CA: Freeman & Co.

Ornstein, R. (1977). *The psychology of consciousness.* (2nd ed.). New York: Harcourt Brace Jovanovich.

Ornstein, R., & Sobel, D. (1987). *The healing brain.* New York: Touchstone.

Owens, C. (1992). Zen Buddhism. In C. Tart (Ed.) *Transpersonal psychologies: Perspectives on the mind from seven great spiritual traditions* (pp. 153-202). San Francisco: Harper.

Oyle, I. (1976). *Time, space and mind.* Milbrae, CA: Celestial Arts.

Parker, G., Tupling, H., & Brown, L. B. (1975). A Parental Bonding Instrument. *British Journal of Medical Psychology, 52*, 1-10.

Pearsall, P. (1998). *The heart's code: The new findings about cellular memories and their role in the mind/body/spirit connection.* New York: Broadway Books.

Peck, M. (1978). *The road less traveled.* New York: Touchstone.

Peele, S., & Brodsky, A. (1975). *Love and addiction.* New York: Signet.

Perls, F. (1972). *Gestalt therapy verbatim.* New York: Bantam.

Pert, C. (2005). *Molecules of emotion: the link between body and soul.* Symposium conducted at the conference What The Bleep Do We Know?!? Santa Monica, CA.

Perry, J. (1989). Spiritual emergence and renewal. In S. Grof & C. Grof (Eds.). *Spiritual emergency: When personal transformation becomes a crisis,* (pp. 63-76). New York: Tarcher/Putnam.

Petrie, J., Giordano, J., & Roberts, C. (1992). Characteristics of women who love too much. *Affilia, 7*(1), 7-20.

Prevatt, J., & Park, R. (1989). The spiritual emergence network (SEN). In S. Grof & C. Grof (Eds.). *Spiritual emergency: When personal transformation becomes a crisis,* (pp. 225-232). New York: Tarcher/Putnam.

Prezioso, F. (1987). Spirituality in the recovery process. *Journal of Substance Abuse Treatment, 4,* 233-238.

Radin, D. (2006). Randolph, Elizabeth. (1985). Children who shock and surprise.

Rathbone-McCuan, E., Dyer, L., & Wartman, J. (1991). Double jeopardy: Chemical dependence and codependence in older women. In N. Van Den Bergh (Ed.). *Feminist perspectives on addictions* (pp. 101-113). NY: Springer Publishing.

Recovery Publications (1987). *The twelve steps for adult children of alcoholic and other fdysfunctional Families.* San Diego, CA: Recovery Publications.

Rice, J. (1996). *A disease of one's own.* New Brunswick, NJ: Transaction Publishers.

Roehling, P., Koelbel, N., & Rutgers, C. (1996). Codependence and conduct disorder: Feminine versus masculine coping responses to abusive parenting practices. *Sex Roles, 35*(9/10), 603.

Rogers, C. (1961). *On becoming a person.* Boston: Houghton-Mifflin.

Rothberg, N. (1986). The alcoholic spouse and the dynamics of codependency. *Alcoholism-Treatment Quarterly, 2,* 73-86.

Ruitenbeek, H. (Ed.). (1962). *Psychoanalysis and existential philosophy.* New York: Dutton.

Russell, B. (1938). *Power: A new social analysis.* New York: W. W. Norton & Co.

Schaef, A. (1986). *Co-dependence: Misunderstood-mistreated.* Minneapolis: Winston Press.

Schaef, A. (1987). *When society becomes an addict.* San Francisco: Harper & Row.

Searle, J. (1994). *The rediscovery of the mind.* Cambridge, MA: MIT Press.

Shapiro, F., & Forrest, M. (1997). *EMDR: Eye movement desensitization and reprocessing.* New York: Harper Collins.

Sheridan, M., & Green, R. (1993). Family dynamics and individual characteristics of adult children of alcoholics: An empirical analysis. *Journal of Social Service Research, 17*(1-2), 73-97.

Shockley, G. (1994). Overcoming the obstacles of co-dependency: An interdisciplinary task. *Journal of Spiritual Formation, 15*(1), 103-108

Shulman, G. (1984). Sexuality and recovery: Impact on the recovering couple. In Health Communications (Ed.), *Co-dependency: An emerging issue* (pp. 71-76). Pompano Beach, FL: Health Communications.

Siegel, D. (2001). Toward an interpersonal neurobiology of the developing mind: Attachment relationships, "mindsight," and neural integration. *Infant Mental Health Journal, 22*(1-2), 67-94.

Siegel, D. (2006, Apr). An interpersonal neurobiology approach to psychotherapy. *Psychiatric Anals. Thorofare, 36*(4), 260-262.

Siegel, D. (2010). *The mindful therapist: A clinician's guide to mindsight and neural integration.* New York: W. W. Norton & Company, Inc.

Siegel, D. (2011). *Mindsight: The new science of personal transformation.* New York: Bantam Books.

Siegel, D. (2012). *Pocket guide to interpersonal neurobiology: An integrative handbook of the mind.* New York: W. W. Norton & Company, Inc.

Small, J. (2000). *Awakening in time: The journey from codependence to co-creation.* Austin, TX: Eupsychian Press.

Spann, L., & Fischer, J. (1990). Identifying co-dependency. *The Counselor, 8*, 27.

Sperry, R. (1995). The riddle of consciousness and the changing scientific worldview. *Journal of Humanistic Psychology, 35*(2), 7-33.

Springer, C., Britt, T., & Schlenker, B. (1998). Codependency: Clarifying the construct. *Journal of Mental Health Counseling, 20*(2), 141-158.

Stenger, V. (1997/1998). Quantum spirituality. *Free Inquiry, 18*(1), 57-59.

Stevens, A. (1995). Jungian psychology, the body & the future. *Journal of Analytic Psychology, 40*, 353-364.

Subby, R. (1984). Inside the chemically dependent marriage: Denial and manipulation. In Health Communications (Ed.), *Co-dependency: An emerging issue* (pp. 25-30). Pompano Beach, FL: Health Communications.

Subby, R., & Friel, J. (1984). Co-dependency: A paradoxical dependency. In Health Communications (Ed.), *Co-dependency: An emerging issue* (pp. 31-44). Pompano Beach, FL: Health Communications.

Svanberg, P. (1998). Attachment, resilience and prevention. *Journal of Mental Health, 7*(6), 543-578.

Szasz, T. (1978). *The myth of psychotherapy.* New York: Anchor Press.

Talbot, M. (1981). *Mysticism and the new physics.* New York: Bantam Books.

Talbot, M. (1991). *The holographic universe.* New York: Harper-Collins.

Tannen, D. (1990). *You just don't understand.* New York: Morrow.

Tart, C. (1980). The systems approach to consciousness. In Walsh, R. & Vaughan, F. (Eds.). *Beyond ego: Transpersonal dimensions in psychology* (pp. 115-118). Los Angeles: Tarcher.

Tart, C. (1986). *Waking up: Overcoming the obstacles to human potential.* New York: Viking.

Tart, C. (1992a). *Transpersonal psychologies: Perspectives on the mind from seven Great spiritual traditions.* San Francisco: Harper.

Tart, C. (1992b). Science, states of consciousness, and spiritual experiences: The need for state-specific sciences. In C. Tart (Ed.). *Transpersonal psychologies: Perspectives on the mind from seven great spiritual traditions* (pp. 9-58). San Francisco: Harper.

Tart, C. (1992c). The physical universe, the spiritual universe, and the paranormal. In C. Tart (Ed.) *Transpersonal psychologies: Perspectives on the mind from seven great spiritual traditions* (pp. 113-153). San Francisco: Harper.

Tart, C. (1992d). Some assumptions of orthodox, western psychology. In C. Tart (Ed.). *Transpersonal Psychologies: Perspectives on the mind from seven great spiritual traditions* (pp. 59-112). San Francisco: Harper.

Tart, C. (1993). The structure and dynamics of waking sleep. *The Journal of Transpersonal Psychology, 25*(2), 141-169.

Tart, C. (1994). *Living the mindful life*. Boston: Shambhala.

Tavris, C. (1982). *Anger: The misunderstood emotion*. New York: Touchstone.

Taylor, E. (1999). An intellectual renaissance of humanistic psychology? *The Journal of Humanistic Psychology, 39*(2), 7-25.

Theriault, S., & Holmberg, D. (1998). The new old-fashioned girl: Effects of gender and social desirability on reported gender-role ideology. *Sex Roles, 39,* 97-112.

Thoele, S. (1991). *The courage to be yourself.* New York: MJF Books.

Tillich, P. (1962). Existentialism and psychotherapy. In H. Ruitenbeek (Ed.). *Psychoanalysis and existential philosophy* (pp. 3-16). New York: Dutton.

Trungpa, C. (1976). *The myth of freedom and the way of meditation*. Boston: Shambhala.

Uhle, S. (1994). Codependence: Contextual variables of the language of social pathology. *Issues in Mental Health Nursing, 15*, 307-317.

Vaillant, G. (1977). *Adaptation to life*. Boston: Little, Brown & Co.

Van Den Berg, J. (1962). Significance of human movement. In H. Ruitenbeek (Ed.). *Psychoanalysis and existential philosophy* (pp. 90-129). New York: Dutton.

Van Den Berg, N. (1991). Having bitten the apple: A feminist perspective on addictions. In N. Van Den Berg (Ed.). *Feminist perspectives on addictions* (pp. 3-30). New York: Springer Publishing.

Van Dusen, W. (1962). The theory and practice of existential analysis. In H. Ruitenbeek (Ed.).

Psychoanalysis and existential philosophy (pp. 3-40). New York: Dutton.

Van Wormer, K. (1989). Codependency: Implications for women and therapy. *Women & Therapy, 8*(4), 51-63.

Vaughan, F. (1980). Transpersonal psychotherapy: Context, content and process. In R. Walsh & F. Vaughan (Eds.). *Beyond ego: Transpersonal dimensions in psychology* (pp. 182-189). Los Angeles: Tarcher .

Von Franz, M. (1971). *Lectures on Jung's typology.* Zurich: Spring Publications.

Wallace, J. (1984). Personality disturbances among co-dependents before...after the onset of alcoholism. In Health Communications (Ed.), *Co-dependency: An emerging issue* (pp. 67-70). Pompano Beach, FL: Health Communications.

Walsh, R., & Vaughan, F. (1980). A comparison of psychotherapies. In Walsh, R. & F. Vaughan (Eds.). *Beyond ego: Transpersonal dimensions in psychology* (pp. 190-220). Los Angeles: Tarcher.

Walter, R. (1995, February). Codependency? Nonsense. (Speak Up!), *RN, 58,* 80.

Walter, R. (1986). Putting the codependent in charge: A compression approach to an alcoholic system. *Journal of Strategic and Systems Therapies, 5,* 1-3.

Walters, M. (1990). The codependent Cinderella who loves too much...fights back. *The Family Therapy Networker, 14*(4), 53-57.

Wegscheider-Cruse, S. (1984). The therapeutic void. In Health Communications (Ed.), *Co-dependency: An emerging issue* (pp. 1-4). Pompano Beach, FL: Health Communications.

Wegscheider-Cruse, S. (1985). *Choicemaking.* Pompano Beach, FL: Health Communications, Inc.

Wegscheider-Cruse, S. & Cruse, J. (2012). *Understanding codependency: The science behind it and how to break the cycle.* Deerfield Beach, FL: Health Communications, Inc.

Wells, M., Glickauf-Hughes, C., & Bruss, K. (1998). The relationship of codependency to enduring personality characteristics. *Journal of College Student Psychotherapy, 12*(3), 25-38.

Wells, M., Glickauf-Hughes, C., Jones, R. (1999). Codependency: A grass roots construct's relationship to shame-proneness, low self-esteem, and childhood parentification. *The American Journal of Family Therapy, 27*(1), 63-71.

Welwood, J. (1990). *Journey of the heart: The path of conscious love.* New York: HarperPerennial.

Welwood, J. (2000). *Toward a psychology of awakening: Buddhism, psychotherapy, and the path of personal and spiritual transformation.* Boston: Shambhala.

Wetzel, J. (1991). Universal mental health classification systems: Reclaiming women's experience. *Affilia, 6*(3), 8-31.

White, J. (Ed.) (1972). *The highest state of consciousness.* New York: Anchor.

Whitfield, C. (1984). Co-dependency: An emerging problem among professionals. In Health Communications (Ed.), *Co-dependency: An emerging issue* (pp. 45-54). Pompano Beach, FL: Health Communications.

Whitfield, C. (1986). Co-alcoholism: Recognizing a treatable disease. *Family and Community Health, 7*, 16-25.

Whitfield, C. (1987). *Healing the child within.* Deerfield Beach, FL: Health Communications.

Whitfield, C. (1993). *Boundaries and relationships: Knowing, protecting, and enjoying the self.* Deerfield Beach, FL: Health Communications.

Whitmont, E. (1991). *The symbolic quest: Basic concepts of analytical psychology.* New Jersey: Princeton.

Wilber, K. (1979a). *No boundary: Eastern and western approaches to personal growth.* Boston: Shambhala.

Wilber, K. (1979b). *The spectrum of consciousness.* Wheaton, Illinois: Quest.

Wilber, K. (1980a). Psychologia perennis: The spectrum of consciousness. In Walsh, R. & Vaughan, F. (Eds.). *Beyond ego: Transpersonal dimensions in psychology* (pp. 74-86). Los Angeles: Tarcher.

Wilber, K. (1980b). A developmental model of consciousness. In Walsh, V. & Vaughan, F. (Eds.). *Beyond ego: Transpersonal dimensions in psychology* (pp. 99-114). Los Angeles: Tarcher.

Wilber, K. (Ed.). (1982). *The holographic paradigm and other paradoxes.* Boulder, CO: New Science Library.

Wilber, K. (1999). Spirituality and developmental lines: Are there stages? *The Journal of Transpersonal Psychology, 31*(1), 1-10.

Wilber, K. (2000). *Integral psychology: Consciousness, spirit, psychology, and therapy.* Boston: Shambhala.

Wilkinson, H. (1999). Schizophrenic process, the emerging consciousness in recent history and phenomenological causality: The significance for psychotherapy of Julian Jaynes. *International Journal of Psychotherapy, 4*(1), 49-66.

Wise, A. (1997). *The high performance mind.* New York: Tarcher.

Woititz, J. (1983). *Adult children of alcoholics.* Pompano Beach: Health Communications.

Woititz, J. (1984a). Chemical dependency: Insidious invader of intimacy. In Health Communications (Ed.), *Co-dependency: An emerging issue* (pp. 55-60). Pompano Beach, FL: Health Communications.

Woititz, J. (1984b). The co-dependent spouse: What happens to you when your husband is an alcoholic. In Health Communications (Ed.), *Co-dependency: An emerging issue* (pp. 83-91). Pompano Beach, FL: Health Communications.

Wolf, F. (1994). *The dreaming universe: A mind-expanding journey into the realm where psyche and physics meet.* New York: Touchstone.

Woodward, L. (2000). Timing of separation and attachment to parents in adolescence: Results of a prospective study from birth to age 16. *Journal of Marriage & Family, 62,* 162-174.

Wright, P., & Wright, K. (1991). Codependency: Addictive love, adjustive relating, or both? *Contemporary Family Therapy, 13*(5), 435-454.

Wright, P. & Wright, K. (1995). Codependency: Personality syndrome or relational process? In S.Duck & J.T. Wood (Eds.), *Confronting relationship challenges* (pp. 109-128). Thousand Oaks, CA: Sage.

Wright, P., & Wright, K. (1999). The two faces of codependent relating: A research based perspective. *Contemporary Family Therapy, 21*(4), 527-543.

Wright, R. (1994). *The moral animal: Why we are the way we are.* New York: Vintage

Yeshe, T. (1987). *Introduction to Tantra: A vision of totality.* Boston: Wisdom Publications.

Zelvin, E. (1999). Applying relational theory to the treatment of women's addictions. *Affilia, 14*(1), 9-23.

Zukav, G. (1979). *The dancing Wu Li masters: An overview of the new physics.* New York: Quill/Wm. Morrow.

Zukav, G . (1989). *The seat of the soul.* New York: Simon & Schuster.